Ronnie's Looking for Trouble

RONNIE HOWARD
with Tim Fennell

RONNIE'S LOOKING FOR TROUBLE

THE TRUE STORY OF BRITAIN'S MOST BRUTAL UNDERCOVER COP

MAINSTREAM
PUBLISHING

EDINBURGH AND LONDON

This book is dedicated to:
Ronald Howard (2 May 1921 – 6 June 1974)
'The gift of love to us God gives.
Someone to love he lends.'

First published in Great Britain in 2007 by
MAINSTREAM PUBLISHING COMPANY (EDINBURGH) LTD
7 Albany Street
Edinburgh EH1 3UG

ISBN 9781845962845

This book is a work of non-fiction based on the life, experiences and
recollections of Ronnie Howard. In some cases names of people and
places, and the sequence or details of events have been changed to
protect the privacy of others. The author has stated to the
publishers that, except in such respects not affecting the substantial
accuracy of the work, the contents of this book are true.

A catalogue record for this book is
available from the British Library

Typeset in Trixie and New Baskerville

Printed in Great Britain by
Clays Ltd, St Ives plc

CONTENTS

prologue

TRUST NO ONE

They say if you want to make your mark on this world, you have to sell your soul to the Devil. Mine ended up somewhere far more troublesome.

I spent a lifetime hunting criminals. And found plenty of them. Some were even wearing the same uniform as me.

I gained a fearsome reputation and enough enemies to fill a phone book. Along the way, I lost family, friends and a lifetime of normality.

And for what? A filing cabinet full of backslaps and commendations that proved to be worthless protection against a force that would eventually turn against me.

This is my story.

one

THE STITCH-UP PART I

It was 6.50 p.m. as I turned onto Washwood Heath Road
on a hot balmy evening in July. The unmistakable smell of a brand-new
car surrounded me as I sped past the chaos of the Asian shops. Ahead
of me was the Fox and Dogs pub. Despite the warm evening, no one
was standing outside drinking.

I eased off the gas and turned into the car-park entrance, a narrow
passageway the width of one vehicle. The tyres squealed against the
hot road. The car park was empty apart from a couple of battered
Datsuns and Nissans, the vehicles of choice for many a minicab driver.
My Saab Turbo stuck out like a hooker at a wedding. A very expensive
hooker: I had £50,000 cash in dealers' wraps sitting in the boot.

As I sat waiting for my supply of drugs, a rush of thoughts went
through my head. Would my dealer turn up alone? Where should I test
the gear? (I could identify heroin by smell alone, but I would have to
burn some on silver foil to check its purity.) If I got out of the car, the
boot would be unlocked by the central locking. Would the money be
secure? Shit. Why hadn't I thought of all this before?

'The money doesn't come out of the car. It stays locked in the bloody
boot.' Those were the final words lovingly imparted by the operational
commander, a portly man with an awesome capacity for losing both
the plot and his temper.

I checked carefully to make sure my escape route out of the car park
was clear. I pictured the view the surveillance team had of the scene.

Suddenly, the headlights of a large vehicle lit up the car park. A blue

Ford Sierra swept in and came to a halt on my near side. It contained three men I'd never seen before. One leapt from the rear of the car and headed towards me. Cradled in his arms was a baseball bat.

I reached for the ignition. As I sparked up the engine, the windscreen exploded in my face. Foot to the floor, I reversed out of the entrance, back onto the Washwood Heath Road, cursing the wheel slip of the front-wheel drive as I jammed it into first and roared away, tyres screaming.

I stormed through Saltley, confident that no one would catch me in the Saab. Dagenham and I had tested it down the Hollywood bypass at 140 mph – no problem.

I was covered in glass like uncut diamonds. As the wind whistled past my head, I went over what had just happened: the bastards had tried to rob me. I never run from trouble. Ever. Had it not been for the 50 grand in the boot, I would happily have stayed around to dish out some mindless violence.

Back at HQ, the operational commander would be going ballistic. I found a payphone and punched in the digits. After four rings, he picked up. 'Surveillance lost you. Where the fuck are you?' he yelled. 'Have you still got the money?'

'Yes!' I snapped. '502 the Chocolate 49.'

The Force Surveillance Unit had devised a code in which we spoke to each other in numbers. This was to prevent eavesdropping on operations by criminals using a VHF radio: 502 was a surveillance code to signify the end of the operation; I was returning to Bournville Police Station, near to the home of Cadbury's chocolate – the Chocolate 49. I wondered if the operational commander knew what that meant? Then his nickname flashed to the front of my mind: TSB (Tell Sir Bollocks). 'He'll work it out,' I thought.

I slammed down the phone and jumped back into the damaged Saab. The next thing I remember was travelling at high speed through the Queensway Tunnel in the centre of Birmingham, heading for home.

Home for me was the Drug Squad office. I lived and breathed the job. When I got there, the office was empty. It was a shambles, with crap everywhere. It looked like the place had been burgled. The silence was broken by the other Drug Squad members clattering along the corridor. They filed in, and Dagenham came over to where I was sitting. 'You all right?' he enquired.

'Yeah. The boss is going mental, I presume.'

'What do you think?' he said, smiling.

Dagenham was five feet ten inches tall and hard as they come. He had a punch that would have made light appear beneath Mike Tyson's feet. Unfortunately, Dagenham couldn't find the switch to turn the boss's lights on.

Moments later, the operational commander barrelled through the large wooden doors like a pot-bellied prophet of doom. He conducted a debrief, informing everyone of what they had done wrong, particularly the surveillance team, who realised that although they could see me they were too far away to offer assistance.

'Well, at least the money is safe,' he concluded.

'Yes, sir,' I replied tetchily. 'And so am I.'

'And the car?' he added, ignoring me.

'Just the windscreen, sir.'

'Get it sorted. And I need a full report on my desk in the morning.'

Dagenham and I adjourned to the pub to conduct our own debrief. 'That was a fuck-up,' I moaned.

'I'll say,' replied Dagenham, laughing.

'Thanks,' I said, swigging my beer. I wasn't used to failure.

Dagenham was one of the rare people I got on with in the job. His ability as a detective was phenomenal. He also had the remarkable quality of being able to bring the mayhem I caused to some form of acceptable conclusion.

I'd been described as a few things in my time. One of the more printable descriptions came from a senior officer, late in my career. 'You are a bit of a Roy Keane,' he said, referring to the former Manchester United captain. To me this was a compliment. Well, it was better than being called a James Hunt.

Roy Keane is a man for whom I have the utmost respect. He is a person who polarises opinion, a man who speaks his mind without deference to those above him or alongside him. He is a winner who demands nothing less than 100 per cent. He drives himself to the limit and expects everyone else to do the same. Most people find such an honest and forthright approach difficult to live with. Not me.

From my earliest days as a policeman, my direct approach put a lot of people's noses out of joint – criminals and coppers alike. Dagenham said that dealing with me was like stroking a rattlesnake. In my line of work, I dealt with every situation in the same manner: don't pussyfoot around a problem, tackle it head on. My philosophy was if you think it's there, then kick the door off and get it. The same applied to getting information from criminals. A cocky and uncooperative dealer could very quickly be persuaded to reveal where their drugs were hidden if they were lifted a couple of inches off the floor in an arm lock – or held over the ledge of the top storey of a multi-storey car park. It was unconventional. But it got results.

I rode my luck on many occasions. In an operation to nail one of the main operators in the Birmingham sauna scene, I followed his car, intending to stop him at the first opportunity. I called for assistance only to find myself with no back-up. Rather than wait, I caved in the driver's-side window and dragged him screaming out of his car. In my hurry, I never actually got round to opening the door. I searched him and recovered two bob's worth of cannabis. We then searched his house and found nothing. As a last resort, we turned his mother's house over and found six kilos of cannabis under her bed.

My appetite for work was boundless. I always hit the office no later than 8 a.m. I always knew when I would start work but never knew when I would finish. My phone bill at home was huge, as I was never off the blower calling informants and chasing people.

I led by example. I was fit, I was fast and I was always the first through the door, regardless of who or what was on the other side.

Dealing with colleagues, I always gave it to them straight. I'd stab them in the chest but never in the back. Praise them in public, bollock them in private. I didn't care about being liked. The world is full of nice blokes in second place. The English attitude of 'it's not the winning, it's the taking part' has always irked me. It's bullshit.

My activities and attitude meant I ended up with plenty of enemies, both in the underworld and under my own roof in the police force. I shouldn't have been too surprised, then, when the heroin bust took a rather sinister turn. Our informant on the job was a weasel of a man called Sahid Mohammed, who was well connected within the drug fraternity. He was five feet five inches tall with a mouthful of gold teeth. A female officer noted that he must have had the largest penis in Balsall Heath, judging by the Polaroid that had been recovered from his house when he'd first been arrested.

Sahid had told us about a dealer who had a large quantity of heroin for sale. We gave him £700 to make a test purchase. Test purchases were a method devised to check the standing of prospective targets before a full-blown operation was staged. It also helped to gain the dealer's trust. An informant would be supplied with a quantity of cash to purchase a small initial quantity of drugs. Undercover officers would then go directly to the dealer for larger amounts.

Sahid returned with a half-ounce of heroin, which oddly contained traces of walnut shell. He explained that this was the method being used to import the drugs. We eventually got a direct introduction to the dealer, whose name was Janay. Posing as criminals, we told him we were interested in buying three kilos of heroin.

'It'll cost you 50 grand,' he told us. 'I'll have the gear a week today. Meet me in the Fox and Dogs car park at 7 o'clock.'

The operation was under way. We rented the Saab Turbo – a car Dagenham and I both longed to own – and senior management authorised the cash. For insurance purposes, this had to be painstakingly photocopied, note by note. It was then made into dealers' wraps of £100 – nine £10 notes with the last tenner wrapped around the bundle.

But the dealer hadn't shown. He'd sent the heavies with the baseball bats instead. Something really didn't smell right. My instincts told me that this was more than a straightforward fuck-up. It was a stitch-up.

The morning after the operation went belly up, I went looking for Janay. This time I wasn't alone.

two

THE COUNCIL HOUSE KID

I grew up on the Wyrley Birch Council Estate, the eldest of three children. My father was a hard-working, loyal husband who idolised his children. My mother was equally hard-working – the brains and the steel of the family.

My father always threatened to do this or that to us for misbehaving. My mother just did it. On one occasion I'd come home full of myself, a probationary constable in half uniform. I'd squared up to my younger brother, only to be brought down to size by a blow from the fireplace poker wielded by Mum.

It was on the estate that young villains served their criminal apprenticeships. It wasn't unusual for one of my friends to disappear for a time after being arrested for some petty crime or other. Not that it was always petty. Paul O'Grady, a local thug, was convicted of murder. Another, Andy Johnson, was found guilty of a number of brutal rapes.

I was never involved in any real criminal activities, mainly through fear of what my mother would have done to me. But I still learned how all the various scams worked.

I won a place at grammar school and wandered through my school career playing football, following Aston Villa and struggling with the guitar. They say if you want to get on in this world, you have to sell your soul to the Devil. I ended up selling mine to something far more troublesome.

In the second week of the GCSE examinations, my father became ill with severe headaches and was admitted to hospital. He died two weeks later from a brain tumour. I remember sitting in bed with my mother when the telephone rang with the news. And I'll never forget the look on my brother's face when he was told the terrible news.

From that day, things were never the same. I'd gone to bed a boy and woken up a man, always feeling alone in the world. I didn't grieve for my father because I didn't know how to. And I never saw my mother cry once. She had too much on her plate.

I left school with two GCSEs and found work clearing builders' rubbish from the recently completed Gracechurch Shopping Centre. I had to earn money for the family. My mother was a school dinner lady taking home a pittance with a nine year old and a thirteen year old to bring up, and she also had to try and keep me on the straight and narrow. I started an apprenticeship with the City of Birmingham Housing Department as a builder. I hated every minute of it.

It was at that time I discovered drugs. I tried them but quickly gave up when a friend, Kenny Heathrington, was found dead, having overdosed on tranquillisers. By then I had already learned the tricks of the drug trade – tricks that would come in handy in later life. I could walk the walk and talk the talk.

On 16 May 1977, I fulfilled a long-held ambition and joined the West Midlands Police. I completed my initial training at Ryton Dunsmore Police Training Centre, a former Second World War refugee camp. In the canteen, the tables were each laid with a large sugar bowl in the middle. On top of each bowl was a saucer to prevent the sparrows that swooped freely around the hall from crapping in the sugar.

I arrived on a Sunday evening to be met by a drill sergeant in a slashed peaked cap. I greeted him with a casual, 'All right, mate?' Big mistake. My feet didn't touch the floor for five weeks. As a junior, I was the lowest form of human life. Students would leave on a daily basis because of the hard-line discipline, but there was no way I was going to crack.

I phoned Mum every night with a lump in my throat, as I had never been away from home before. Home was 27 miles away – not exactly the other side of the world. The lump in my throat moved to my trousers when I met a policewoman from Avon and Somerset, and I didn't feel quite so homesick.

My first posting was Queens Road Police Station, Aston. I was sitting in the parade room on my first day when one of my new colleagues, a man known as Piggy Johnson (because of his appearance and his eating habits), greeted me. He asked me if I would be prepared to go on strike, which I found puzzling, as I hadn't actually done any work yet. The reason was that police were paid less than milkmen at that time. In fact, a complete shift at Queens Road had left to become milkmen. I hadn't given much attention to the salary I was getting because I just wanted to be a copper and lock up thieves. My first pay packet for a month's work was £175.

The Labour Government had at that time appointed Lord Edmund Davies to carry out an inquiry into police pay, and he subsequently recommended a 40 per cent pay rise, which the government said it would implement that autumn. This recommendation coincided with a forthcoming general election. Margaret Thatcher, the leader of the Conservative Party, made it known that if she came to power she would implement the pay rise immediately, thus securing the votes of all members of the police force. The pay rise was awarded by the Conservatives, who had swept to power, a full six weeks before the date the Labour Government had set.

I clearly remember my first working day because I left my leather gloves and special-issue torch in the parade room only to return and find them missing. That's the trouble with police stations – they're full of thieves.

When my first two-till-ten shift finished, I was asked if I wanted to work some overtime, which I jumped at. At that time, the National Front were active in Handsworth, an area with a large ethnic community. That evening, we had the job of policing a National Front meeting at Bolton Road School in Handsworth, which was under siege by demonstrators. The night ended with us standing in the playground of the school with truncheons drawn, being stoned by demonstrators on the other side of the iron school railings. One officer had a dustbin lid, which he used to deflect rocks being thrown at us. 'What the hell am I doing here?' I thought to myself.

Things got worse as the National Front activity escalated. There was a large-scale demonstration outside a meeting held at Digbeth Civic Hall. Once again, we were called in to protect the bad guys. We came on duty at 7 a.m., were fed steak and kidney pies and given a packed lunch that consisted of a Penguin biscuit, a pork pie and a ham sandwich. The ham was so thin that it looked like it had been photocopied.

A short coach trip took us to Digbeth Civic Hall, where we were lined up, three deep, to surround the front of the hall. Riot shields had been borrowed from the army: there were 12 of them to go around the whole force.

Lucky me, I was on the front row with Boggie Howes. He was known as 'Boggie' because his black hair stood on end like a toilet brush. Also, he was barking mad.

Before the demonstration started, the front row were instructed to file around the corner into Milk Street, where we were each issued with a strip of clear plastic on elastic and instructed to put them in our pockets. Special Branch had received information that demonstrators would spray ammonia into our eyes. We were not to put the plastic over our faces until instructed to by officers who would do so with loudhailers from the safety of the roof of Digbeth Coach Station across the road.

(The standard of Special Branch information was legendary. When the investigation was being made into the Birmingham pub bombings in 1974, officers were supplied with warrants to search premises based on Special Branch information. When they arrived, they found themselves at derelict bombsites from the Second World War.)

The demonstration kicked off, and we were nearly stoned to death. The main problem was that we couldn't protect ourselves because our arms were linked together to keep back the demonstrators. Eddie Oldham, one of the officers with the riot shields, suffered a fractured skull from a house brick. But second-rate public-order policing wasn't the West Midlands Police Force's only shortcoming, as I was about to find out.

Back on normal duty, I was posted to the D Division, which covered the area in which I'd grown up and still lived. I knew most of the criminals in the area and quickly began to collect information, which

I then passed on to a detective sergeant on the Serious Crime Squad. This resulted in some worthwhile arrests. One in particular was a soldier serving in Northern Ireland who was bringing guns home to sell to his friends.

It was around that time I first met Dagenham. He got his nickname because he spent a lot of time with his face pressed against the windscreens of high-performance cars he couldn't afford to buy. We worked at the same station. An astute inspector thought we'd work well together, and he was proved right. We quickly ended up bonding over a dead body.

Our first day working together was during the ambulance strikes. That morning, a fresh-faced Dagenham and I were standing on parade waiting for the inspector to brief us on the shift ahead. 'Right, you and you, listen in,' the inspector said, pointing a finger at us. 'Report to the controller and you will be given the keys to a transit van parked in the yard. It's fully kitted out. You are now an ambulance.'

We both sighed with disbelief. This wasn't why we'd joined the police force. Inside the transit there was a first-aid kit and a large green plastic coffin. 'If we're going to be real ambulance drivers, we won't be patrolling the streets looking for punters,' Dagenham announced. 'So I suggest we adjourn to the snooker room till we get a call.' I liked him instantly.

As we were perfecting our snooker techniques, we received a call. 'Foxtrot Ambulance One, please attend 54 Martineau Tower, Newtown. Report of man collapsed.'

With our makeshift siren blaring, we drove to Newtown, where we parked at the bottom of one of those charmless 1960s tower blocks. We took the lift to the fifth floor and arrived to find an old lady looking very distressed.

'What's going on, love?' I asked.

'It's my husband. He's collapsed in the toilet.'

I stepped into the hallway and pushed at the toilet door. It was locked. I shouldered it open and came face to arse with an old man bent forward with his arms and legs twisted around the pan. I felt his neck. He was cold. I checked for a pulse. Nothing.

It's remarkable the number of people who die on the toilet. A doctor once told me that all that concentrated effort puts as much strain on the heart muscle as it does on the sphincter.

As the first officers at the scene of a sudden death, we would have to remain with the body to ensure continuity of evidence. This would ultimately mean witnessing the post-mortem examination. It was always a pleasure to watch someone having the top of his head removed with a bone saw.

'We'd better go and fetch the box, mate,' I said to Dagenham.

'I'll just put the woman straight first,' he replied. He went back outside the flat and told the woman the bad news. 'I'm sorry, love, but your husband has passed away.' The lady began to cry, and a neighbour took her away to comfort her.

Dagenham and I took the lift back down to the van to get the coffin. The only way it would go in the lift was to stand it on its end. Back at the flat, we unclasped the man from the toilet and carried him out into the hall. 'There is no dignity in death,' I thought to myself as I pulled up his trousers. We opened the coffin and tried to lift him. His arms and legs were stiff. We managed to straighten out all of his limbs except one of his legs, which was still bent. This meant we couldn't get the lid of the coffin on properly. Dagenham took a sheet from the airing cupboard and wrapped it around the protruding leg. I then grabbed a length of washing line from the balcony and wrapped it around the coffin to secure the lid. 'Right,' I announced. 'Let's get him out to the lift.'

We manhandled the coffin onto the landing, then stood it on its end inside the lift. 'I'm going to tell the old lady that we're off now,' I said to Dagenham. 'Check we've locked her flat.'

As I came out of the neighbour's flat, Dagenham was standing on the landing with his mouth open. 'What's the matter?' I asked.

'The lift. It's gone,' replied Dagenham. And so had the coffin.

The lights above the lift indicated that it was headed down. We made a lung-bursting dash down five flights of stairs to intercept the runaway coffin. All the way down I could hear Dagenham laughing. We arrived at the ground floor at the same time as the bell pinged announcing the arrival of the lift.

Dagenham was still laughing as the doors opened and the coffin slid out, much to the horror of the two ladies who were about to get in. As I was about to have a heart attack of my own, Dagenham calmly announced, 'Sorry, girls. Lift's out of service.'

Dagenham was a kindred spirit. Like me, he liked to keep fit. He thought nothing of going out for a 40-mile cycle ride during an afternoon. He was also immensely strong for his size. Late one night, we were called to a suspected break-in at a house in Handsworth. I was told to cover the back of the house and saw someone trying to climb out of the transom window. I jumped up, grabbed the burglar around the head and tried to pull him out of the window. He screamed blue murder and resisted. I remember thinking to myself that if I did get this bloke through the window he was going to be a right handful.

I was grunting away almost ripping his head from his shoulders. The burglar continued to squeal. Suddenly, a light came on in the kitchen. There, on the other side of the window, was Dagenham holding onto the man's legs to stop him getting out. The poor villain must have come away from our little tug of war a good six inches taller.

Dagenham and I kept each other sane and entertained. One time, we confiscated a dead adder from a bunch of school kids who'd beaten it to death with a tennis racquet. Back at the station, we put the snake in the cap of a duty sergeant who'd left his headgear on his desk while he took a coffee break. On his return, he screamed even louder than the burglar we'd stretched through the window.

During one arrest, Dagenham found a handful of Polaroids of the suspect's wife in all sorts of exotic poses. The man complained bitterly about the arresting officers ogling the photos. I played good cop, took the photos from Dagenham and instructed the suspect to put them in his pocket, for which he was most grateful. At the police station, he was told to empty his pockets, at which point the whole station got to see the porno shots of his wife.

Dagenham and I learned to cover each other's backs whenever things got out of control, which they did on more than one occasion. We worked nights once a month, which we both found tough, as we had difficulty sleeping during the day. The shifts would begin at 10 p.m.

and finish at 6 a.m. the following morning. I'd often end up crying with exhaustion because I'd had no sleep for a week. One night, Dagenham and I were patrolling Newtown, a hotbed of small-time criminal activity, where robbery was something of a sport. Our main responsibility was to ensure that all commercial premises were checked for any sign of break-in. This meant we had to go through a procedure called pulling locks in which we'd try the doors and windows to make sure they were secure. To cover more ground, Dagenham and I split up.

After ten minutes of rattling doors, I heard the controller calling my partner on the radio: 'Foxtrot One to 9782. Foxtrot One to 9782. Do you copy? Over.' Dagenham didn't reply. 'Foxtrot One to 9782. Foxtrot One to 9782. Do you copy? Over.'

'He's probably gone for a crap,' I thought.

'Foxtrot One to 9782. Foxtrot One to 9782. Do you copy? Over.'

This went on for another 45 minutes. Still Dagenham didn't reply. 'That's one hell of a crap,' I concluded.

Control then started to put out calls to individual officers: 'Any officer knowing the location of 9782, please copy.'

No one had seen him. Things were starting to look serious. Where the hell was he? I tried radioing him myself. Nothing. I was getting calls from everyone, right up to the duty sergeant.

'He's supposed to be your fucking patrol partner. Where the hell is he?' bellowed the sergeant.

'I don't know, Sarge,' I answered, my mouth dry and my guts in a knot as I started to feel genuinely concerned for Dagenham's welfare.

A few years before, a young constable called David Green had been stabbed to death while on night shift after getting separated from his partner. The attacker stabbed him in the chest and twisted the knife as he removed it, splitting Green's heart and killing him instantly. Every year, there was a service to commemorate him. Every year, we would all turn up to shed a private tear.

As the sergeant ordered a full-scale search, I continued to comb the streets and back alleys, fearing the worst. As I wandered along another badly lit road, I saw the silhouette of a man up ahead of me in the distance. He seemed dishevelled and a little unsteady on his feet. My heart began to race. It was Dagenham, but was he all right? I ran towards him, and as I got closer I saw the whiteness of his teeth as he broke into his trademark smile.

'Where've you been?' I squeaked, my voice rising as I spoke, trying to catch my breath at the same time.

'Calm down, mate,' he grinned. 'You know that traffic warden we met the other night? Well, she lives round here, and I thought I'd pop in and pay my respects.'

In the early days, Dagenham and I were both ladies' men. Quite a team, in fact. But this was during our own time, never on duty. 'Fucking hell, man, the whole of Birmingham Police Force has been looking for you. If they find out you've been shagging in the firm's time, you'll be up the road.'

'Shit,' said Dagenham, realising he'd lost all track of time. So, we hatched a plan. I called through to HQ to say that I'd found him. The story we concocted was very simple: Dagenham had disturbed some thieves trying to steal bits off cars; he had then confronted them and had been knocked unconscious.

To make it look authentic, we took some wheels from a parked car and lobbed them into a bush. For the assault part of the story to stand up, Dagenham had to look like he'd been battered. 'Make it look good,' Dagenham said as I lamped him with my best right hook. He staggered to his feet with a black eye and a nose like a blood orange.

The cavalry arrived to find a shaken Dagenham sitting on the kerb nursing a bruised face and sporting a bloodied shirt. Instead of being caught with his pants down, Dagenham returned to the station a hero.

That night taught me a valuable lesson about myself: when things were looking bleak, I could think on my feet. I knew I could always get myself – and those around me – out of a tight spot. In the years to come, it would prove to be an invaluable skill. In fact, it saved my life on more than one occasion.

As Dagenham and I went up through the ranks, our paths started to diverge. Dagenham's fascination for cars saw him specialise in tackling motor theft, which was rife in the Midlands at that time. I had my eyes on CID. Eventually, we were moved to different stations.

I ended up at F Division, which was responsible for policing the city centre of Birmingham. I finally achieved a transfer after an interview with Her Majesty's Inspectorate of Constabulary. I complained bitterly about the amount of travelling – four miles – I had to do to get to work and the strain this was causing me financially.

One Monday evening, I arrived at Steelhouse Lane, the main city-centre police station, to parade for night duty. The inspector was a short man with an aggressive personality who barked out his orders. I introduced myself to him, and he set about lecturing me on how hard-working F Division officers were and how it was going to be a shock to my system coming to Steelhouse Lane. I took on board what he said and was posted to walk the city centre.

After a few nights, I noted that I rarely saw another officer on the streets after 11 p.m. One night when I was walking back to the police station to take a refreshment break at 2 a.m., I came across an officer who had clearly already taken his refreshments in the pub. I watched as he went into the station and staggered into the lounge of the single men's quarters. After a short time, I went to investigate and found him, along with half a dozen others, asleep in the lounge. At the end of the shift when all the officers assembled to book off duty, the smell of stale beer was overwhelming.

The sergeant who booked everyone off duty was a loud man with an enormous beer belly. One of my new colleagues with lager breath winked at me and whispered that I should watch out for the sergeant: 'If he catches you in a pub drinking while you're on duty, he'll come down heavily on you. He'll make you buy everyone a drink!'

That was the way it was. Even the superintendent at the station would go out on patrol once a month and would have to be escorted back to the police station when he couldn't drink any more beer. I refused to join the drink-during-work culture. I enjoyed a drink but had never been very good at holding it. As an ex-girlfriend once told me, 'After a couple of pints, you're nobody's.'

I was super fit. I had discovered long-distance running. Physical exercise was my way of dealing with stress, because when I was running my mind was empty. I began to enter marathons that were being staged all over the country. The best time I ever managed was three hours and ten minutes.

One of my proudest moments came in later life when I was asked to run the Severn Trent Challenge with some lads from the SAS. It was a team event similar to orienteering, with check points at various stages. The race was run over 32.5 miles of hills in the Peak District National Park. It also had to be run in army-issue boots.

I was doing undercover training with a sergeant from the Counter Terrorist Cell at the time. He said he was looking for a fourth team member. I was flattered but said I didn't know whether I would be up to running with members of the SAS who could run hundreds of miles with wardrobes on their backs. But I could never resist a challenge, even one as stupidly tough as that.

The race started at 7 a.m. Breakfast that day was a bar of chocolate and two bananas. We covered the first twelve miles in under two hours, which doesn't sound that fast until you consider the severity of the terrain. The views in the Peak District National Park are beautiful – or so I'm told. All I saw was the ground, as I spent the entire time looking where I was putting my feet. We completed the distance in seven hours eleven minutes and came second, nine minutes behind the winners. I sprinted the last hundred yards and then crawled from the finish line to the shower. The pain in my feet was excruciating. It felt as though I'd run without any boots on.

In the early days, running gave me the physique of a stick insect. To combat this, I started lifting weights. This built my muscles and also my aggression. I was six feet two inches tall with a forty-four inch chest. I rarely had to raise my voice – just a look was enough. A friend of mine once commented that I had an air of violence about me. It wasn't something that I cultivated. It was just something that was there.

Half of any physical battle is won in the mind. If you know you'll never back down in the face of a threat, people can sense it. And that makes you twice as dangerous. I always felt that a fit body would give me a sharp mind, so I trained hard. Sadly, most of my colleagues in the police force at that time were carved from blancmange.

I took the same attitude towards work. Instead of wasting my time getting drunk on duty, I preferred to concentrate on locking up thieves. I quickly earned the respect of my more experienced colleagues.

One charming aspect of working at Steelhouse Lane was that the Central Mortuary was situated just around the corner from the station. It would often be a young officer's duty to open up the mortuary and await the arrival of a body. The entrance was in a dimly lit street, which was secured by heavy iron gates. Beyond the gates there was a long unlit drive that led down to the mortuary. The entrance was a heavy refrigerator-type door secured by a large padlock. The building was Victorian, and inside the mortuary it was pretty grim. In the winter, with old people dropping like flies, it wasn't unusual for bodies to be piled up on top of each other. I quickly discovered that mortuaries aren't silent places. The escaping gases cause the bodies to sigh and moan. It's very disconcerting.

The officer who briefed me on the procedure of opening up the mortuary advised me to put the padlock and keys securely in my pocket. This was to stop me getting locked inside by one of the shift comedians. Another favourite wind-up was for the radio controller to call an officer who was alone in the mortuary on his personal radio. When the officer answered the call, he would be greeted with an eerie 'Wooooooooo!'

The mortuary had a large register in which the belongings of a deceased person were recorded. It was interesting to note the wobbly style of most of the writing. Many a nervous officer would have to strip a corpse alone before filling in the details.

Back at the police station, I was having my eyes opened on a daily basis. I couldn't believe the number of nutters out there on our streets. There was one chap who would turn up at the station once a month and produce a notebook. This notebook would have to be stamped three times on two pages, and he would then go quietly on his way.

On another occasion, a lady came into the police station and announced she had murdered her husband. The experienced duty officer, wary of the types of lunatics who wander in and out, told her to fuck off, which she did. She then went to the next police station she could find and made the same allegation. Officers went to her house, and found her husband pinned to the bed with a bread knife between his shoulder blades.

Court was another eye-opening experience, especially the summary justice meted out by the dock sergeants. On Saturday mornings, a court was held for what were known as 'lock-up cases'. These were people who had been arrested on Friday evening but could not be released on bail. Most had been arrested for being drunk and disorderly. The court would usually be run by an old sweat of a sergeant, who was the dock officer. One Saturday morning, it was my duty to escort all the drunks into the court. They all sat on a bench before the magistrates. Their names were called out, and they were asked how they intended to plead to the charge of being drunk and disorderly. This was after the sergeant had read out the evidence to the magistrates, which he did just once, as it was the same for each person: 'Shouting, swearing, eyes glazed, speech slurred, drunk, your worships. He was drunk.'

The sergeant then went down the line of people on the bench saying, 'How do you plead?' To which each person said, 'Guilty.' That was until one idiot uttered the words 'Not guilty'. To which the sergeant said, 'Not what?' And the man replied, 'Guilty.' The sergeant in a flash said, 'Guilty, your worships.'

I learned very early on not to be affected by the sentences handed out to the criminals I'd arrested. It was my job to put them before the courts. What happened to them afterwards was out of my hands.

I noticed that in the judicial system no one ever considered the victim. The punishments for offences against property, such as stealing, were always harsher than for crimes of violence against a person. A deal would usually be done between the defence and prosecution lawyers to reduce a charge to a lesser offence. The criminal would then plead guilty to this and receive credit from the judge for saving the expense of a trial by getting a reduction in his sentence. No one would ever enquire how the old lady was whose house had been broken into or who'd been dragged up the street by her handbag.

Mind you, old people were just as capable of perpetrating crime as being victims. I remember investigating what appeared to be a simple fraud – a clever scam operated on loan companies. The offences had been uncovered by a sharp employee of one of these companies, who'd recognised that the writing was the same on loan applications made in the names of two different people.

The offender, a man in his early 60s, had been to prison for the theft of some jewellery a few years before. He'd learned the scam while he was inside. He found vacant houses in good areas that were being sold by estate agents. He then went to the central library and found the name of the previous occupier from the list of voters. He then went to the post office and had the mail to the address of the empty house redirected to another address, and from there to a second address. The offender then photocopied an income tax return form, which he completed fictitiously, showing earnings for the previous year in the name of the former occupier of the empty house. He then opened a building-society account in the former occupier's name and made an application for a personal loan. This was for no more than £2,000 so as not to draw attention to the scam. When the loan application was processed, a cheque would be issued and forwarded to the empty house, which would be redirected by the post office and then again to the safe second address. The scammer would then recruit a vagrant from the city centre, who would collect and hand over the cheque for a couple of quid.

I went and arrested the con artist, a timid little old man. He cooperated and told me that there was a locked bedroom at the flat he shared with his wife in which a book could be found containing details of the various frauds he had committed. I went to the flat. In the locked room I didn't find a book with a few details in it, but a ledger detailing hundreds of frauds totalling many thousands of pounds. His poor wife knew nothing about it and had been working hard every day to save a deposit for a house for them both to live in. Her old man had squandered £25,000 betting on the horses. He was charged and remanded in custody but eventually given bail to return home.

In the course of our enquiries, we had identified a particular vagrant the man had used to collect his mail. This vagrant approached us and told us he had been asked by the offender to collect post for him once again. He passed an envelope to us that contained a cheque from a loan company for £2,000. He said he had to meet the offender at the Rose and Crown pub in Moseley that evening to hand over the envelope. We obtained another envelope from the loan company, placed a handwritten note in it and sealed it.

We waited outside the pub until the offender came outside, opening the envelope as he did so. I had written him a note with two words on it: 'You're nicked'.

The scammer was only one of the many people I collared. The arrests I was making began to get me noticed by management. The superintendent at Steelhouse Lane was called Pip Pulsman. He was a legendary detective known and feared by the population of criminals involved in serious crime. He gained a reputation for the ruthless tactics he used to lock up 'untouchable' villains. His philosophy was ruthless men must be dealt with ruthlessly. It was a philosophy I bought into wholeheartedly.

Pulsman had noticed that I had a reputation for being a thief taker. He rewarded me with a posting as a resident beat officer with responsibility for one particular district. I set about tearing apart the criminals who lived in that area. I worked hard, locking up thirty-three in a period of five months. This resulted in a residents' meeting being called to complain about the unrest I was causing.

One morning, Pulsman called me into his office and told me there was only one place for me and that was CID. I was attached to the department for a six-month period to establish whether I was detective material. I set about the job in my usual manner, locking up everyone in sight. I was soon appointed to the position of detective constable and worked on various squads and on high-profile murder inquiries.

One case in particular was the murder of an Indian diplomat called Ravinder Mhatre. He was kidnapped by a group of terrorists known as the Jammu Kashmir Liberation Front. It was my responsibility to set up the incident room, which meant putting up tables and plugging in telephones, one of which rang immediately. There was a woman on the other end who said her name was George. With no taste for time wasters, I hung up. It rang again, and the female told me not to put the telephone down but to shout out that George was on the telephone, at which point a detective chief superintendent came scurrying over and took the telephone from me. George, I soon found out, was an MI5 code name.

As the kidnapping was a political incident, the resources devoted to the investigation were phenomenal. The Yorkshire Ripper inquiry computers were installed in the incident room along with staff from Yorkshire. At the time, these were the only police computers available in the country. There was also a fax machine, which had been supplied along with a civilian operator, who spent most of his day demonstrating its use, as none of us had ever seen one before.

The kidnappers eventually put forward their demands: to secure the release of their leader Maqbool Bhat, who was in prison. They gave a final deadline of 8 p.m. on a Wednesday evening. I remember sitting in silence watching the clock until it reached and passed 8 p.m. Mhatre was found dead some hours later on a farm drive in Leicestershire. He'd been shot twice in the head.

The inquiry rumbled on, and I worked from 7 a.m. to 11 p.m. every day for six weeks. I was taking overtime home in a shopping trolley, until a superintendent asked me when I had last taken a day off and ordered me to take two days' leave.

It turned out that a man named Ansari was responsible for the murder. Information was received from an informant who identified the group responsible. Another member of this group was arrested and interviewed. His solicitor made an application to the crown court for a writ of habeas corpus, which claimed there was no case to answer, and so he was released. Ansari fled the country to Pakistan, where he remains. He was never prosecuted. A number of his associates were prosecuted for conspiracy to murder and received long prison sentences, but the man who pulled the trigger was never brought to justice.

During the course of the Mhatre incident, I got to work with an officer nicknamed Doc Holliday. He had been moved to work beside me after punching the detective inspector at his previous station. Doc was a stocky Scot from Edinburgh with a straightforward approach. I liked him immediately.

We worked from 7 a.m. until 11 p.m. After that, we'd indulge ourselves. The computers from the ill-fated Yorkshire Ripper inquiry arrived with a full complement of female operators, so we zeroed in on them. They'd all been put in a hotel owned by Quakers, so they couldn't get a drink. We introduced them to the famous Elbow Room Club owned by Albert Chapman, one-time manager of Black Sabbath.

One morning we got a phone call to say a fellow officer called Spike had collapsed and been rushed to hospital. Spike was diagnosed with cancer. Over the next week, we watched in agony as he slowly deteriorated.

One afternoon, Doc and I arrived to find Spike sitting up in bed with tears in his eyes. 'What's wrong, pal?' I asked.

'They want to cut my fucking arm off,' Spike replied.

'What do you mean?' I said.

'The cancer is spreading, and they want to amputate my arm,' he explained. We stood in silence not knowing whether either of us would share his tears. Then Spike broke into a smile. 'Thieving bastards aren't having it, though,' he said, laughing through his tears. 'I came in with two. I'm going out with two.'

Spike kept both arms. Two days later, he was dead. At his funeral, the lesson was read by a 20-stone, rugby-playing superintendent who sobbed like a baby. A plaque in Spike's honour still hangs at Digbeth Police Station.

The worst day of my career happened while I was working in Digbeth. One Saturday, a mother and father came into the police station, accompanied by a male friend, to report that they had lost their three-year-old daughter in the city-centre Rag Market. The Rag Market was a gaggle of stalls selling clothing, dress-making materials and other cheap merchandise. The place was always very busy. A three-year-old child wandering alone in such a busy place would quickly have been picked up and handed to security.

Unknown to anyone at the police station, the father of the child had been previously arrested for abusing a young girl. Not in the sexual sense but physically. It seemed he had a dislike of female children – he had a son with whom there had been no problems. Social services were fully aware of the man's past, but, unfortunately, social services do not work on a Saturday.

When she was born, the little girl had been placed in the custody of a foster family for protection. The father of the foster family was an officer with the West Midlands Police. When the little girl reached her third birthday, some half-wit in social services decided that it would be a good idea if she was reunited with her birth family.

A large-scale search of the area came up with nothing. This was then broadened to take in the remainder of the city centre. The mother, father and the friend were separated and interviewed individually. Their accounts of the day's events were recorded. I had the task, with another officer, of speaking to the male friend. He was a little runt of a man with a previous history of petty theft. I spent two hours going over and over the day's events, and his account became more and more vague.

It was a wintry evening, and it was getting dark. I repeated a question that I had asked earlier, and the runt gave me a completely different answer. This caused a twitch in the reflexes of my left hand, and I planted a hook on his jaw, dumping him onto the floor. I was about to follow up with a right when he began screaming that he would tell us what had happened to the girl. I'd never before resorted to violence to obtain a confession, but I had a three-year-old daughter of my own, and this had shortened my fuse.

The runt began gibbering that the child had been handed back to the family on the Wednesday and that the father had begun to systematically abuse her. The mother had told him that the father had held the girl's head under water in the bath. He had then hit her in the face with a piece of wood. Finally, he had placed a ball of wool in the child's mouth and tied a handkerchief around her face. The runt said that he had gone to the family home on the Saturday morning and had been told that the child was dead. Her body was then placed in a black bin liner, and he and the father had gone out into the countryside to bury her.

After a further persuasive chat, he agreed to show us where the body was buried. We were taken to the Clent Hills, a beauty spot about 12 miles from Birmingham city centre. By the time we arrived, it was pitch black. I dragged the runt through the undergrowth, stopping at various spots where he thought the body was buried. Eventually, we found a place where the soil had been disturbed, and I scraped the surface with my hand. I shone a torch at the ground and saw a pink ear and three small pink dots that I realised were the tips of three fingers in the soil. I shouted to the other officers that we had found the body, to which one of them shouted, 'Good.' I retorted that there was, and I quote, 'FUCK ALL GOOD ABOUT IT.'

The scene was preserved and the coroner's officer summoned. The coroner, a pot-bellied man known as Quincy, named after the television series about the pathologist who solved more crimes than Sherlock Holmes, soon arrived. Quincy set about digging up the body, which he then put into a clear plastic sack. I remember seeing the child's feet, which resembled my daughter's. He then put the sack over his shoulder and strode off to his estate car, placing the little girl's corpse in the rear. I had to accompany him with the body to the Central Mortuary.

I was present when the post-mortem examination took place. Quincy prised open the little girl's mouth. Inside were bits of wood and a ball of wool. The cause of death was suffocation. I then had to watch while she was cut to pieces.

The father eventually pleaded guilty to manslaughter and received ten years' imprisonment. He should have gone down for life.

three

HELLO DRUG SQUAD

'You're a bit of a star, aren't you?' announced the detective superintendent. One of my informants had come up with a top-drawer tip-off that had resulted in the recovery of three ounces of heroin, unheard of at that time. The detective superintendent suggested I apply for a post with the Drug Squad. I'd smoked a bit of dope and tried LSD when I was 16, so I figured I was qualified for the post.

The Drug Squad was part of A Division, as was the Serious Crime Squad. It was a long-held ambition of mine to transfer to A Division to work alongside the cream of the force's detectives, and I was posted to the Drug Squad. My partner was a dapper chap who was very good on the social side of the job, which was mainly drinking and womanising.

Such was our standing in the force that one day, not long after I joined, it was announced that Princess Diana would be visiting us. She would be entertained with presentations detailing the successful operations we'd been responsible for and then taken on a tour around the building and shown the types of drugs we'd seized.

We were warned to be on our best behaviour and that bad language would not be tolerated. 'I can keep my mouth shut,' I said, 'but can Diana?'

We were also instructed to be suitably dressed. No one was to wear cowboy outfits. This was a dig at Bernard Dinnis, one of the members of the squad. Bernard was the classic medallion man who always wore his shirts open, accompanied by jeans and cowboy boots. He had wavy dark hair, and someone had once remarked that he looked like Tom Jones.

Whenever a female was around, I would say to Bernard that she had remarked that he looked like Tom Jones, to which he would respond, 'It's not unusual.'

Princess Diana arrived at the station. She was stunning with blue eyes that sparkled when she looked at you. I felt a strong urge to take her out for a meal. Not for anything romantic, more to fatten her up a bit. She was as skinny as spaghetti.

Halfway through the visit, she took a break for a bacon sandwich. This was made in the station canteen with the crusts cut off. She then used the loo, which had been specially sanitised for her. The toilet was later removed and destroyed to prevent it being captured by souvenir hunters.

Yet behind all the gloss and prestige of the Drug Squad, something wasn't right. A few weeks after Diana's visit, my team was asked to investigate the owner of a shop in Birmingham city centre. The suspect was under investigation for allegedly dealing in cocaine.

Arrangements were made for a tap to be put on the suspect's phone. I set about getting copies of his telephone bills, which showed he was a heavy phone user. One night after work, I arranged to meet other members of my team in a pub called the Queen's Head. The pub was a favourite haunt of the market-trading fraternity, many of whom were known to the police.

I arrived at the pub and began talking to a well-known detective who was working on the case. He was drinking heavily with a blonde, brassily dressed girl whose roots were starting to show through. The two of them were worse for wear and were having a good time laughing and joking. I wasn't a good drinker, so I didn't stay long.

Within a couple of days, the telephone tap went live. Despite this, the operation seemed to be getting nowhere. A meeting was called to plan the way forward. We needed to have a snoop inside the suspect's shop, but no one could come up with a method that wouldn't raise his suspicions. 'Why don't we screw the place?' I suggested.

My partner went purple and looked at the superintendent for guidance. 'Care to enlarge on that?' asked the super.

'It's simple,' I explained. 'Wait till the shop closes, then I'll smash one of his windows to set the alarm off. When the local boys turn up, we can join them in a search around the premises.'

The room went silent. The super looked at me, his eyes wide as billiard balls. 'Brilliant,' he said. 'Let's get on with it.'

A few days later, we put the plan into action. I was to break the window with a lump hammer and then disappear. The others would keep watch for the uniformed officers to arrive and then assist them with a search.

We all set up in position at about midnight. It was at that point I realised I hadn't done my homework, because right next door to the shop was a 24-hour snooker hall. There were punters going in and out, and I struggled to find an opportunity to break the window undetected.

After half an hour of fannying around, I chose my moment and launched the hammer at the window with all my strength. It broke a small hole in the glass but failed to set off the alarm. Pissed off, I pulled up a broken paving slab and crashed it into the shop window, shattering it into a million tiny pieces. I then walked coolly away.

It worked like a dream: the uniformed officers turned up, followed by my colleagues who carried out a systematic search of the shop, resulting in the recovery of valuable intelligence.

The trawl for evidence continued. One afternoon, I positioned myself in a café opposite the suspect's shop for a spot of surveillance. I hadn't been there long when I saw the brassy blonde who'd been with the detective in the Queen's Head go into the shop. She chatted with the staff like she was a long-lost friend. 'Something's not right,' I thought.

The suspect's telephone bills suddenly became very small, and the only conversations tapped were those with his wife. It seemed that the operation's secrecy had been blown. The finger pointed at the boozy detective.

I reported my suspicions to the operational commander, who sighed long and hard and said he would bring the operation to an end. This rattled me. Why not investigate why the cover was blown? My protests fell on deaf ears.

I began to take closer interest in the other operations I was involved in. One involved a drug dealer whose flat we raided. We searched the property and found ten bags of amphetamine sulphate hidden in a chair. The *Birmingham Evening Mail* reported the dealer's conviction at the Crown court for possession of 27 grams of amphetamine sulphate. Twenty-seven? That was a fraction of what I'd seen recovered. What had happened to the rest of the gear?

On another occasion, I was asked if I would take part in an operation to arrest members of the group UB40. The operation was code named 'There's a Wrap in Me Kitchen'. It soon became quite apparent that the group were being fitted up. The officer concerned was a Drug Squad legend who was having a hard time. He thought that making a high-profile arrest would be good for his career. I told him I would have nothing to do with fitting up innocent people. Mercifully, the operation was cancelled.

Along with fit-ups, I found myself struggling to come to terms with police officers around me openly dealing in drugs. It was an often-heard remark that the best drug dealers around were on the Drug Squad. I had joined the police force to lock up criminals, not to become one. The rumour was that one officer had bought a house on the proceeds of the drugs he'd siphoned off. I was so poor I didn't even own a car at that time.

I heard other stories of police officers committing burglaries in the days before the huge pay rise of 1978. Police pay was so poor that it would have been difficult to support yourself, never mind a family. I supplemented my income by working as much overtime as possible and using my labourer's training to do building work in my spare time. I stayed as far away from anything dodgy as I could. And there was no way I could report what was going on, because the police culture was such that you never ratted on your colleagues.

There was a well-documented case from a few years before of a young police officer who arrested a factory worker for stealing from his employers. It was customary to inform the CID of any arrest for theft, as they would carry out the necessary interviews. Three CID officers who had spent the afternoon in the pub set about interviewing the factory worker, but he would not cooperate. Tempers rose, and the prisoner was punched. He was led from the interview room with blood all over his face. The young constable saw this and made an official complaint of assault against the CID officers. The three detectives were arrested, sent to trial at Crown court and ended up in prison. The young constable was ostracised by his colleagues. On one occasion, he was being assaulted, and he called for assistance. No one responded, and he was beaten to a pulp.

I was young and idealistic. I decided my best policy at that time was to keep my head down and my mouth shut. But with all this going on around me, I started getting despondent. Then things started to look up.

One morning, I heard the news that Dagenham was joining my department. While I'd been barging my way up the Drug Squad ladder, Dagenham had been busy waging a one-man war on organised rings of car thieves throughout the West Midlands. His record was so impressive that the powers that be thought he was perfect Drug Squad material.

Dagenham was to be my partner. It was exactly what I needed – an ally. Once again, we became inseparable. It was odd, because even though we'd been really close before, when our professional lives had started to drift apart, so had our social lives. As soon as we hooked up again, it was like we'd never been apart. It all slotted back into place easily.

Early on in our renewed partnership we were tipped off about a prostitute who wanted her pimp put in prison. In return, she would become our informant. Prostitutes are trusted by criminals and often used as couriers for drug dealers. They are some of the best informants a copper can have.

The girl's name was Debbie. She was a coffee-skinned girl, about 20 years old. Her mother was white; her father was West Indian. Her pimp, Winston Sloane, earned around £800 a week from her. This was at a time when I was taking home £800 per month.

When Debbie first met Sloane, he wined and dined her like a girlfriend, showering her with gifts. Then one day he asked her how she would repay him for his kindness. Pressure was applied continually until she finally gave in, becoming a prostitute. To secure the payments, Sloane would administer savage beatings. Over the years, the violence and abuse increased. Finally, Debbie turned to the police for help. We agreed that if she turned informer, we would help to lock up Sloane, who was also a cocaine dealer. I told Debbie to tip us off when he was in possession and we'd bust him.

Early one morning, we hit his house. Sloane was in bed, and after a violent struggle he was subdued and ordered to dress. As he was doing so, his clothing was searched. Two wraps of cocaine were found in his pockets. Sloane went mental. Suddenly, he launched himself full length through a closed window. He hit the porch with his head on the way down, before landing on the garden path.

An ambulance was called, and Sloane was taken to hospital with me as the escort. He refused treatment and was discharged. I carted him to the police station, where he was charged with possession of cocaine with intent to supply. After a messy trial, he was convicted and sent to prison for three years.

Debbie became our informant, and the floodgates opened. Her knowledge of the drug trade was phenomenal. Her tip-offs about other local drug dealers produced result after result. The information Debbie was supplying was so good that Dagenham and I quickly became the busiest partnership in the Drug Squad office, eclipsing all the other legends.

Debbie was also great company and could drink like a fish. She would always insist on spending her tip-off money in the pub with us. Her party trick was opening beer bottles with her teeth. She offered to sleep with me as a way of saying thank you, but I declined. I have to admit, it was tempting, but why spoil a working relationship?

She even offered to work for me if I ever wanted to take up pimping and supplement my measly income with some of her earnings. Again, I turned down the offer. I was as straight as they come.

I still bent the rules a bit when it came to helping out a fellow officer. Late one night, I got a call from Dagenham on my radio: 'Meet me behind my neighbour's rabbit hutch.' Without asking why, I headed for the rendezvous. I found Dagenham exactly where he'd said he'd be, smelling of beer. We'd spent many hours in crooks' gardens on surveillance, so it didn't feel as odd as it could have. (What was odd, however, was the garden that he was hiding in belonged to a married woman I'd been shagging when I was 15 years old. But that's another story.)

'Forgotten your keys?' I asked him.

'No, mate, had a bit of a prang.'

He'd wrapped his car around a lamppost. A pint over the limit, he couldn't afford to hang about waiting for a career-threatening breathalyser test. Instead, he'd walked home across the fields only to find a patrol car already waiting for him outside his house. I drove him back to mine and gave him an alibi.

Seeing his neighbour's rabbit hutch was as close as I ever got to Dagenham's house. Even though we were partners, there was so much I didn't know about him. I spoke to his wife regularly on the phone but never actually met her because he never invited me round. If I ever gave him a lift home, he would make me drop him off at the end of his road, never directly outside his house. And it wasn't only me he kept at arm's length on the domestic front. I got to know his brother, who said that even he had no idea where Dagenham lived.

The truth was, Dagenham and I were both loners. Work was our life. Some days we'd spend eighteen hours on duty and six at home. A lot of the time, work was an escape from home life. The more of myself I ploughed into the job, the less I invested in my relationship with my own wife. Hardly surprising, then, that as my career started to go into orbit my marriage began sliding down the pan. And so, as it turned out, was Dagenham's. We both ended up divorced. As a result, we threw ourselves even harder into our work.

four

THE SECRET BEGINS

'You lot can forget your Friday night out', announced the operational commander. 'We've got a job on tonight.'

'What is it?' I asked.

'Can't say,' he replied.

'Bollocks,' came the collective response.

It was the end of another long, hard, Drug Squad week. Instead of heading out for a relaxing Friday night, our evening would be taken up with a secret operation involving the Darlaston office.

The Darlaston office was part of the West Midlands Drug Squad with responsibility for the Black Country. Officers from the Darlaston office were very similar to the locally brewed Banks's beer, whose marketing slogan was 'Unspoilt by Progress'.

The operational commander said that he could not divulge the exact location of the operation. This instantly told us that it was to be a pub raid. We'd be in the boozer after all, but not in the way we'd had in mind.

A pub raid involved Drug Squad officers together with uniformed officers from the Operational Support Unit – affectionately known as 'Hitler Youth' – being crammed into the back of a large furniture van. These Operational Support Unit officers were usually employed at football matches and other public-order events. The level of violence they encountered was well reported in the media. Their method for dealing with football hooligans was legendary and was partly responsible for the decline in violence at matches. (The other main cause of the decline in terrace violence was the increase in use of Ecstasy, which mellowed everyone out. The return of cocaine as the drug of choice has seen a re-emergence of the old-style aggression.)

Plain-clothes officers would already be in place in the pub to identify the drug dealers. The raid officers would pile out of the van into the pub and drag everyone to the ground. The floor usually ended up covered with packets of drugs thrown down by the dealers. This would then require the implementation of the 'Five Foot Rule'. Anyone found to be within five feet of a discarded packet of drugs would be awarded ownership of them and arrested.

We were instructed to go to Tipton Police Station, where we got into the furniture van and were transported to a large pub near Dudley Zoo. I tumbled out of the van like a piano falling out of a window and stormed into the pub to find the customers outnumbered by undercover police officers. It was practically empty.

Back at Tipton, the operational commander conducted his angry debrief. It was clear that the drug dealers knew we were coming. 'Somebody must have said summat,' he screeched. 'If I find out who it was, heads'll roll!'

We adjourned to a pub, where the operational commander began to entertain us with anecdotes of his glorious past. Being a lightweight, the lager began to take effect on me, and the yarns began to grate, until I suddenly piped up with, 'Blimey, gov. The way you tell it, you've had more successful operations than the NHS.'

'How dare you speak to me like that!' he erupted.

I was dragged from the premises by Dagenham before a retaliatory attack could be mounted. Over the weekend, I decided that an apology, although out of character, was the best course of action to keep me out of trouble. On the Monday morning, I strode into the operational commander's office. 'I was out of order the other night, boss,' I confessed in the most sorry manner I could muster. 'I apologise. And I hope you are big enough to accept my apology.'

Never one to bear a grudge, the operational commander immediately stopped Dagenham and me from working together. I was assigned to work with a new female detective and told to show her the ropes. She was a slim blonde with an amazing chest and was fresh from working in murder incident rooms.

Murder incident procedure had been standardised since the Yorkshire Ripper investigation, during which Peter Sutcliffe had twice slipped through the net after being interviewed by the police. All investigations throughout the country were now carried out in the same way: salient points were highlighted; actions were raised and given to officers to investigate. This brought about a breed of detectives who lacked initiative and relied on being told what to do.

The Drug Squad was different in that it was driven by informant-led intelligence. But the Slim Blonde had no informants, and my new partnership turned out to be more of a babysitting exercise. On one occasion, I asked her to make a note of all the registration numbers of the cars outside a premises we were investigating. I then told her to check the vehicles against the computer and obtain the owners' details. She'd written down every number incorrectly.

To liven things up, I squeezed one of my informants. He tipped me off about an amphetamine dealer, telling me that one of his associates was scoring speed at a premises in Erdington. We would follow the suspect, arrest him in possession and then raid the address.

I briefed my team and gave each of them his or her responsibilities. We set up surveillance and sighted the target as he drove to a terraced house in Slade Road, in the middle of Erdington. Half an hour later, the target left. We followed him for half a mile to a spot known as Stockland Green, where he stopped at a set of traffic lights. We quickly boxed in his vehicle, and I dragged him out of the driver's seat. I searched his pockets but found nothing. I then dragged him into a side street. The Slim Blonde began to climb out of the front of the car. 'Get back in the car,' I told her.

'Why?'

'You might not be comfortable with what's about to happen,' I explained. Moments later, I emerged from the side street clutching a paper wrap in one hand and the target in an arm lock in the other. 'Caution him,' I told the Slim Blonde, 'then arrest him.'

'For what?' she muttered nervously.

'Possession with intent to supply.'

'I'm not sure I can,' she started to babble.

I didn't have time for this, so I arrested the target myself. Back at the police station, I interviewed him, and he put his hands up to possession with intent to supply. We then raided the house in Slade Road, recovering several thousand pounds' worth of speed.

After the raid, I collared the Slim Blonde. 'What the fuck was all that about?' I asked.

'I wasn't comfortable with what went on,' came the reply.

'What do you mean?'

'With where the drugs came from.'

'You think I planted the drugs on him?'

'I didn't say that,' she spluttered.

'Well, I'll tell you where I found the drugs – Sellotaped to the end of his cock.'

'Oh.' The Slim Blonde's mouth dropped open.

'Just because he was a criminal didn't mean he had to go through the indignity of you staring at him with his trousers round his ankles.'

I couldn't work like this. Seething with anger, I immediately applied for two weeks' leave. Things were serious. I lived and breathed police work, and annual leave was something I took reluctantly.

Not being able to work with Dagenham was devastating. He was the one person in the world I could trust. Not just with work, but my life. Compared to me he was quiet. But he could be just as tough, just as ruthless.

On one occasion, we had a tip-off that there was some heavyweight drug dealing going on at a party. A raid was duly organised, with the Operational Support Unit drafted in as back-up. Dagenham and I arrived first to find the person holding the party was a well-known boxer. We tried to talk our way into the club, but the bouncers were having none of it. I started off by being polite. I could charm the birds out of the trees if I needed to. (I always say if you start off nice, you can then get nasty. If you start off nasty, you've got nowhere to go.)

It was time to get nasty. With my usual gift for dealing with the threat of violence by threatening even more violence, I made the situation worse. The verbal insults turned into a physical game of push and shove. Normally, Dagenham could iron out my rough approach, but this time the usual diplomatic channels were very quickly shut down.

It was five against two. Five of the handiest-looking doormen you've ever seen versus two gnarly coppers whose back-up was nowhere to be found. The sensible thing would have been to have backed off. But that wasn't in my nature. Dagenham knew this and stood firm, even though the odds were stacked heavily against us.

To reduce the odds a little, I nutted one of them on the bridge of his nose, knocking him backwards. Dagenham took a swing at another, who swerved and aimed a steel toe cap at my partner's head, missing by an inch. I caught the kicker's standing leg behind the knee, and he went down. The other three doormen piled in, and Dagenham and I ended up fending off a flurry of fists. In the melee, I managed to crack Dagenham full in the mouth.

Back-up finally arrived and arrested us. We were thrown into a prison van until someone identified and uncuffed us. I emerged with a four-inch cut on my forehead. Dagenham lost his two front teeth. He never once complained. That was Dagenham.

He never said a word when part of a door I was battering down during a drug raid swung up and caught him full on the chin. As the rest of us piled into the premises, Dagenham lay there quiet as a mouse – as people tend do when they've been knocked unconscious. This was a type of camaraderie that the operational commander who had split us up would never understand, the type of loyalty he could never inspire in others.

A few weeks after our partnership was disbanded, Dagenham and I met for a drink in the Gunmaker's Arms, a small bar two minutes from police headquarters. The pub doubled up as the senior-officers' mess, where the most important decisions affecting the West Midlands Police were made. Also in the pub was Superintendent Bob Harris, head of the Drug and Serious Crime Squad. Harris was a nice chap with a ruthless streak.

As Dagenham and I were engaged in plotting revenge, we were joined by Superintendent Harris, who listened sympathetically to our plight.

Harris and I shared a good relationship. That night in the pub he told me he might have something that would interest me, but he wouldn't say what. 'Keep in touch,' he added as they rang for last orders.

Towards the end of the second week of my leave, the telephone rang. It was Harris. 'How are you?' he asked.

'Bored,' I replied despondently. My leave had consisted of moping around the house all day, then joining Dagenham in the pub in the evening.

'DCI Sleek is running an assets-seizure course. He's struggling to make up the numbers. Do you fancy it?'

'What's an assets-seizure course?' I asked.

'It's a training course for undercover police officers.'

'How could I be an undercover officer?' I laughed. 'I'm six feet two with eyes of blue. I've got Old Bill written all over me.'

'It's a two-week course with maximum expenses,' Harris added.

'Sounds right up my street,' I declared. 'Where do I sign?'

On a bright Monday morning, I arrived at Tally Ho, the police training centre. I walked with my usual confident swagger into the reception, where the notice board gave details of the classes and the relevant room number. I made my way to the room and took a seat near the front. This was partly a ploy to show that I was confident. It was also because my eyesight was deteriorating, and I wanted to be able to see the blackboard.

At about 9.20 a.m., the door of the classroom opened, and Detective Chief Inspector Leslie Sleek stepped in. Sleek was an excellent public speaker with a fetish for odd photographs of himself. One photo he showed us was of him standing next to the Lord Mayor of Walsall with a big grin on his face. Another was of him after he'd been thrown through the windscreen of a car.

Sleek had worked for a special Metropolitan Police department known as SO10, which was responsible for all undercover police operations in London. He'd now been given the responsibility of setting up a similar department for the West Midlands Police. I was about to become part of that new set-up.

Sleek introduced us to a stocky, bearded man called Detective Sergeant Peter Odessa, who also worked for SO10. He was a charming, sharp, streetwise man with vast experience. As such, he was regarded as the high priest of police undercover operations. Odessa taught us the scams he'd used to trap criminals and recover large quantities of contraband. He then asked us to role play scenarios to see how we'd behave in certain situations. In one, I acted as a buyer for a consignment of stolen CDs. My aggressive demeanour went down well, particularly when giving evidence in the fake court room with Odessa cross-examining me.

I'd given evidence many times and had earned the nickname 'The Bully' because of my refusal to be manipulated in the courtroom. My philosophy was that attack was the best form of defence. And always answer a question with a question.

One of the main problems with infiltrating criminal set-ups is keeping yourself on the right side of the law. To remind us of this we were shown a pocket notebook, which we would use to record our meetings and conversations with criminals. Inside the front cover was a set of guidelines. These stated that no undercover officer was allowed to aid, abet, counsel or procure the commission of a criminal offence. In legal terms, it was known as being an agent provocateur. In other words, we could engage in a conspiracy of criminal activity that was already organised, but we couldn't actually initiate such a conspiracy in the first place. This was trickier than it sounds. To get round this, an undercover officer would have to record himself saying to a criminal something along the lines of, 'Now, then, I don't want you doing something you wouldn't normally get involved with on my account.'

Detective Chief Inspector Sleek outlined the back-up facilities that had been put into place to allow us to develop fictitious identities so that we could operate undercover: fake companies had been formed that could be used as references to open bank accounts; and premises were rented with telephone answering facilities that could be used for a business address. We were then each given £250 to set up a bank account. I went to a NatWest Bank and persuaded them that I'd spent years working in Lanzarote repairing timeshare property and had never held a bank account. They opened an account for me that day.

We each had to come up with an undercover name so that we could be provided with false driving licences. Mine was Ronnie Howard – my father's first and middle names. I was also given the address of a safe house that I could use as my home address. I later learned that this address was the home of Detective Chief Inspector Sleek's recently deceased father.

Our false driving licences eventually materialised, but on closer inspection the box on the document where the type of licence was indicated contained four zeros instead of the word 'Full'. They could easily have blown our cover with anyone who had any knowledge of driving licences.

Some of the group wanted every conceivable document available to back up their fake identity. There was clearly merit in sometimes carrying identity documents but not all the time. I felt that the likelihood of being compromised was increased should such documents fall into the hands of a criminal during an operation. Out there in the real world, most villains travel light. When arrested, they often only have cash, a packet of fags and a single key in their possession.

Sleek had also arranged a deal with a second-hand car business to lend vehicles to the department, many without road tax. An informant of mine told me that the only way to move with the top criminals was to look like you had money. They always stayed in the top hotels and wore the best suits. But there we were driving second-hand cars with no rent on. Not exactly a good look.

At the end of the course, Sleek set up a siege scenario. It was very elaborate, with hostages being taken away in a car that had to be followed by a surveillance unit. They ended up inside a barn on a farm. A team of negotiators – us – was then called out to bring the siege situation to an end. For authenticity, the hostage scene was even attended by the Tactical Firearms Unit. The siege went on for several hours, with the hostage takers negotiating for food and drinks. As their morale began to deteriorate, one of the hostage takers asked for the services of a priest.

'Anyone want to have a go at negotiating?' asked one of the trainers.

I jumped at the chance. 'How hard can it be?' I thought.

I entered the siege house and introduced myself as Father Flanagan. I was asked various questions to verify my identity, which I dealt with comfortably. I was then asked to recite the Ten Commandments – suddenly, I was snookered. The more bullshit you come up with in a situation like that, the more chance you've got of getting caught out, if not killed. Hostage negotiation is a very delicate skill.

When I was coming up through the ranks, one of my colleagues was faced with a jumper on the roof of a block of flats. He'd had no training as a negotiator, and the man was threatening, for the umpteenth time, to jump. Thinking that the man was bluffing, the negotiator casually encouraged him to get it over with. 'Go on then, mate,' he advised. 'Then we can all get back to work.' The man promptly did and jumped to his death. From that day on, the officer was known as Geronimo.

With training completed, each of us was sent back to our day-to-day jobs, waiting to be called upon to start undercover operations. Carry on as normal was the instruction. We weren't allowed to discuss anything with our fellow officers. Even our superior officers weren't automatically privy to what we were up to. The theory was that the fewer people who knew what was going on, the less chance there was of our cover being blown. This would later cause a lot of friction with senior officers who felt they couldn't keep a track on me.

We were each issued with pagers. Some officers wore them like a badge of office. Mine stayed in my pocket out of sight. I was careful that my photograph was never taken, and this remained the case for ten years. It is still something I am uncomfortable with.

To put me in a criminal frame of mind, I began to look for different areas I could educate myself in, such as cheque and credit-card fraud, firearms and counter-surveillance. I also signed up for an SAS training course in countryside surveillance techniques. Late one afternoon, I was dropped off in the middle of a field wearing lightweight kit with no food or water. I dug in behind a hedgerow and was told to observe a road junction, reporting anything that happened.

I remained in position all night as the ground frosted over. In the early hours of the morning, an instructor appeared out of the darkness and enquired if anything had happened. I told him nothing had. He handed me a tin of tuna fish and crawled back into the undergrowth.

So there I was, freezing to death with a tin of tuna fish and no can opener. At 10 a.m., two cars stopped at the junction, and the occupants got out and stood beside the vehicles talking. I had no means of recording the numbers of the cars other than scratching them into the ground with a stick. I remained in position throughout the day and into the following night.

At 4 a.m., an instructor appeared from the undergrowth and asked if anything had happened. I told him there had been two cars, and I had recorded the numbers by scratching them into the mud. Neither of us had a torch so we couldn't see what I'd written. He said I would have to remain in position until morning so we could record the numbers. He crawled away after tossing me another tin of tuna fish.

I lay in the dark, hungry and thirsty, for another two hours until the instructor reappeared and told me that the exercise was over. I was removed from my position, and as I got into the vehicle to take us back to base one of the instructors threw me a tin opener.

Back on duty at the station, I got stuck into routine police work, still without Dagenham. One morning, after weeks of day-to-day duties, my undercover pager received a message telling me to go to the Specialist Operations HQ. 'Welcome to your first assignment,' announced Detective Chief Inspector Sleek. 'You're going to Gloucestershire.'

We travelled to Cheltenham to be briefed by the operational commander, who was a West Midlands officer on exchange with the Gloucestershire Constabulary. He was a keen man whose enthusiasm was infectious. The task was to infiltrate the drug-dealer network in a pub called the Brewery Tap, which seemed to be selling more cannabis than beer.

I persuaded the operational commander to allow Dagenham to partner me on the operation. If I couldn't work with him on regular police work, then at least we'd be able to team up on the odd undercover operation. Dagenham was the only officer I trusted completely. He was also excellent at surveillance. His calm and unassuming demeanour meant you hardly noticed he was there. He was one of those blokes who could never get served in a pub.

Our cover story was that we were working on a new housing development on the outskirts of Cheltenham. To add to his look, Dagenham had a pretend ponytail stuck to the back of his head, which made him look like Fu Manchu – but with Popeye's forearms.

At the Brewery Tap, the cannabis fumes hit us full in the face as soon as we entered the bar. The decor had long-since deteriorated, and the furnishings were tatty and worn. The carpet was brown and sticky and made you feel like wiping your feet on the way out. In our filthy building-site attire, we fitted in well with both the decor and the soap-dodging locals.

We headed for the pool table, where virtually every opponent offered us cannabis. As the week wore on, people became increasingly relaxed and open around us. After a fortnight, we were part of the furniture. We'd also managed to identify all the main dealers.

A few nights later, I noticed a guy sitting near us with a very pale complexion. My immediate thought was that he was a smackhead. He was drinking beer, but he was also eating sweets, a classic sign of a drug addict. They all develop an insatiable sweet tooth.

'All right, mate,' I said to him. 'Fancy a game?'

'No thanks. I'm not much good,' he replied. His hands trembled so much he'd never have been able to hold a pool cue, let alone chalk the end of it. His name was Lenny, and he turned out to have a whizz habit.

Whizz is a street term for amphetamine sulphate, the poor man's cocaine. It is more commonly known as speed and was originally produced as an appetite supressant and given to troops in the Second World War and Vietnam War to keep them going. It was also used as a slimming aid for a while, until it was discovered that while dieters lost weight they also gained an unhealthy drug habit.

One thing about whizz addicts is that once they start talking they don't know when to stop. I couldn't shut Lenny up: 'You want some speed? I can get you speed if you want speed?'

'I might be interested,' I said and then hedged my bets. 'But I'm not interested in piddly grams. I'm after ounces.'

'I can get ounces for you no problem, no problem,' ranted Lenny. 'I'll get something for you for Friday. No problem.'

'If it's good gear, I'll be interested in getting hold of a lot more,' I said.

'I can get you a quarter kilo,' said Lenny.

'Only if the gear's good and the price is right,' I answered.

'Well, they usually go for £140 an ounce,' added Lenny.

'You'll have to settle for £70 on the ounce,' I said.

'I don't know about that,' Lenny replied, squirming.

'Take it or leave it,' I said, nonchalantly.

At closing time, Dagenham and I rolled out with the rabble and wandered around until the streets became quiet. When we got to the car, we found a wino asleep on the back seat. He didn't even stir as we dragged him out of the car and left him lying in the middle of the pavement.

With all the information we'd gathered, plus the overtime we'd clocked up, the operational commander was anxious to arrange a raid on the pub as soon as possible. With the patented West Midlands method for raiding pubs as our guide, we drew up a game plan for the local bobbies. 'When I go to the jukebox, that's the signal to start the raid,' I explained at the briefing. 'You lot hit the place. We'll take care of ourselves.'

The raid was set for a Friday night. Dagenham and I took up our customary positions in the Brewery Tap and waited for the evening's business to commence. The resident dealers arrived at about 8.30 p.m. and trade was brisk. Deals of cannabis were openly being cut up and parcelled on tables in the pub. As ever, the air was thick with spliff fumes.

Lenny came shuffling into the pub and headed straight for the bar. Eventually, he came over. 'Ronnie?'

'Yeah, what's the problem?' I said.

'I spoke to you last week, didn't I?'

'That's right. What do you want?'

'You said you wanted something.'

'Yeah.'

'Well, I've got it for you.'

'What have you got?' I asked.

'A quarter kilo.'

We went into a toilet cubicle, and from inside his jacket Lenny produced a freezer bag of white powder. 'I haven't got the money on me now,' I said.

'What are we going to do, then?' asked Lenny, shuffling nervously.

'Hang on to it until tomorrow. Then I'll have the cash and we can do a deal,' I assured him.

'It'll have to be tomorrow or the deal's off,' said Lenny.

Back in the bar, I gave the prearranged signal for the raid to start. But nothing happened. The two plain-clothes policewomen who were to make the first move were too busy chatting to one another to notice what was going on. In frustration, I walked across to them and said, 'Have you got any change? I'm going to the fucking jukebox.'

They quickly jumped to their feet and left the pub. Moments later, the local storm troopers burst in and dragged everyone, including me and Dagenham, to the floor, which had mysteriously become covered in packets of drugs of all sorts. Some of them were perilously close to me, but the five-feet rule didn't apply in Cheltenham, so I was searched and released. As I left, I saw Lenny being dragged from the pub bitterly complaining about his stroke of bad luck. The operational commander was beside himself at the success of the operation.

Back at HQ, we were asked to recount the details of our heroics on such a dangerous operation. If going undercover was always going to be as easy as this, then I, for one, wasn't complaining.

five

GUN TO MY HEAD

'You still having it off with that brief?' asked Sleek.

'Yes,' I replied.

'She comes from Liverpool, doesn't she?'

'She does.'

'Merseyside Special Branch need some assistance. You up for it?'

'Does Michael Palin have a passport?'

The job was in Toxteth, the scene of serious race riots in 1981. Police heavy-handedness and racial harassment had been blamed for the disturbances, which had led to black youths bombarding officers with petrol bombs and paving stones. Nine years on and parts of Toxteth were still no-go areas. Three roads – Upper Parliament Street, Croxteth Road and Granby Street – formed the notorious 'Golden Triangle'. Drug dealing was rife, and it continued to be a popular place for dumping stolen vehicles, as the police still weren't keen to show their faces around there.

Intelligence had been received that tensions were again on the rise and that the pot was about to boil over. Dagenham and I were chosen to move into the area to monitor the situation. The Merseyside detective superintendent in charge of the operation set up a meeting with us at a place called Port Sunlight, a development built by the Lever Brothers company at the end of the nineteenth century to house the firm's employees. It had been converted into a museum and café. Dagenham and I arrived early for the meeting. It was a hot sunny day, and I lay on the grass and fell asleep.

I was awoken by a Vauxhall Cavalier coming to a stop on the gravelled car park. I watched as the occupants got out of the vehicle. They were clearly policemen. They were both wearing grey suits and club ties denoting their affiliation to some CID fraternity.

After a few minutes, Dagenham and I followed them into the café and sat down in silence at a table about ten feet away. We sat there for about five minutes checking out everyone in the room, making sure that none of the pensioners that had stopped for a cream tea were likely to kick off.

The detective superintendent clearly didn't want to make the first move for fear of blowing our cover. Undercover work is hard. Perpetuating the mythology is even harder. To break the ice, I went over and introduced myself. Then we set about putting a plan into action.

Only a handful of people would know we were on the operation. We were given a special telephone number to call should we require assistance. A clapped-out gas-board van – cost £100, top speed 71 mph – completed our cover as a pair of plasterers. It was another skill I'd picked up during my days working on building sites.

On our first morning in Liverpool, Dagenham and I wandered into Toxteth and asked the locals if they knew of anywhere we could rent. We were given the address of a slum landlord who overcharged for poor-quality property. He had a flat in Bentley Road that he was renting for £70 a week. We knocked him down to £40 and moved in. The flat was in the loft of a house overlooking the street, and the location was perfect. It was at one end of Granby Street, the main road into the heart of the badlands.

Our first night in Liverpool was spent in the Philharmonic pub near Liverpool University, famous for its toilets. These are made from Victorian marble and are one of the wonders of the civilised world. The following morning, we rose early to make a reconnaissance of the area.

We walked down Granby Street and found a café. It was eight in the morning. As we were about to step inside, I was approached by a skinny mixed-race lad. 'Wa 'appenin, lah?' he said in a mix of Jamaican patois and Scouse. 'Do you want any grass?'

'Have you got any black?' I answered, asking for some cannabis resin, trying to appear streetwise.

The lad looked at me for a second, then jabbed a finger in our direction. 'Dicks. You's dicks,' he spat and walked off.

Dicks was slang for detectives. Was it that obvious? Had he really sussed us out? Or was it because we were two unfamiliar white faces? The only thing to do was front it up and stick with the plan. It was a risk but far less embarrassing than admitting to HQ we'd blown our cover after less than half a day on the job.

As we wandered around the area in search of work, I noticed a peculiar thing about Toxteth. Many of the streets seemed very dark, even in daylight. The trees that lined the roads were all overgrown and blocked out the light. Many parks in the area were in the same state. Liverpool Council couldn't afford to carry out maintenance work, as no one living in council property had paid rent for over three years.

If the local council wasn't very resourceful, the local people certainly were. 'We've got company,' Dagenham said. As we rounded the corner, I looked back and noticed that we were being followed. Two young girls, whom I remembered from the café, had been tailing us. We took them on a guided tour of the area before losing them and returning to the flat.

It was a little unnerving that the criminals were that organised. I once had a conversation with a soldier who was operating in the twilight world of terrorism in Northern Ireland. He told me how the IRA had checked him out by sending a 14-year-old boy to follow him.

My girlfriend at the time had a sister who was living in a terraced house on the edge of Toxteth that was in urgent need of renovation. We set about plastering the house from top to bottom and soon became a familiar sight in the local area. The neighbours began to enquire if we could carry out similar renovation work to their homes. We were only too happy to oblige, as it helped maintain our cover story. To hammer it home, we wore the same boots and clothes – caked in plaster – we had been working in when we went out in the evening. One bar we frequented was called Peter Kavanaghs. At the time, it was well populated by the drug-dealing fraternity. They were understandably cagey around two rough-looking blokes from Birmingham.

One evening, we went to Kavanaghs to watch the football. It was the summer of 1990, and England were playing Cameroon in the World Cup finals in Italy. The pub was filled with black lads all rooting for Cameroon. It was the first time in my life that I'd been subjected to racial abuse. The atmosphere became really aggressive when England got a very dubious penalty seven minutes before the end. When our second penalty was awarded in extra time, Dagenham grabbed my arm. 'I think that's our cue to leave,' he said, steering me towards the door.

Nothing really fazed me, as I knew I could handle myself. Back in the Midlands, I had a reputation amongst criminals for being a copper you didn't mess with – not unless you wanted to run the risk of having your teeth knocked out or a lump of your scalp pulled off. But there are some things that you just can't defend yourself against. Bullets, for example.

Sitting in the flat late one afternoon, Dagenham and I heard two gunshots right outside our window. We went outside and saw the body of a man lying in the gutter with one arm on the pavement. The street was deserted. As we walked towards the body, a young girl appeared from the front garden of a house and stood beside it. She began screaming hysterically. As I got closer, I saw a dark red pool forming under the man's head, like lava seeping from a volcano.

'Is he dead?' asked Dagenham.

'Very dead,' I said. 'Shot twice in the head. He's been executed.'

We returned to the flat and contacted Special Branch to report what we'd seen. We then returned to HQ for an update and to strengthen our own security, which we felt wasn't what it could be. If there were to be any problems, we needed to know there'd be back-up.

Back in Birmingham, Detective Chief Inspector Sleek was no longer head of the Specialist Operations Department. He'd been moved to concentrate on the Force Intelligence Department. The new head of Specialist Operations was Detective Chief Inspector David Donovan, who had been my detective inspector while I was serving with the Drug

Squad. He had arrived at the Drug Squad with a reputation for being a ruthless pursuer of top-drawer criminals. There were a number of legends in the squad who insisted that drug-related crime was different from dealing with conventional criminals. Donovan refused to accept this and questioned them about the long-term operations they all seemed to be engaged in, which mostly apppeared to be an excuse to go to the pub. Donovan brought this to an end by instructing each legend to take out a search warrant on the homes of their target, bringing the shams to an end. In many cases, this also coincided with the termination of the legend's Drug Squad career.

Now on Specialist Operations, Donovan told us that the Merseyside Force were impressed with the intelligence we'd been providing. I was quite surprised by this, because we'd only passed on information about low-level drug dealers. There didn't seem to be any sign of civil unrest. The population of Toxteth were far too stoned to start a riot. I suggested to Donovan that, with the help of an informant, I might be able to dig a bit deeper.

My main informant was a man called Billy The Truth. I nicknamed him this because when I asked him for information about crimes, he could never resist the temptation to tell me. Once he started, you'd have to shoot him to shut him up.

Billy was into house burglary, stealing only cash or jewellery, which was easy to shift and virtually untraceable. Any victim who was properly insured would always get their goods back in some shape or form.

Billy The Truth could tell a good story, too. Like the time the house owners returned while he was in the living room. He had to lie behind the sofa for four hours whilst the owners watched television before retiring to bed. Or the time he was disturbed by a noise while he was in the garden of a house he was about to burgle. He hid behind a garden shed only to find his brother there about to burgle the same house.

Billy was an excellent informant, but the only way to remain a good informant was to be involved in criminal activities. His information helped me to solve some major crimes. He very rarely let me down. I always treated him with respect and paid him well. He would come to me for advice on many things, and I managed to keep him out of prison for a number of years.

I asked Billy who he knew in Liverpool, and he told me about a man called Joe Amobi, who dealt in powder cocaine. He said Amobi could usually be found at the community centre. Our surveillance of Toxteth had already taken us into the community centre, a place with sentries on the door and a very unwelcoming atmosphere if your face didn't fit in. One night, Dagenham and I had played ignorant, strolled in and started to play pool. The locals had tried to intimidate us, but we had acted like two idiots from out of town who didn't understand that we were being threatened. It had seemed to dissipate the air of menace. Had we reacted aggressively, it could have got very messy. For them, I mean, not us.

I asked Billy The Truth to introduce me to Amobi. After I gave him a number of assurances concerning his own safety, he agreed.

Amobi was a member of a large drug cartel and his family were well known in Liverpool for their sophisticated drug-distribution network. They were operating on such a large scale that they had become engaged in similar activities to the Mafia. They'd launder the profits of their drug trade by setting up legitimate businesses that created employment for people in the area. They were considered untouchables. The Merseyside Drug Squad were understandably enthusiastic about the possibility of infiltrating the family.

I was adamant that I didn't want any surveillance team following me, because being found out could place me in serious difficulty. I reasoned that I should be safe, as my informant was known and trusted by Amobi. I also argued that there was no point in overcomplicating things by bringing Dagenham along.

The plan was for Billy The Truth to introduce me to Amobi. I would then arrange a deal directly with Amobi at a later date. This would distance Billy The Truth, who would be out of the way by then, from the bust. After the rendezvous with Amobi, I was to make my way through Liverpool to the M56 motorway, where I would be met at the Little Chef diner to debrief the superintendent.

At 10 p.m. the following Thursday, Billy The Truth drove me into

Toxteth. We were lucky we weren't arrested for dangerous driving on the way, as Billy's control of the car was shaky to say the least. 'Have you ever passed a driving test?' I asked him as he narrowly avoided another collision.

'No,' he replied. 'I paid one of my mates to take it for me.'

We pulled up to the community centre and parked outside. We waited, but there was no sign of Amobi. Billy rang Amobi's mobile phone, but it was switched off. As we were waiting, the rear door of the car opened and someone climbed into the back seat. Without even introducing himself, he produced a small freezer bag of white powder. 'Look, this is great gear,' said the man. 'I can do you a very nice deal.'

'We're not interested, mate,' said Billy politely, 'so fuck off out of our car.' With that, he turned around and punched the dealer in the mouth, sending him scrabbling back out of the door.

We drove off to look for Amobi in some of the pubs around Toxteth, but there was no sign of him. Half an hour later, we returned to the community centre and made our way inside. A group of teenagers around the pool table stopped playing and stared at us. My training had taught me that there were certain rules when walking into strange, potentially hostile, surroundings. The first was not to make eye contact with anyone. The easiest way to induce a hostile reaction is to eyeball people. Ordinary people don't look each other up and down. It's a trait too often displayed by police officers and is a dead giveaway.

One of the pool players recognised me from before and held out his fist in greeting. I met his fist with mine, and the tense atmosphere immediately subsided. Billy asked if Amobi was around, and we were directed to a closed door at one corner of the room. Standing by the door was an enormous black man. 'Who you looking for?' asked the man mountain.

'I'm looking for Joe,' said Billy.

'Wait there,' said the mountain, and he put his head round the door.

A minute later, the door was opened to reveal a tiny broom cupboard that doubled as an office. Inside was an old school desk and chair taking up most of the floor space. Behind the desk sat a heavy-looking man in his early 40s. Standing next to him was a wiry, younger man in his 20s. Neither of them spoke.

Billy The Truth broke the ice. He greeted the older male in Jamaican patois: 'Wa 'appenin, Joe? Tell me now, tings good or what?'

'Yeah, man, good, good,' said the older man, nodding.

'Joe, this is my friend Ronnie. He's looking for some charlie. He's after powder.'

'Ain't got nothing,' said Amobi with a shrug.

This was for my benefit: a white man with a permed Third Division footballer's hairstyle in a black man's club trying to buy cocaine. Billy then began to give references. 'Look,' he insisted, 'this man's good for it. He's got money.'

I seized the opportunity to set out my stall: 'Look, I want something regular. I don't want no credit. It's straight cash. It will be just me and you, nobody else. I don't want no one knowing my business. You get me? I'll come and collect the parcel myself.' This effectively took Billy The Truth out of the loop, distancing him from any future bust.

'Maybe we can do something,' Amobi muttered. 'You got to call me and tell me what you want, and you come straight away. I don't want nothing laying around here, you know?'

'No problem,' I assured him. 'Whatever you say. But I need a weighed gram of powder for me to take back to Birmingham so we can wash it and make sure it's safe.'

'That'll be £80,' Amobi answered.

'Look, d'you want to do business with me or not?' I asked, sneering. 'I'm talking big business. Ounces, not grams. Give me the sample for nothing. You can stick the money on top when I come back.'

'Fucking hell, man, I never even seen you before and you want me to lay the stuff on you for nothing?' snapped Amobi.

'Look, I wouldn't have come all the way up here if I was going to rip off a gram,' I replied, firmly going into bully mode. 'I'm coming back with big money. I got to know we've got some trust. Otherwise this is a waste of fucking time.'

This lively conversation went on for about ten minutes, until the bully finally wore him down. Throughout my undercover work, I always refused to pay for any samples of merchandise. If a criminal would part with a sample without cash changing hands, it provided a good indication of his position in the hierarchy of a criminal conspiracy. Also, obtaining a free sample was the first real negotiation with the criminal, and if this battle was won, the upper hand had been gained at an early stage.

The request for a weighed gram of cocaine was a simple tactic to ascertain the purity of the drugs, which were often stepped on, i.e. mixed with impurities to bulk up the weight and inflate profits. A favourite ploy was to put glucose or bicarbonate of soda into powdered cocaine. A gram of powdered drug would be 'washed up' into a rock of crack cocaine and then weighed. If the rock weighed almost a gram, the powder was of high purity.

'Meet me back here in an hour,' Amobi said.

Billy The Truth and I returned to the car and went to a nearby pub for a drink. An hour and forty minutes later, Amobi arrived back at the community centre, and we were shown back into the broom cupboard. His companion produced a wrapped gram and handed it to me. 'I'll get this checked and call you in a few days,' I said. Amobi's companion gave me his pager number.

Billy and I then made our way out of Liverpool, through the Mersey Tunnel, to a Little Chef, where the detective superintendent was waiting. I handed over the gram of cocaine. 'I'm gobsmacked. I never expected this to happen so quickly,' the superintendent said.

I returned to Birmingham, and the following day I contacted the detective superintendent in Liverpool to discuss how to progress the operation. This was the point at which undercover operations usually became difficult. Dealing with criminals was child's play. It was always the police bureaucracy that caused the problems.

I suggested that I negotiate the purchase of half an ounce of cocaine from Amobi at a cost of £600. I explained that I couldn't order a kilo of cocaine from a man whom I'd just met. This he accepted, but he said he would have to seek higher authority to sanction the spend before we could progress. West Midlands undercover operations were blighted with the same reluctance to spend money, particularly Drug Squad operations.

It took several days before the Merseyside Drug Squad granted the authority. I paged Amobi and arranged to purchase half an ounce of cocaine the following Thursday. When that evening arrived, I met the detective superintendent and the detective inspector at motorway services off the M62 for a briefing on the night's proceedings. I was handed the cash, which I folded into dealers' wraps of £100.

'Can't you just negotiate with Amobi to get a larger package of cocaine?' the superintendent asked. 'I can't see the point of spending this money with him first.' I explained that I had to build up a relationship first. Then we could go for the big one and get him put away properly for 12 years.

I drove to the community centre. I arrived at 10 p.m., and, once again, there was no sign of Amobi. I paged him and got a message saying he'd be there within the hour. I went inside the centre to wait. At 11.20 p.m., Amobi arrived with his young sidekick who was at our first meeting. I followed them into the broom-cupboard office.

'What is it you want?' asked Amobi.

'A half-ounce of powder.'

'It's £700 for half.'

'Look, mate, I thought we were trying to set up a relationship here. It's no good if you're going to try and rip me off from the start.'

'You can have an ounce for £1,200, but it's £700 for the half. You still owe me for the gram.'

We haggled for several more minutes until I got him to accept £600.

'Wait here,' Amobi instructed me. He left the office with his sidekick and locked the door. The office was eight feet by six feet with no windows. The only way out was through the locked door. I was trapped. I swallowed hard and began to wonder what I'd got myself into. As security, I'd taped a flick knife to my leg, but I would have been better off with a lock pick. I sat down at the desk, my mind racing. I began to sweat. This was *serious* shit. After 20 minutes, I heard a key in the door. It was opened by Amobi and his companion.

As ever, I believed that attack was the best form of defence, so I flew into a rage. 'What the fuck d'you think you're doing, locking me in here?' I ranted.

Amobi stuttered an apology: 'I don't want no one coming in here while I am away. This is my business.'

'I hope for your sake you've fucking got what I came for,' I raged, half in annoyance and half in relief.

'It's here,' he said, producing a small bag of white powder. I opened the bag, removed a tiny quantity of the powder and rubbed it between my thumb and first finger. Cocaine hydrochloride (powder cocaine) has its own distinctive smell and bitter taste. When rubbed between the thumb and first finger, the powder has a soapy feel. Cocaine is also completely soluble in water, so if a small amount is dropped into a glass of water, it should immediately disappear – anything remaining would be an adulterant. I could feel the soapy texture of the drug on my fingers and it had a bitter taste in my mouth.

'Is this good gear? Because if not, I'll be here tomorrow for my money back. You understand me?'

'It's good gear,' Amobi assured me. 'Now, where's the money?'

'I've got to go and fetch it. I ain't walking in here cold with cash in my pocket.' (It was, in fact, in the sole of my shoe.) 'You can come with me if you want.' He declined.

I placed the cocaine in a brown envelope I'd brought and sealed the envelope with Sellotape. I then handed it to Amobi. He looked perplexed by this until I reminded him that we were still learning to trust one another. Wrapping up the drugs made it more difficult for him to switch the merchandise. It also made the drugs more difficult to dispose of when an arrest took place.

I left the club and took a drive around Toxteth, returning 20 minutes later. I removed the flick knife from the tape on my leg and put it into my trouser pocket. I went to the office and counted out £600. Amobi's minder was standing on the opposite side of the desk. He maintained eye contact but said nothing. I had the impression he was attempting to be menacing, but I was eight inches taller and fifty pounds heavier. There was a short pause, and I found myself looking between Amobi and the kid.

Suddenly, I had a gun in my face. 'So you want this regular?' the kid said, pushing the silver semi-automatic into my cheek.

I felt a mix of anger and fear. I was angry that I'd let myself get into such a situation. I thought about the flick knife but realised I'd be a dead man before I even got it out of my pocket. I could feel the barrel of the weapon beneath my right eye. I looked along the slide on the top of the weapon, searching for the calibre of it in the hope I would see '8 mm' – the sign of an imitation firearm. The markings were on the other side of the slide, the side I couldn't see.

I didn't know whether to shout or shit myself. I tried to maintain a defiant glare – difficult when your head is pounding ten to the dozen. My natural reaction was to give the kid a mouthful. Then I had a flash of the man in the road with blood oozing from his head. I gritted my teeth and breathed heavily through my nose.

'There's a war going on around here,' the kid said. 'People are trying to move in on our yard. If you want something, you come to us. You get me? No one else.'

I said nothing until he removed the gun from my cheek. 'You know what?' I said when the gun was finally back in his pocket. 'This fucking deal is off. First you lock me up. Then you stick a gun in my face. Give me the fucking money. I'm out of here.'

This caught Amobi by surprise. 'Hey. It's cool, man,' he stuttered, raising his hands in some sort of apology. 'We got to protect ourselves. You are a stranger, man.'

'Another stunt like that and I'll give you a fucking war,' I shouted.

At that point, I heard raised voices coming from the club. The kid opened the office door, and I could see that five angry-looking men were trying to push past the enormous bouncer, who was knocked to the floor and kicked. Things were getting really nasty. The club had erupted into one very violent brawl.

Amobi and the kid retreated back into the office. I took the opportunity to push past them, through the crowd of flying fists and feet, and outside onto the steps. I ran to the car, floored it and sped off along Upper Parliament Street. Out of the back window I saw a dozen or so men spill out of the club. Suddenly, there was a flash, followed by the thud of a shotgun being fired, then the sound of something hitting the rear of the car.

I accelerated away into Liverpool city centre, then through the Mersey Tunnel and Tranmere until I reached the Little Chef restaurant. The detective superintendent, who was accompanied by his inspector, climbed wearily out of his car as I approached. 'We were beginning to give up hope for you,' the superintendent said. I looked at my watch: it was 3 a.m.

'Sorry about that, but time keeping is low on the criminal agenda,' I said. I produced the half-ounce of cocaine, at which point I was asked if I had spent all the money. I said I had, which was greeted with obvious disappointment. I then gave a detailed account of what had just happened. There were indentations in the boot lid where the pellets from the shotgun had hit the vehicle. The superintendent said that the safety of the operation would now have to be reassessed in the light of the developments.

The following day, I was informed that the operation was to be terminated. I received a commendation for my undercover work. It read, 'By performing duties in difficult circumstances with ingenuity, commitment and enthusiasm, the objective of the operation was successfully achieved.'

A few weeks later, Amobi was found executed in a similar fashion to the man we'd seen shot in Bentley Road. The front page of the *Liverpool Echo* reported this as the brutal murder of a Liverpool businessman. The truth was that he was the victim of a drugs war the police didn't know how to handle. No one was ever charged with the murder.

six

THE PHANTOM PHOTOCOPIER

I returned from Liverpool a very different man. Life on normal police duties seemed very quiet in comparison. Detective Chief Inspector Donovan was using his informants to set up undercover operations, and I made myself available to the departmental HQ to assist in running them.

One afternoon, I bumped into Terry Heath, a fellow undercover officer whom I'd known for many years – we'd risen through the ranks together. Terry was a first-rate detective with vast experience, and he was a very capable handler of informants. He was also a very sociable bloke, but I never managed to get him into the pub once in all the years we worked together. He was either very health conscious or very under the thumb.

As time went on, Terry and I were to work together on a number of successful operations. He was excellent in the role of being the first man in, paving the way for me to follow. He always struck up a friendly relationship with criminals, leaving the hard nut and violent stuff for me to handle.

Terry had gone undercover to investigate the theft of high-end photocopiers, which were worth thousands of pounds. He'd been approached by criminals to rent office space to set up a scam. This involved the con artists making a personal visit to a showroom to order a machine. The copier would then be delivered in pieces to the business address rented by Terry. An engineer would follow an hour later to assemble the machine and deliver the invoice. By the time he arrived, the copier would be long gone.

On one occasion, the criminals were in the process of removing a photocopier from an office, but the engineer arrived early and caught them in the act. The thieves ran off. Unless we caught them in possession of the machine, we had no evidence to arrest them.

I suggested to Detective Chief Inspector Donovan that I should be introduced as Terry's business partner so we could continue the operation. Terry arranged a meeting at a pub called the Orange Tree near Warwick, where I was introduced to the two scammers, known only as Roger and Bryan. Roger was a skinny rodent of a man with a bald head and a wispy moustache to go with his rat-like features. Bryan was a younger, quieter individual who had an enormous black eye, which he said he'd got playing rugby.

'If I'm putting money into this,' I said, 'I need to know it's not going down the pan.'

'There'll be no hitches, I promise,' Roger replied confidently. 'As soon as the machine comes in the front door, we're straight out the back door with it.'

The problem was that their faces were now known locally, so they'd decided to shift their operation down to Cornwall. 'There's a copier place in Truro,' Roger explained. 'They're all yokels down there, and they won't be very switched on. Also, renting an office will cost nothing.'

Terry and I reported back to the operational commander. His first question was how the West Midlands Police could get involved in a scam taking place 300 miles away. I pointed out that the original conspiracy had taken place in Birmingham, which gave the West Midlands Police jurisdiction.

The Regional Crime Squad offered to send two officers to Cornwall as back-up. I had two weeks to complete the operation, as I was due to travel to New York with Dagenham. With this time constraint in mind, I set off with Roger and Bryan in their Ford Sierra, accompanied by Roger's collection of George Michael cassettes. The journey down the M5 was broken with a stop in Exeter.

'Let's make a few quid while we're here,' Bryan suggested.

'What have you got in mind?' I asked.

'Watch,' said Bryan, who went into a pound shop and bought a roll of bin liners. He then walked into a store selling jeans and casually started browsing through the racks. I sat on the public benches outside the shop and watched an expert shoplifter at work. His anti-surveillance techniques were quite good. While he was browsing, he turned the hangers around so they could be removed easily. Then he took a couple of pairs off the rack and dropped them into the bin bag. He left the bag in the shop and walked out of the door. If no one followed him, then he hadn't been spotted by the cameras. He waited a few minutes, returned to the shop and then took a dozen more pairs off the rack in one sweep. He dropped them into the bin liner and walked smartly out. It was ridiculous to watch so many pairs of jeans just disappear. And no one said a thing.

We continued on to Cornwall, heading for Penzance, where we'd chosen to rent an office. We found rooms above a pub called The Castle. That evening, Bryan got amongst the customers to sell the jeans he'd stolen. This was good for integrating with the locals, but wasn't that clever, as it drew too much attention to us. Things could backfire on us before we'd even got the photocopier scam up and running.

At closing time, we finished our drinks and went to our rooms. I was in a single room, and Roger and Bryan were sharing the room next door. I thought nothing of this until I'd been in bed for about half an hour and was disturbed by strange noises coming from the next room. As I listened, I realised it was the sound of two men wrestling naked on a bed, one of whom was having his back door kicked in with some gusto. Roger and Bryan were closer than I thought.

The next morning, the two of them turned up for breakfast wearing suits and ties. This was in complete contrast to the two toerags I had driven down with the day before. 'You two look like you just fell out of Burton's window,' I said, laughing.

'If you're in business, you've got to look the business,' smiled Roger, delivering a line I'm sure he'd used a hundred times before.

Most of the day was spent searching for premises. We found an office in a converted garage that we got for next to nothing. The next morning, Bryan and Roger went to see Roger's ex-wife, who lived nearby. 'She could be useful if we need any extra help,' explained Roger. 'Her new husband has got a van, and he said we can borrow it if we need to move anything.'

'Fuck me, how many people have you told about this scam?' I snapped. 'The more people that know, the more the chances of it going tits up.' They both went quiet. It was the first time they'd seen my temper. It wouldn't be the last.

I took advantage of their sheepish mood. 'Look, where is this machine going to end up?' I asked. 'We're going to have a right pain trying to move something that big around without getting noticed.'

'It's in bits when it's delivered, which will make it easier to transport,' Bryan explained. 'We're going to take it back to my sister's garage in Coventry.' Obligingly, he scribbled the full address and even a contact phone number on a scrap of paper I'd torn out of the Yellow Pages. This was all very casual, but it would later become evidence of his involvement in a conspiracy to steal.

The next day, Bryan and Roger asked me to drive them over to the photocopier dealer in Truro to set up the scam. 'I'll drive, but I'm not coming in,' I said. 'I'll leave the negotiation to you two.'

I dropped them near the Canon showroom. After an hour, they returned in a sombre mood. 'They've gone a bit safe on us,' Bryan said. It seemed that their bungled attempt at theft in Birmingham had echoed around the copier dealers. The delivery procedure had now changed, and the engineer had to accompany the copier. They also wanted payment on delivery.

That evening was spent with Roger and Bryan in dejected silence in the bar of The Castle while they tried to work out how to get their hands on a copier. 'What about a forged bank draft?' I suggested.

'Brilliant. But where do we get one?' asked Bryan.

'I might know someone who can sort us out,' I said. 'Leave it to me.'

The next morning, they weren't at breakfast. I went to their room, but they weren't there, and they hadn't checked out. An hour later, there was a knock at my own door. 'Told you she would come in useful,'

Roger said, smiling smugly as he entered the room with one of his bin bags over his shoulder.

'What do you mean?' I asked.

Roger responded by emptying the plastic sack onto the bed. Out tumbled a sawn-off shotgun. 'Borrowed it from my ex's new husband,' smiled Roger. 'We can use it to stick up the engineer and nick the copier!'

'Are you off your fucking heads?' I asked. 'We'll get 20 years if we get caught with that. Take it back or I'll wrap it round your neck.'

'But they're away till the weekend,' said Roger.

'Well, you'll have to hide it,' I ranted. 'I want it out of my sight by the time I get back.'

I went to a payphone and called the operational commander, who didn't like the idea of firearms being involved. He said we would have to abort the operation. The problem was that if I pulled out now there was no way of knowing if they'd go ahead with the hold-up. 'They don't even know which end of the shotgun makes a bang,' I said.

'It's too risky,' said the operational commander. 'We'll have to arrest them.'

The local police were contacted for assistance. They said that if they arrested the two men, they would release them on bail pending a decision by the Crown Prosecution Service. There was a good chance they'd be freed. Then I had an idea. I contacted the back-up team and told them to get over to Penzance. I returned to The Castle, where Roger and Bryan were in their room, looking despondent.

'Where's the gun?' I asked.

'It's in the boot of the car,' said Bryan.

'I thought I told you to get rid of it.'

'We don't know what to do with it.'

'Take it to the office,' I ordered. 'Now, here's the plan. I've just spoken to a mate who says he can forge a bank draft. We need the full details of the company the draft needs to be made out to.'

Bryan called the photocopier dealer to confirm that a bank draft would be acceptable. Then he scribbled the payment details on a page of the company's brochure that showed the model of the copier we were after. More evidence.

'How soon can we get the draft?' asked Roger.

'Couple of days. But we're not doing anything till that gun's gone back. Now, get that fucking thing hidden.'

I sent them off to the office we'd rented and said I was going to pick up an extra padlock to stop the landlord wandering in unannounced. 'Wait for me there,' I instructed them. 'Don't leave the gun until we can lock up properly.'

Half an hour later, Roger and Bryan answered a knock at the office door. They were expecting to see me. Instead, they were greeted by my back-up team who had followed them from the pub. They searched the premises, found the gun and arrested them. By that time, I was on a train on my way back to Birmingham.

Roger and Bryan appeared before the Crown court, facing charges of conspiracy to steal and possession of a firearm. They were sentenced to seven years' imprisonment.

Immediately after the operation, I spent a week in New York with Dagenham. The trip was financed by the Broad National Bank of New Jersey as a thank you for the arrest of an Iranian criminal called Hamid.

Hamid was studying in Britain at Birmingham Polytechnic. He lived in a house in the Erdington area with his wife, who he regularly beat up. His nephew also lived with him. The nephew had relatives in New Jersey, one of whom went into the Broad National Bank and arranged to wire $670 to his uncle. The employee carrying out the transaction left a finger on the zero button, and $67,000 was sent to the nephew's account at the Midland Bank in Birmingham by mistake. When the money arrived, the manager of the bank asked if he could be of service by investing the $67,000 (about £45,000 at that time) on Hamid's behalf. However, the nephew was told to draw out the money in a bank draft made out in his uncle's name.

Realising its mistake, the bank in New Jersey contacted the police in Birmingham. That evening, Hamid was arrested and interviewed. The bank draft was nowhere to be found, and he refused to disclose what he'd done with it. He was eventually charged with theft and received three years' imprisonment, but the money was never recovered.

After his release, I received information from an informant that Hamid was dealing in heroin. Dagenham and I got a warrant to search his house. There we found heroin and an extensive collection of pornographic Polaroids featuring his girlfriend. We also found a catalogue from the Swiss Banking Corporation. Beside the Manchester branch was a small pencil mark. I contacted the branch, and it was confirmed that Hamid had deposited the bank draft with them.

The Broad National Bank recovered their money and offered us the trip to New York to show their gratitude. And who were Dagenham and I to turn them down? It was one of the very rare perks of the job. It wasn't particularly well looked on, but it certainly wasn't corrupt.

The one and only other time I accepted more than a thank you was from a millionaire who had his car stolen. Harry Bramble was a steel stockholder. One night, he took his wife to a restaurant in the centre of Birmingham. At the end of the evening, he went outside to find his car had been stolen. The car turned up a few days later in the Perry Barr area of Birmingham. It was up on bricks and had been stripped of anything of value.

When Bramble was told about the state of the vehicle, his first remark was, 'So it's gone then?'

'What's gone, sir?' asked the officers in charge of the investigation.

'The £7,000 cash and box of my wife's jewellery that were in the boot.' The total value of stolen goods was nearly £20,000. This made it a CID matter, and I was put in charge of the investigation.

I immediately arranged for the vehicle to be fingerprinted, but the scenes of crime officer was a clumsy twat. His shoes were permanently silver from all the metallic fingerprint dust he spilled. There was a rumour that he'd once attended the scene of a burglary at a scrapyard and had got his foot stuck to the electromagnet they used to pick up damaged cars. To my surprise, he found a single fingerprint on the rear arch of the car. It belonged to a criminal from Perry Barr, which was where the vehicle was recovered.

I took out a search warrant on the villain's home address. The suspect, who was unemployed, was out. The lad's father, an ex-para who had served his country, was completely unaware of what his son had been up to. We searched the lad's bedroom and found a locked wooden box. We forced this open and discovered £4,000 in cash. A search of his sister's bedroom uncovered a leather pouch stuffed with the most amazing jewellery I had ever seen.

The crook's dad – who was potless and unemployed – was pissed off when we told him how much money we had found. We waited for his son to return. When the lad arrived, he gladly pointed the finger at his two accomplices, who had already begun to spend the money on cars and holidays. One was due to fly out to Greece the very next day. We soon put a stop to that.

We contacted Bramble and arranged to return the jewellery and what was left of the cash. We were invited round to his house, which was amazing. It had expensive-looking furniture, a full-sized indoor swimming pool and a better-stocked bar than any pub I'd ever been in. His prized possession was a photograph of himself with his fist under the chin of Muhammad Ali.

I handed over the cash and the leather pouch containing the crown jewels. I asked Bramble what the true value of the jewellery was. He said £30,000 was a conservative estimate. That's the equivalent of about £90,000 these days.

'I would like to reward you for all your efforts,' he then said gratefully.

'Well, you're more than welcome to make a donation to the police benevolent fund,' I suggested.

'But none of you will necessarily benefit from that,' Bramble pointed out.

'That's true, sir,' I acknowledged.

'How many detectives were involved in this recovery?'

'Five,' I said in a flash. He then invited all five and their families to a meal at the Galleria restaurant to say thank you. That was my first and last night as a bent detective.

seven

MILKING IT

Early one morning, before the streets were aired, I stood blinking on a doorstep with a sledgehammer in my hands. A nod from a fellow officer and I sent the hammer crashing against the door on a level with the lock. The lock gave in, the door swung open and half a dozen of us piled through the gap and into the darkness.

'Police! Nobody move!' was the advice offered free of charge to anyone – but hopefully a criminal – who happened to be on the premises . . .

I'd returned to my day job with the Drug Squad. I was posted to work in operations that involved taking off a suspect's front door in the early hours of the morning and trusting to good fortune that there'd be drugs on the premises. While there'd been plenty of action, recovery rates had been down of late.

One morning, I was summoned into the detective inspector's office. 'How are you getting on with your new posting?' he asked.

'With all due respect, sir, I'd be getting on much better if I could team up with Dagenham again and do some proper detective work,' I replied. 'Just a suggestion, sir,' I added. 'You know best.'

A week later, I was informed that I was to remain independent but could work alongside Dagenham if operational requirement demanded it. Result. I quickly began to pull together an operation into a group of Asian milkmen who were suspected of dealing in heroin. The main target was a man known as Tariq Shaffi. Every member of the Shaffi family had been flagged by the Regional Drug Unit, but, as yet, nothing had been followed up.

The Regional Drug Unit was, at that time, a newly formed arm of the Regional Crime Squad. Senior management were finally beginning to accept that the heavyweight criminals of the 1960s and '70s, those who favoured robbing with the aid of a sawn-off shotgun, were now turning their attentions to the profits to be made in drug dealing. At the same time, police forces were forming dedicated firearms units with improvements in training techniques. It was becoming more and more likely that criminals carrying firearms would be shot dead by armed police officers.

Search warrants were taken out for the home of Mushtaq Shaffi, Tariq's father, and the rest of the family addresses. If drugs were found at one address, common sense would suggest the others should be searched.

In the early hours of a cold rainy morning, we assembled at the station, where I conducted the briefing. 'Dagenham and I will go with Officers Flarty and Rogers to execute the warrant at the home of Mushtaq Shaffi,' I barked. 'The remainder of you will observe the remaining addresses until we know the result of the initial search.'

Officer Flarty was a six-feet-tall, eleven-stone ex-Royal Marine who was as hard as nails. He was totally reliable, provided he had not been anywhere near his local watering hole, The Brit in the Acocks Green area of Birmingham. When on leave, Flarty would often visit his father in Ireland for a Guinness binge. The village in which his father lived only had one telephone, which was in the chemist. If ever I needed to contact him to remind him to come back to work, I would ring the chemist and leave a message. Flarty would turn up in Birmingham so saturated with booze that if we took him to the pub, he would be dribbling after two pints of beer. The two of us had disagreed on a number of occasions, usually when the demon drink was involved. We'd often squared up to fight, only to be dragged apart by Dagenham.

We left the station in separate groups and headed to Mushtaq Shaffi's home, a council property in a quiet grove off the main Alum Rock

Road. We parked short of the entrance to the grove and made our way towards Shaffi's house on foot. I was carrying a sledgehammer to open the front door.

I checked my watch: it was 5 a.m. The lights were on in the house. This was no real surprise, as Shaffi would usually be up at that time because of his job. We made our way quietly to the front door. I belted it with the sledgehammer, and we all piled into the house.

'Police! Nobody move!' I yelled. Nobody did move, mainly because the house was empty, with the exception of a small dog who was cowering in the corner of the living room. Our search eventually took us into the kitchen, where Dagenham went into a small pantry and found a tall freezer. Moments later, he held up a large plastic bag containing some brown powder. 'Well that's the business, that is,' he declared quietly. If it was heroin he was holding, it would have a street value of at least £1 million.

'The big fat hairy business, I'd say,' I replied, laughing.

This now meant that we could nail Tariq and Mushtaq Shaffi. The rest of the team then executed the search warrants at the other premises. No drugs were recovered but large amounts of cash were found. This would easily be explained away as the proceeds from the milk-round business.

We scoured the streets until we found Tariq Shaffi and, finally, his father Mushtaq, who were both delivering milk. Each was searched, and they were found to have a gram of heroin on them. This heroin was later examined together with the kilo we'd recovered and found to be similar in composition. Tariq and Mushtaq Shaffi were arrested and taken to Steelhouse Lane Police Station, where they both asked for legal representation.

Mushtaq Shaffi admitted that the kilo of heroin was his property. Tariq Shaffi only admitted possession of the gram found in his pocket. At HQ, I was met with a steady procession of officers who had never seen a kilo of heroin and had come to gaze.

Mushtaq Shaffi pleaded guilty at the Crown court, where he received a sentence of 12 years' imprisonment. Tariq Shaffi was granted bail and fled to Pakistan, never to return.

At one time, Iran was the largest producer of heroin. It was from this that the Shah of Iran obtained a large proportion of his wealth. When the Ayatollah Khomeini came to power, heroin producers were stood against a wall and shot. Some managed to flee across the border to Pakistan to continue their trade. They were welcomed with open arms into villages where there was no real industry or employment.

A few weeks after the milkman bust, I was executing a search warrant at the home of a crack dealer who was a particularly violent individual. As we burst into his bedroom, the dealer picked up a knotted polythene bag containing three large batteries and began to attack us. 'Yarrrrrgggggghhhhh!' he yelled, swinging the makeshift mace.

'Rarrrrrgggggghhhhh!' we yelled back, as Dagenham and I launched ourselves at him like a pair of savages.

In the confusion of the struggle, I punched one of my colleagues in the mouth, Dagenham kicked someone in the face and Rogers bit my leg. The dealer was finally subdued after someone picked up a large bag of builders' sand and threw it on his chest. What a bag of sand was doing in the living room of a flat on the 15th floor was anyone's guess, but it did the trick. And that, as far as we were concerned, was reasonable force.

When he had eventually calmed down, I noticed a large burn scar on the side of his face. 'Did you answer the phone while you were doing the ironing?' one of the officers asked him with a smirk.

'No,' replied the dealer, stone-faced. 'My mother did it to me when I was a kid.' No wonder he'd turned out so violent. And no wonder we'd had such a struggle to subdue him.

The question of reasonable force has always been a double-edged one. Chief Constable Geoffrey Dear once asked me what I would do if I had to assault a criminal for my own defence or to further an operation. In reality, I wouldn't have thought twice about it. Punch first, ask questions later. 'Well . . .' I said, struggling for the legally correct response.

Dear quickly put me out of my misery. 'Provided the assault is justified, then you should never worry about it,' was his take on the matter.

Dear was one of the most forward-thinking chief constables of the day. He had dragged the West Midlands Police, once known as the 'Force of a Thousand Mackintoshes', out of the 1960s and into the '90s.

Despite this, the 1990s was a turbulent time for the West Midlands Police. A Crown court case collapsed amidst allegations of criminal corruption made against officers of the West Midlands Serious Crime Squad. The squad had carried out investigations into serious crime with phenomenal success, particularly thefts of cash in transit – security-van robberies. But they were coming under increasing media pressure concerning the methods being used by squad members to achieve results. Allegations ranged from fabrication of confessions to torture. One such torture method was to place plastic bags over the heads of criminals, who were then starved of oxygen until they signed false confessions.

All these allegations were thoroughly investigated by the South Yorkshire Police. The inquiry cost the taxpayer £1 million and produced no evidence to support any charges. Even so, our Serious Crime Squad was eventually disbanded.

To this day, criminals are still being released from sentences because they were originally arrested by the Serious Crime Squad. The Birmingham Six were released partly because confessions had been recorded by members of the squad. Their convictions, for planting two IRA bombs in Birmingham city centre, killing nineteen people and seriously injuring nearly two hundred others, were deemed to be unsafe.

The disbanding of the Serious Crime Squad had a traumatic effect on the force. Chief Constable Dear was overlooked for a knighthood that he had been in line for and was sidelined into a civil-servant job. Senior officers throughout the force who had served with the Serious Crime Squad earlier in their careers were placed in non-operational posts, their careers in ruins.

One officer I knew on the squad was called Larry Shaw. Larry left the police force and ended up committing armed robbery on a post office two miles from where he used to work. During the robbery, he apologised to a customer, saying, 'Sorry about this, love.' He was eventually arrested and sentenced to 12 years' imprisonment at Warwick Crown Court.

A new chief constable, Ronald Hadfield, was appointed and given the task of steadying the force and restoring confidence. He was an old-fashioned copper from Yorkshire, whom we nicknamed 'Biffo', which stood for 'Big Ignorant Fucker From Oldham'. Hadfield quickly devised the 'Three Year Plan' for reorganising the force, which appeared to be based upon the working practices of Marks & Spencer, linked as it was to providing a good service. My interpretation of this was that if crooks broke the law, then I would lock the bastards up by whatever means. That, in my book, was providing a good service. Sometimes it was easier said than done.

One Sunday morning after a heavy night on the lager, I was sitting in the living room when the phone rang. 'Hello, mate. Got a tip-off for you . . .' It was Dave Donovan. By that time, he was a chief superintendent. He still maintained contact with his informants, unlike some people in senior management who felt that dealing with such dirty business was far beneath them.

'There's a premier-league villain staying in a suite in the Midland Hotel,' he explained. 'He's dealing top-drawer cocaine. The informant said the villain has got ten ounces of coke. He says it will be hidden either above the ceiling in the bathroom or in a suitcase in the wardrobe. He has got a young prostitute with him. He will be in the bar of the hotel at lunchtime.'

The target's name was John MacPhee, a Glaswegian who was moving down to the Midlands to set up a protection racket to extort money from the owners of saunas and massage parlours.

To obtain a search warrant for the hotel suite on a Sunday morning would be a long process, which would involve contacting the Force Control Room, who would then contact the out-of-hours magistrates clerk, who would then contact a Justice of the Peace at home. We would then have to go to the home of the Justice of the Peace to swear out the search warrant. This would eat up several hours, and we'd miss the opportunity to nick MacPhee.

I remember one occasion when I needed an out-of-hours search warrant. The magistrate in question invited me into his house and offered me a malt whisky, which I had to decline. The normal procedure was for me to take the oath on a Bible and give information on the premises we wished to search. The magistrate would then grant a search warrant by signing the document. I asked if he had a copy of the New Testament. He was Jewish, so he didn't have one. We stood around for a few moments, considering what to do next. Then the magistrate piped up. 'Will this do?' he asked, holding up a copy of a well-known magazine.

'Fine by me,' I answered. 'I won't tell if you won't.' I then swore out a search warrant using the *Radio Times* for a Bible. Well, it is for some people, I suppose.

To avoid taking out a search warrant, the plan was to nick MacPhee outside his room. Once he was arrested, we had the power to search any premises of which he was the occupier.

I called a team together, including Dagenham, and arranged to meet them at the Drug Squad offices. We made our way in convoy into the city centre and entered the hotel by a rear entrance. Inside the bar, I saw an oak tree of a man with a red beard and a small blonde girl in tow. Talk about the stereotype of a Scotsman.

In an instant, Dagenham and I had a grip of him by both his wrists. 'I am arresting you on suspicion of intent to supply drugs,' I informed him. As I did so, something fell to the floor: a piece of silver foil folded neatly into a small oblong. It was a wrap of cocaine. MacPhee and the girl were whisked away to Steelhouse Lane Police Station.

We then made our way to MacPhee's palatial suite and began to make a search. There were all sorts of drug-dealing paraphernalia in the room: silver foil, scales and a blackened dessertspoon that had been used to wash up cocaine. There were piles of cash everywhere.

Dagenham removed the suspended ceiling in the bathroom, and I began to search the wardrobe, which was full of expensive clothes. At the bottom was a suitcase. Packed in amongst the clothing there was a large freezer bag containing ten smaller bags of cocaine. Each bag contained about an ounce of coke that was hard as rock, similar to a pumice stone.

The phone in the suite rang continually. The callers were customers trying to place orders for cocaine. It appeared that MacPhee had a real cottage industry on the go, selling cocaine from his hotel suite.

MacPhee admitted to possessing the cocaine that was in the wardrobe, but he would not admit that he had been dealing. He was charged with possession with intent to supply and scheduled to appear before the courts the following day.

The blonde had come from an escort agency. She'd been with MacPhee for two weeks and had been paid by the day. She would not assist with any information about MacPhee's activities, but she did say that, during all the time she'd spent with him, he hadn't laid a finger on her. She was released from custody without charge.

MacPhee agreed to assist the police by giving them information. When he appeared before the courts, we made an application to have him remanded to police cells for three days. He was then taken to Chelmsley Wood Police Station, where there were facilities to house supergrasses.

The intelligence on MacPhee was enormous. He was a premier-league drug dealer, suspected of involvement in firearms incidents back in Manchester. He had reportedly fired a shotgun out of a car at rival criminals. He was also suspected of the murder of a criminal who had been shot in the face with a sawn-off shotgun.

MacPhee kept us entertained for three days but came up with little information of use. He told us how he'd doctored the firing pins on firearms to alter their identity after they had been used in crimes. He also told us that his brother Billy had been photographed on the drive of the home of John Stalker, the former deputy chief constable of Greater Manchester Police, to give the appearance that he was leaving Stalker's house. Stalker was involved in an investigation into the activities of the Royal Ulster Constabulary, and this was an attempt by supporters of the police in Northern Ireland to discredit him. And that was all he came up with. Useless, really.

A police officer from Manchester then called to say that he wanted to interview MacPhee but would not say what about. We suspected that the officer might be on MacPhee's payroll, such was his evasiveness.

We spent the next few weeks trying to prevent him from being bailed from custody. On a number of occasions, he produced sureties for his bail – people willing to guarantee his appearance at court. They were all criminals, so we knocked him back each time.

MacPhee eventually appeared before the Crown court. I gave evidence for two days. This culminated in the defence making an application for our informant to be named. This would have meant revealing the identity of Dave Donovan's grass. The prosecution withdrew the case, as the naming of an informant was sacrosanct. If they revealed who had given the information, the whole informant system could grind to a halt. People could get killed.

There is nothing worse than watching a criminal who you know is guilty walk free, or having to return cash, knowing full well the money is from the proceeds of drug dealing. MacPhee walked away a free man thanks to a clever barrister willing to try his luck. The irony is that the trial judge said he was disappointed that the prosecution had folded so easily, as he might not have been sympathetic to the application to reveal the name of the informant.

MacPhee went on to fight in Bosnia as a mercenary. He spent three years fighting for the ultra-violent wing of the Croatian army. Several years later – 3 May 1998 – he appeared on the front page of the Scottish newspaper the *Sunday Mail* under the headline 'Monster'. He'd been trying to sell the story of his exploits in Kosovo in which he admitted to killing innocent women and unarmed men. He boasted, 'I did my job, killing all who came before me. Enemy after enemy. I never looked for a uniform.'

Had we managed to lock him up when we had the chance, he wouldn't have been free to butcher people in a conflict that had nothing to do with him. You win some, you lose some. Unfortunately, we weren't the only losers on that occasion.

eight

CANNABIS GANG BANG

'You mustn't follow him,' came our instructions. 'If he spots you, it'll go off quicker than a fireman's hose on fireworks night.'

Dagenham and I had received a tip-off about the importation of a large consignment of cannabis from Amsterdam, the clearing house for most of the drugs in Europe. Our target was Leroy McCoy, a well-known and much-feared face in the drug fraternity. Our informant insisted that surveillance could not be used on McCoy, as he was ultra wary. 'He's sly as they come,' continued the informant, 'and he isn't the sort you want to mess with.'

'If we can't follow him,' I said, 'then we'll have to befriend him.'

It was time to send someone in undercover. It was too risky to use anyone from the Midlands force in case the target recognised them. Instead, we sent in two officers from the Met who posed as potential buyers for the drugs.

McCoy took the bait. He confirmed that a large importation of cannabis was coming, but he could not give any firm dates. The undercover officers took a trip to Amsterdam to meet the suppliers, who gave details of the different types of cannabis being imported. Frustratingly, they would not reveal the delivery date.

At that point, we were duty bound to inform Customs and Excise. The first thing Customs did was to put a surveillance team on McCoy. (When he was later arrested, McCoy informed us that he knew he was being followed. One snowy evening, he noticed seven vehicles parked in the same street with no snow on their roofs. To top that off, one Customs officer walked past him, nodded and said, 'Good night.') We eventually persuaded Customs to withdraw the surveillance on the understanding that we would keep them fully informed of any developments. We also had to withdraw the undercover officers, as Customs had made it too dangerous for them to operate. We went back to relying on our very reliable informant for information.

The intelligence we received was that McCoy was working alongside a man called Earl Ivanhoe. Earl was the son of Kenneth Ivanhoe, a well-known drug trafficker who had recently been jailed.

On 14 December, our informant contacted us to say that the drugs had arrived. He didn't know the exact location, only that they were in a garage somewhere near St Andrews, the Birmingham City football ground. Dagenham and I spent the evening touring round all of the industrial developments in the area. At 10.30 p.m. we came across the Imex Trading Estate, a honeycomb of small factory units. We parked the car and went on foot into the poorly lit estate. It was a bitterly cold night and raining heavily.

On first impression, the place seemed deserted, but as we walked deeper into the complex we heard the sound of voices coming out of the darkness. We backtracked to the car and drove into a quiet side street. This gave us the opportunity to observe the entrance of the estate without being seen. As we watched, a man appeared carrying a large cardboard box, which he placed in the back of a white van. He was joined by three others who were also carrying boxes. Behind the white van, I noticed a black Golf GTI. A large Rastafarian came out of the darkness carrying a box, which he placed in the boot of the Golf.

'Let's clobber them,' I suggested, keen to get the job over and done with as quickly as possible.

'There's too many,' Dagenham replied, ever the voice of reason. 'No point in blowing it. We need back-up.' This was easier said than done, as the rest of the Drug Squad were getting trousered at the annual police Christmas party. All except me and Dagenham. For us, work came before everything else, even socialising.

The van and Golf GTI started to drive off. I wanted to follow. 'Let them go,' Dagenham suggested. 'We need to find the source of the gear. Then we can sit and wait for them to come back.'

We radioed through the registration numbers of the van and the Golf. They checked out as false plates. We then went back into the darkness of the trading estate, where we eventually found a unit with a large blue Ford Transit van parked inside. There were wet tyre marks up to the entrance, indicating that the van had been driven recently. On one side of the warehouse was a long bench covered with tools that were kept neatly in a row. The opposite wall of the unit had shelves labelled with the names of vehicle parts. I climbed through a window at the rear and let Dagenham in. We peered through the window of the Transit and could see that it was full of large cardboard boxes. A closer examination revealed Dutch writing on the boxes. We'd found the gear.

It was now almost midnight. 'Where the fuck is our back-up?' I wondered aloud. A lack of sleep was catching up with me.

After another half-hour of frustrating calls, all we could come up with were two officers from Customs and Excise. I was detailed to remain inside the factory unit, while Dagenham and the others secreted themselves along the approach road outside. And then we waited.

Just after 5 a.m., my radio crackled into life. A middle-aged West Indian was approaching the factory unit. He parked his car outside, and as he was about to enter the unit, I dragged him through the door, swung him round and put him in an arm lock. 'You're under arrest . . .' I began.

Before I could finish what I was saying, one of the Customs officers stormed into the unit and declared, 'I claim these drugs in the name of Her Majesty the Queen.'

'You and Her Majesty can fuck right off,' I growled, irritated that he should try and claim the glory for all my hard work. Even more annoying was the fact that the bloke I'd just pinned against the wall wasn't McCoy.

Customs backed off, the interloper was removed and the trap was set once again. We returned to our positions and waited. At that point, I realised I had been at work for 24 hours. I had eggy breath and was badly in need of a shave.

I was daydreaming a little when the door of the unit opened and in stepped Leroy McCoy. He was a large, well-built man of about fifteen stone, and he was well over six feet tall. His reputation as a hard man meant nothing to me. If you hit the hardest bloke on the planet hard enough, he's going to go down. I'd lamp him first, and ask questions about his reputation later.

I once spent an entire afternoon locking horns with a criminal who was one of the biggest meatheads in the Midlands. He was one of the infamous Birmingham Zulus, a group of football hooligans responsible for many nasty acts of violence. Some of them also made a tidy living out of all sorts of scams, including ram raids and drug dealing. The meathead Zulu was trying to offload a quarter of a million pounds' worth of stolen tax discs on me but wasn't making a very good job of it. I got more and more annoyed, yelling and screaming and pushing him around. Afterwards, the surveillance crew told me that they couldn't believe that the thug hadn't decked me. It just didn't occur to me that I was in any real danger.

In order to infiltrate the Zulus, I'd had to hang out with them and go through some heavy interrogation. As a final test of my allegiance, one of my interrogators waved a knife in my face and told me to prove how committed I was by stabbing someone in the bar. I took the knife from his hand and stuck it straight back into his shoulder.

Stabbing is not a silent act – not like in films. I know this because he squealed the pub down. But instead of bearing the brunt of his anger, I earned his respect. I suspect if he ever finds out who I really was, there might be a blade with my name on it somewhere in the vicinity of St Andrews.

Yet no matter how fearless you feel, you always have to be on your guard. Criminals are dangerous animals. In 1985, a Metropolitan Police officer called John Fordham was staking out the criminal Kenneth Noye. Noye was under surveillance as a suspect in the Brink's-Mat robbery. A gang had broken into the Brink's-Mat warehouse at Heathrow Airport expecting to find cash. Instead, they found gold bullion worth £26 million. The criminals then had to dispose of the haul. Noye was brought in to help smelt the gold down to make it untraceable.

Noye stumbled across Fordham and a colleague in his garden. One officer escaped, but Fordham was stabbed fifteen times and died. Noye was arrested and charged with murder but put forward a case of self-defence. He said that he'd come across a man on his property wearing a black ski mask and had feared for his own life. Noye was acquitted. Eleven years later, he was convicted of stabbing to death a motorist who cut him up on the M25.

Coming face to face with drug dealer Leroy McCoy in a darkened warehouse held no fear for me. I've never been afraid of physical violence, no matter the size of my opponent.

For a second, we both stood there just looking at one another. Then I came to my senses and slammed him against the wall by shoving my forearm under his chin. He was slow off the mark, and I didn't need a second invitation. I caught him with an uppercut just below his ribcage. Then I fell into him with all my bodyweight, driving the air out of his lungs. As I landed on him, I felt something hard in his jacket under his left arm. He'd come tooled up.

McCoy was winded and gasping for breath. With no time for niceties, I head-butted him, catching him full across the bridge of his nose. With a crack, it split open. His head snapped back and hit the wall with a sickly thud. I followed up with a punch to his now broken nose. Then another, and another. Each time, his head bounced back up off the brick wall and back into my waiting fist. I spun him over and pulled his arms behind his back, giving him a whack on the back of the head with a pickaxe handle that was lying on the bench.

'Stop! Stop!' McCoy screamed. He'd gone down like a pile of Lego. As the saying goes, the harder they come, the harder they fall. But I was still taking no chances. I gave him a final crack with the pickaxe handle and reached inside his coat for the weapon. What I pulled out was a mobile phone. I threw it across the factory, and it broke into pieces as it hit the floor. On another day, it could have been a loaded pistol.

McCoy's pockets also yielded a set of keys to the Transit, which incriminated him nicely. He was arrested and taken to Steelhouse Lane. We then went for his partner Earl Ivanhoe, who was dragged from his bed. The two were charged with conspiracy to import cannabis.

At the debriefing, the operational commander announced that a press release had been sent out detailing the success of the operation. 'That's ridiculous,' I argued. 'We haven't finished locking up any of the other people involved.' The reason for such an early press release was so that those in charge could beat their chest in public. The West Midlands Police had suffered such bad publicity with the demise of the Serious Crime Squad that it was considered a nice change to have some good news to report.

West Midlands Police made a habit of this, often to the detriment of the undercover set-up. The Metropolitan Police once ran a hugely successful operation from a second-hand shop that they set up to buy stolen goods in an area with a burglary problem. The shop was wired with video and audio equipment to record all the transactions. After they collected sufficient evidence, people were arrested and prosecuted. This idea was adopted by West Midlands Police. However, we used a van fitted with video and audio equipment to act as a mobile second-hand shop at a fraction of the cost. An advert was placed in the local papers offering to buy electrical goods. We were inundated with stolen gear. It was phenomenally successful and dozens of arrests were made. Then management made the outrageous decision to release video footage from the van to the media. This was all very well for senior officers who wanted to get their names in print, but it put an end to a very effective method of tracking down stolen goods.

This latest announcement could jeopardise our chances of catching those involved in distributing the marijuana. Pissed off, Dagenham and I adjourned to the pub. This was a mistake, as we were both exhausted.

'How long have we been at it?' Dagenham asked.

'Forty hours,' I announced after a very slow totting up.

The lack of sleep and the booze quickly took effect, and I got slaughtered. I awoke in the early hours of the following morning sitting in an armchair in the Drug Squad office. I went home to clean myself up and then returned to work to find the whole floor of the office covered in cardboard boxes from the bust.

It was the largest recovery of drugs the force had ever had. Each box was full of all types of blow: resin, herbal cannabis, Moroccan cannabis. The resin was in nine-bars – blocks that weigh nine ounces, four of which make up a kilo. Each of the nine-bars had a strip of lead tape on it. If the boxes were X-rayed, the drugs would look like electrical components.

The Super then informed everyone that he was closing the office over Christmas for two weeks. I spent several days lying on the settee at home alone, catching up on my sleep. The day after Boxing Day, I was bored, so I decided to go for a drive. I'd had a tip-off about the Golf GTI we'd seen outside the industrial estate.

I drove down Dudley Road towards Handsworth. The black GTI was on a petrol-station forecourt with a 'For Sale' sign on the windscreen.

I asked the garage owner about the GTI. He said that a guy called George Erskine had put it on the forecourt and had left a phone number where he could be contacted. I flashed my police ID and persuaded the garage owner to give me the keys. I also left a note for Erskine to contact me. The number I left was an ex-directory number into the Drug Squad office. This number was used by police informants so that they didn't have to go through a police switchboard or use a regular police number.

A week later, I received a telephone call from a solicitor. He said that he understood we were looking for the Erskine brothers and that they would present themselves at Steelhouse Lane at 9 a.m. the following morning. This was quite a surprise to us, as we didn't know Erskine had a brother.

The following morning, the Erskine brothers turned up at Steelhouse Lane with their solicitor and were arrested. Their home was searched, and officers found a cardboard box with Dutch writing on it, the same type in which the cannabis had been imported. Both the brothers denied any knowledge of such a box in their house. They also denied owning a black GTI. We went ahead and charged them with conspiring with Leroy McCoy and Earl Ivanhoe to import the cannabis.

The case was heard before the Birmingham Crown Court. I had two days in the witness box, as did Dagenham. It was amusing watching Leroy McCoy jumping up and down in the dock when he thought the defence had achieved something in their cross-examination. Then came the point in the trial at which the Erskine brothers put forward their defence. The first Erskine brother said that he knew nothing about the cardboard box found in his house and that he had never owned a black GTI. An application was made by the defence that there was no case against him, which the trial judge accepted, and he was released.

George Erskine also denied knowledge of the cardboard box or having been present when the cannabis was unloaded at the Imex Trading Estate, and he denied owning a GTI. It wasn't registered in his name, so we couldn't prove it belonged to him. As he stood in the witness box looking smug, I seized the opportunity to bury him.

I walked to the front of the court and handed a letter to the prosecution barrister, who read it and handed it to the defence barrister. He also read it and threw the pen he was holding down on the bench. He sighed and said, 'I have no further questions.'

The letter was then read out to the court. It had been sent by Erskine's solicitor after I'd picked up the keys to the GTI. It said that he was representing George Erskine and that the police had possession of his car, a black GTI, which he demanded be returned to his client. Erskine's own solicitor had effectively got him successfully prosecuted.

McCoy was convicted of importing 443 kilos of cannabis and received 12 years' imprisonment. Earl Ivanhoe and George Erskine were convicted of conspiracy to import cannabis. Ivanhoe received eight years' imprisonment and Erskine seven years'. Erskine was convicted on the grounds that he owned the GTI. Ironically, that was the only real evidence against him. If he had admitted that he owned the car but had lent it to someone else on the night of the drug pick-up, he might have walked.

Criminals, and their representatives, aren't always as smart as they think they are. A few years previously, I had arrested a criminal called Hubert Phillips, together with Lionel Webbon, Wesley Stephens, Leo Moran and John Bullman, a gang that was regarded as the top armed-robbery team in the north of England. I arrested them for conspiracy to rob a Lloyds Bank in the Hockley area of Birmingham. The tip-off came thanks to the alert observation of an officer who had spotted the four men standing at a bus stop. The officer had also noticed a yellow

Security Express vehicle delivering cash to the nearby Lloyds Bank. A surveillance operation was set up, and three weeks later the four of them were arrested. Phillips' home was searched, and £13,000 in cash was recovered, along with a kilo of cocaine.

In court, the gang put forward the defence that they were standing around near Lloyds Bank for three consecutive Thursdays discussing a proposed drugs deal. They claimed that the presence of the Security Express vehicle on each of these days was a coincidence. Despite photographic and observational evidence, the jury believed the defence, and the four men were acquitted. Phillips pleaded guilty to another charge of possessing cocaine with intent to supply and was sentenced to 12 years' imprisonment. (Webbon was later murdered, shot in the face with a sawn-off shotgun after ripping off other criminals in a drug transaction. John Bullman is now serving 25 years for a bungled armed robbery.)

Prior to the trial, Phillips had been concerned that the court would seize his assets, so he had asked a friend called Thomas Sutherland to sell a couple of his houses and hide the money.

Phillips and Sutherland were convicted of conspiracy to dispose of the assets of drug trafficking. It is ironic that the Drug Trafficking Act 1986 came into force in 1987, and Phillips was arrested for possession of the kilo of cocaine a year before. The law was not retrospective, so Phillips' assets were actually safe from seizure. Had he not tried to sell them, he would not have faced further charges and would not have lost both his homes.

As a postscript to the McCoy case, our informant told us that the criminals who supplied the drugs in Holland sent someone to watch the trial. When a consignment is seized by the police or Customs, criminals usually write off the loss. However, the Dutch gang heard our evidence regarding the boxes of cannabis being removed from the factory unit. Not all of the gear had ended up in the raid, so McCoy was presented with a bill from the Dutch mob for the outstanding cannabis.

As a result of McCoy's conviction, Dagenham and I were commended by the chief constable. We attended his suite of offices, where we were given tea and biscuits. He thanked us sincerely for the good press the operation had brought on the West Midlands Police in difficult times. The certificates he gave us bore the following inscription: 'For dedication, resilience and professionalism displayed during Operation Longline, which resulted in arrests and the recovery of £3 million of drugs.'

nine

MIAMI NICE

'Scotch, anyone?'

'Don't mind if I do, sir, thank you.' We had a new boss. And he liked a decent whisky.

The chief constable had recently set about getting rid of some of the senior managers. Detective Chief Inspector Donovan had moved on, and Inspector John Gretton, an intelligent man with a law degree, was given command of the Specialist Operations department. Gretton was popular throughout the force for his dry sense of humour. He was also open-minded enough to listen to lower-ranked, but more-experienced, undercover officers. At departmental meetings, he dished out decent amounts of single-malt whisky, which eased proceedings along nicely.

As part of our development, Gretton arranged for a visit by two officers from the Miami Police Department Street Narcotics Squad. It wasn't unusual for us to swap information with police in America. Once, we had the legendary Joseph Pistone, otherwise known as Donnie Brasco, come to visit us. Back in the 1970s, Brasco had infiltrated the Mafia, gathering crucial evidence relating to murder, blackmail, protection rackets and drug trafficking. He was so accepted by the Mafia that he was on his way to becoming a made man.

While Brasco's undercover record was better than mine, I was uneasy with some of the stories he told. Perhaps it was my own experience of working with people who were legends in their own imagination. They tended to exaggerate the truth.

The Miami officers, Detective Pablo Camacho and Sergeant David

Riggs, were a little more down to earth. They came to lecture us on crack cocaine, an emerging drug in the UK back then. Crack is made by washing cocaine. Washing is a process in which powdered cocaine is dissolved in water and then mixed with an alkaline substance, such as bicarbonate of soda. A small amount of heat is applied – a microwave oven will do – to drive out any impurities, leaving the base cocaine behind to congeal into rocks. It is called crack because of the crackling noise it makes when it is smoked.

After the lecture, I took the officers out for a drink to talk about American football. I was a huge fan. It turned out that Riggs had been a successful college player and was now coach of his force team. Each January, the Miami police played at the Orange Bowl against a team from either New York or Los Angeles. The game was known as the 'PIG Bowl' – 'PIG' stood for 'Pride, Integrity and Guts'.

'Why don't you come over?' suggested Riggs. 'Come and have a look at how we do things. We'll show you around. Watch a bit of football. You could call it research.' I didn't need to be asked twice.

I flew to Miami seven days after the Lockerbie air disaster. Dagenham and Frankie 'the Dog', the Drug Squad dog handler, were with me. We were on the sister aircraft of the one that got blown up by the Libyans. Our flight was understandably empty, so we drank plenty of beer to calm our nerves.

We arrived in Miami jet-lagged and more than a little drunk. We were taken to a hotel suite, paid for by the Miami police department, where we had 24 hours to adjust to the time zone and sober up.

At the Street Narcotics Squad offices the following day, we were immediately made to feel at home. There was a bloke called Billy Perry from Birmingham working there. 'Yow alright?' he asked in a broad Brummie accent. Back in the UK, Billy had spent a great deal of time supporting schoolboy soccer. He'd brought a number of teams to Miami. He liked it so much that he stayed and became involved with the narcotics department.

Billy took us out on patrol to witness an undercover sting operation in progress. Officers posed as dealers selling drugs to potential buyers, who were then arrested. I couldn't quite see the point of this, because no drugs were actually being removed from the streets. I told Billy what I thought. He didn't seem that bothered. 'Never yow moind,' he said, laughing. 'It keeps everyone on their toes.'

The next day, Billy took us out on a more conventional drug bust. Members of the 'narc squad' pulled up alongside a drug dealer, jumped out of their cars and piled on top of him. Although not very sophisticated, it was a little bit like watching American football, so I quite enjoyed it.

On the evening before the PIG Bowl, Pablo treated us to a dinner cruise to the Bahamas. In reality, it was a floating casino. Once the ship left American waters, those on board were legally allowed to gamble. I wasn't a gambler, so I kept myself entertained by bothering the celebrity guests on board. Gloria Estefan was there, as were television actors Fred Dryer (from the show *Hunter*) and Michael Talbot (Detective Stan Switek in *Miami Vice*). Dagenham and I ended up propping up the bar with Michael Talbot at 7 a.m. the following morning. At that point, the ship's captain politely asked if we'd get off his boat, as everyone else had gone home and he wanted to do the same.

Later that day, as guests of honour at the PIG Bowl, we were introduced to Don Shula, the then coach of the Miami Dolphins and a bit of a hero of mine. Halfway through the game, there was a full-scale display by SWAT teams with helicopters, dogs and lots of guns – all favourite subjects of mine. In the end, the cops from Miami won the game comfortably.

That night, I went to dinner with a young lady I'd met on the gambling cruise. We ended up in bed, and she invited me to stay with her for the rest of the trip. She was a district attorney, who also turned out to be a nymphomaniac. After two days, I called Dagenham to help me escape, and I spent the last two days hiding at the other end of Miami.

At the end of the week, we flew home, trying to recall if we'd actually learned anything new to improve our investigation skills. 'Maybe it's our memory skills we should be working on,' suggested Dagenham, shortly before he fell asleep. Perhaps we should have paid more attention.

The day after we left, Pablo Camacho recovered 64 pounds (30 kilos) of cocaine in an undercover operation. The same day, a death threat was made against him by a drug dealer. A week later, the same drug dealer was found dead following a bust. He had the imprint of Pablo Camacho's training shoe on his face. Pablo and another officer were charged with murder but were later acquitted by the grand jury.

Back in the less glamorous surrounds of the Midlands, Dagenham and I met Billy The Truth for a drink. He listened wide-eyed to our accounts of Miami Beach. The conversation then turned to the subject of crack cocaine. 'It's already taking over,' Billy said. 'Handsworth is drowning in the stuff. I'll see what I can come up with.'

Within a couple of days, Billy was on the phone. A well-documented criminal called Roger Blackford was dealing crack. The real reason Billy knew about the drug was that he was using the stuff, and Blackford was supplying him.

Blackford was placed under surveillance, and one afternoon we intercepted his car only to find Billy The Truth behind the wheel. 'What the fuck are you doing in this car?' I asked him.

'I'm not sure,' answered Billy, clearly stoned. 'Blackford is in his kitchen preparing his crack deals,' he added hazily. 'You'll catch him at it if you move quick enough.'

It wasn't that simple. We could end up compromising Billy if Blackford found out that we'd stopped his car. 'Fuck it. Who knows when we'll get such a clear opportunity again. Let's put his door in.'

At Blackford's, we tried to smash our way in with sledgehammers, but the door wouldn't budge. I ran into the back garden and hid beneath the kitchen window. Sure enough, an alarmed Blackford opened the window and threw out bags of crack cocaine. I picked them up as evidence. Meanwhile, the front door finally caved in and Blackford was arrested. He was sentenced to five years' imprisonment, and we recorded the first recovery of crack in Birmingham.

I've since met Blackford in the street, and we shook hands. He even managed a smile. Top-drawer criminals don't make complaints. Blackford knew he was due an arrest.

While I had the grudging respect of the criminals I busted, it didn't always follow that I had the respect of the people I worked for.

Despite my record, my bosses didn't always back me up. One day, me and my big mouth suddenly found ourselves on the transfer list.

I was caught slagging off some fellow officers whom I felt weren't pulling their weight. Rather than kick the slackers off the squad, management shunted me off to Erdington CID in an effort to keep the peace. Fat chance. My bullish reputation went before me. The bosses at Erdington found it difficult to deal with my forthright attitude. They were also unhappy about my lengthy disappearances on undercover operations, because they were never told where I was going or what I was doing.

For me, those undercover operations were a lifeline. It was what I was good at, and I had the commendations to prove it. But their secret nature meant only a few people knew exactly what I was up to and what I was capable of. The other downside was that working undercover could be a very lonely existence. I found myself spending a lot of time in hotel rooms on my own, unable to discuss anything with family, friends or even work colleagues for fear of compromising the operation. All I had to turn to was the mini-bar or the porn channels, which were about as hardcore as *Blue Peter*.

Even though I thrived on pressure, in hindsight I realise that it would have been good to have had some form of release. It's the one thing they never trained me for or counselled me in. I saw many a good officer crack under the strain.

Relationships were few and far between as a result of all the secrecy. I went missing for long periods and could never explain where I was. Any woman with half a brain would become suspicious. Not that women were hard to find. The trouble was I was so preoccupied with work, I couldn't be bothered to make the effort to make a serious commitment. One failed marriage had put an end to all of that. Emptying my kit bags when I needed to would do for me.

There were always a few groupies from the Crown Prosecution Service in a time of need. The Crown Prosecution girls were an odd group of pear-shaped ladies who would never miss an opportunity for a drink and a bit of afters. And the annual Christmas party was always packed with young women. At times, it was like shooting fish in a barrel. One year, I charmed a young lady, who I then escorted back to her place. There was even enough time to return to the function to pull another one.

When I was in the Drug Squad, we were regularly moved from office to office, as there were over 50 of us and we were difficult to accommodate. On one occasion, we were put on the third floor of HQ, right beside the Midland Fingerprint Bureau, which was crammed with gorgeous young women and male anoraks. One of the girls was about to be married, and she made the mistake of inviting us to her hen night. The alcohol took effect, my hunting instinct took over and I started to survey the talent in the room. I started chatting to the bride-to-be and noticed a glint in her eyes, but I put this down to my own predatory instinct and brushed it to one side.

A couple of weeks later, I walked past her office, and she called me in for a cup of tea and a chat. I detected that everything wasn't rosy on the marriage front. As time wore on, I found that she was seeking me out every time I walked past her door. She began to confess that she was having problems with her new husband, so I said I would go out for a drink with her. The main problem was that she wasn't getting any sex, so I offered to help sort her out. Which I did. And she was very grateful.

This was all good fun, but it only served to highlight the flaws in my personality. I had no idea how to form a relationship. Dagenham was in three relationships, which caused him untold grief: he had a daughter on whom he doted; an ex-wife to whom he showed remarkable loyalty; and a girlfriend who also wanted a piece of him. She would do things like book a table for dinner at eleven in the evening after he'd been working since five in the morning. On top of this, I was putting pressure on him to work in more and more undercover roles. He was tearing himself apart.

One afternoon, I was summoned to the Specialist Operations HQ for yet another briefing. A team of local businessmen had discovered how easily the new laser photocopiers could replicate banknotes and had set up a cottage industry forging cash. I was introduced to the informant a few days later, and we went to a pub on the Cannock Road to meet one of the suspects. His name was Martin, and he had a small

...ying and selling wooden pallets. As soon
...vay out of his depth.

'...nitting about all the different scams I was
...n here,' I finally revealed, lowering my voice
...here's a chance there might be some funny

'...mebody who can do something,' Martin

...k later, and we arranged to meet in the same pub.
...re?' I asked. 'Are we on or what?'

...my friend, and he can do some notes,' whispered
...y casing the room.

...tens and twenties,' I told him. 'Anything bigger is no
good to me.'

'He can do those,' came the answer. 'He wants five pounds for a
tenner and ten for a twenty.'

'Not a chance,' I replied, laughing. 'I'll give him a quid for a tenner
and two quid for a twenty.'

With forged currency, the price was always a good indication as to
how close a criminal was to the source of the notes. The lower the
price, the closer they were. I'd gone for broke and offered him 10 per
cent of the face value.

'I'll have to go back to him,' Martin said.

'I'll need to see some samples,' I insisted, still on the offensive. 'Get
me a hundred quid in £10 and £20 notes.'

'I-I-I don't know about that,' stuttered Martin.

I decided to squeeze him further. 'I need the samples in three days
or I'm not interested.'

'I've got some notes at home if you want to see them,' he meekly
offered.

'Let's have a look, then,' I suggested.

Minutes later, I was driven by Martin in his battered old saloon to a
small semi-detached council house half a mile from the pub. The place
was a bachelor pad decorated with beer cans and dirty clothes. In the
living room, there was a fireplace with a coal fire. I watched as Martin

reached up the chimney and brought down an envelope covered in soot. From inside the envelope he produced three £20 notes, two £10 notes and a £50 note, which he handed to me. The notes were shiny with no watermark on them and of very poor quality – the work of novices.

The paper is often the first give-away of a counterfeit note. They tend to be a lot floppier than the real thing, whereas a genuine banknote has a very crisp, distinctive feel. The print on a genuine banknote also produces a unique texture. This is because the print is raised on some areas of a banknote. This is most noticeable on new notes. And although some counterfeiters will attempt to simulate a watermark, the way of telling the difference is that the watermark on a forged note will be visible at all times, not just when held up to the light.

'These are bollocks,' I said. 'Where's the metal strip?'

'Don't worry, these are just samples. That can be sorted out.'

'I want to see the finished product in the amounts I asked for,' I insisted. Martin said he would see what he could come up with. I gave him my mobile number and told him to call me.

This was in the early days of mobiles. Telephones were always a problem in undercover duties, as there was extreme difficulty persuading the telephone companies to provide lines. There was a system known as 'Cascade', which provided out-of-town numbers to give the impression that an undercover officer was from another part of the country. But these were as rare as teddy-bear shit and were exclusively available to SO10 and Regional Crime Squads. Senior management was reluctant to purchase new mobiles due to the cost, so we were continually operating with old equipment. You could always tell who the real criminals were, as they always had the latest phones on the market.

Two days later, Martin called. 'I've got the sample.'

At 7 p.m. that evening, accompanied by a full – but invisible – surveillance team, I met Martin. West Midlands Surveillance Team were without exception the best exponents of the art in the country. The Regional Crime Squads always fancied themselves but were amateurs compared to our lot, who had a full-time dedicated unit.

As I sat in the car park waiting for Martin, I could see him parked across the road behind a row of bushes watching me. To coax him out, I got out of my car and walked into the pub. As I returned to my car, Martin pulled up alongside. He beckoned to me to get into his car and then drove off at high speed. We did a tour of the nearby housing estate.

'What are you doing?' I demanded.

'I'm just being careful,' he replied. He reached behind the lining of the driver's door and threw an envelope on my lap. It contained forged notes similar to the ones I had received previously except that they had a silver line drawn on them to resemble the metal security strip on a genuine banknote. Martin said that he wanted half the face value of the notes, to which I told him to fuck off.

'Deal's off, mate,' I said. 'Take me back to my car.' There was a long silence before he relented and said I could have the notes for nothing. He returned me to my car, and I told him to contact me when he was able to produce a larger parcel of notes.

Two weeks later, I'd heard nothing, so I telephoned him. 'What's going on?' I asked. 'I need £50,000 in mixed £10 and £20 notes. I've got five grand on me now.'

'I'm g-g-g-going to need a few days to get a parcel like that together,' he gibbered, clearly off-balance but unable to resist the chance of some easy money.

So I dangled a carrot: 'If you can get it in three days, I'll make this a regular deal.'

'I'll sort it,' he promised before hanging up.

During the next three days, the surveillance team clocked him scurrying in and out of several different premises. Two days later, he was back in contact. 'Everything's sorted,' he said. 'We just need to arrange a time and a place to do the deal.'

'There's a petrol station on the Holyhead Road by the Bells pub,' I said. 'I'll be there at 11 tomorrow morning.'

The following morning, with Dagenham and £5,000 in cash as flash money in tow, I headed for the rendezvous point. We got there before Martin arrived, with the usual complement of police surveillance.

One of the surveillance team was a female officer called 'Nonetoo'.

Her nickname was derived from the fact that she was 'none too bright', which was a description given to her during her surveillance training. Nonetoo favoured married men. She went on to have an affair with a senior officer who was asked by Nonetoo to leave his wife. He refused, and, tragically, Nonetoo ended up taking her own life.

An Audi pulled into the petrol station. I got out of my car and walked across to it. Martin hadn't come alone. In the driving seat was a heavily built man in his late 40s. Martin was in the back with another man, whom I'd also never seen before. On the seat between them were two shoe boxes. As I got into the car, the driver put his foot down. We roared off and began a tyre-screeching tour of some nearby factory estates.

'What the fuck's going on?' I yelled.

'Just a precaution,' snarled the driver aggressively. 'You could be Old Bill for all we know.'

'Listen, fat boy,' I snapped. 'For all I know, *you* could be Old Bill. I don't know who the fuck you think you are, but stop the fucking car, or I'll stop you fucking breathing.' I could feel the veins in my neck bulge as I waved a fist in his face.

'Calm down,' Martin interjected. 'We're just a little jumpy. This is the biggest deal we've done.'

The driver and I exchanged a few more personal insults until he stopped the car. Martin opened one of the shoeboxes. Inside were white envelopes containing bundles of forged £10 and £20 notes. 'How much is there?'

'Fifty grand, like you asked for,' Martin replied.

I began to count the notes. 'It's all there,' said the driver.

'You'd better hope it is,' I said, reaching into the contents of the second shoe box, which I also counted. As I got to £45,000, Martin put his hand on mine and stopped me. He opened the last envelope and showed me that the rest of the notes didn't have the metallic strip on them. 'What the fuck is this?' I ranted. 'You know I can't use these. I asked for 50 K with strips on. This is bullshit. The deal is off.'

I often adopted this tactic when criminals suspected I might be a police officer: I refused the commodity. Criminals knew the police would want to make the bust as big as possible and get it over with quickly. In the real criminal world, deals start off small until there's enough trust between the parties to go for a bigger deal. By turning it down, I hoped to throw them off the scent.

Once again, Martin stepped in. 'Look, I'm sorry,' he pleaded. 'We've been up all night putting the metal strips on. We just ran out of time to get them all ready.'

'I'll give you three grand for the good notes,' I offered. 'Take it or leave it.'

'We'll take it,' said Martin wearily.

'Now drive me back to my car.'

'Why?' growled the driver.

'To get the money.'

'You haven't got it with you?'

'I'm not stupid enough to get into a car full of meatheads with that sort of cash on me.'

Mumbling to himself, the driver headed back to the garage at a more sedate pace than we'd left it, giving surveillance a much easier job. At the far end of the forecourt, I saw Dagenham in the red Rover 3500 we'd borrowed for the occasion. I asked Martin to give me a forged note.

'Why?' he asked.

'See that man over there?' I said, pointing to the Rover. 'He's not going to let me have a penny until he sees what you've got.' The truth was, I wanted a souvenir of the operation. Martin handed me the note. 'Now wait here,' I said as I got out of the Audi and sauntered across the petrol-station forecourt. I handed Dagenham the note and walked to the boot of the car to get the case containing the cash. This was the signal for the arrest team to descend, which they did with all the subtlety of a sumo in a cake shop. With a screech of tyres and the shouts of a dozen fired-up policemen, Martin and his accomplices were dragged from the car, slammed against the bonnet and cuffed. While they had their faces squashed against the paintwork, Dagenham and I made our exit.

The £50,000 of forged notes was recovered, and a search of the premises that Martin had been seen visiting resulted in the recovery of two Canon laser copiers and a load of forgery-related paraphernalia. Martin and his co-conspirators appeared before Wolverhampton Crown Court, and each received five years' imprisonment.

During the investigation, the aggressive driver of the Audi revealed that his brother was a policeman. This could have had serious repercussions for my undercover status. As a result, I was moved to yet another station. In their wisdom, senior management posted me to Queens Road. It was just four miles from Erdington.

ten

TEN TIMES THE WORK FOR HALF THE GLORY

I arrived at Queens Road under something of a cloud. The reason for my transfer wasn't explained to anyone at the station. I, of course, said nothing. This was poor timing, because within one week of my arrival a large-scale corruption inquiry began centred on Erdington CID, where I'd just been transferred from. I was immediately, and wrongly, singled out as the grass. Queens Road instantly became an unpleasant place to work, with everyone distrusting everyone else. The inquiry went on for three years without producing a scrap of evidence, although it ruined many careers.

I continued to work in a difficult atmosphere. The only way I could get a move was by gaining promotion, so I set about studying for the necessary examination, which I passed. I was given the role of acting detective sergeant and immediately put in charge of a sexual-abuse investigation. The victim was a 40-year-old woman with Down's syndrome who lived with her sister. She attended a day centre and once a week she went to a club for people with learning difficulties held in the evenings at Erdington Bilateral School.

One morning at the day centre, she broke down and told one of the staff members that the driver who took her to the club had been interfering with her. The account she gave to staff amounted to allegations of a number of serious sexual assaults. The victim gave details as best she could, but these were sometimes confused. She noted

111

that she'd seen the driver with what she described as a pink balloon, which turned out to be a condom.

The allegations were reported to the police and passed to the Family Protection Department. The papers were then passed to the Crown Prosecution Service, who decided that the matter could not be prosecuted. They did not view the evidence of someone with Down's syndrome as being reliable enough to support a prosecution. The victim's family complained to their local MP, who took up the case. The case was referred to CID, and I was instructed to investigate the matter.

I began to make enquiries. The driver of the vehicle was called Mason. He had a conviction for theft and had been placed on probation. As part of his probation order, he ferried members of the club between their homes and the school. After his probation, Mason continued to act as a voluntary driver and had become a committee member of the club.

The more I dug into Mason's background, the more suspicious I became. He was a married man with two children and had already had an affair with the mother of one of the girls with Down's syndrome from the club. At one stage, the girl made an allegation that he'd got into bed with her. This was investigated by the police, but, again, as there was no corroborating evidence, no action was taken.

Mason's latest victim was getting dropped off at home two hours after the club finished. She only lived four miles away.

I visited the Probation Service depot where the vehicles were stored. One of the drivers said he'd seen Mason with a girl with Down's syndrome in his car late in the evening on a number of occasions. This was not a great deal of evidence. However, when all other avenues of investigation have been exhausted, the best bet is to nick whoever you're investigating. Frequently, they assume that you've got more evidence than you actually have. This loosens them up, and they often become extremely cooperative.

Early one July morning, along with two of my colleagues, I went to Mason's home. The house, on the well-to-do estate, was huge. We were met at the front door by his wife, who told us that Mason, an electrician, had already left for work. 'What's he done now?' she asked.

'I'm arresting him on suspicion of rape,' I told her.

'Oh no, he can't have,' she said. Dismayed, she added, 'I'll bloody kill him if he has.'

She phoned her husband at work and told him to come home right away. When he did, I arrested him and drove him to the police station in his own car, which gave me the opportunity to apply gentle pressure to secure an early confession. 'All right,' I began. 'There are two ways we can deal with this. We can make a big fuss about it. Or we can keep it nice and low key.'

'I don't know what you're talking about,' Mason replied.

'Are you taking the piss?' I asked. 'Because if you are, I can assure you you've chosen the wrong copper to take the piss out of.'

Mason didn't even blink. 'I've no idea what you're on about,' he answered with a straight face.

At the station, he was put in a cell ready to be questioned. Some years earlier, I'd attended an interview development course, at which I had received instruction on interview techniques perfected by the Royal Ulster Constabulary when dealing with terrorists. We were encouraged to observe body language, which is steered by a person's subconscious and is almost impossible to control. We all have occasions when we instinctively know that someone is lying, but we don't know why. Often this is because we're picking up on physical signs. A simple example is the movement of hands towards the face or the mouth. This is caused by the subconscious mind attempting to prevent a lie coming out. It's very apparent in children but can be modified in the case of an adult to the scratching of a nose or the touching of an ear.

There are other signs to look out for. For example, most people think in pictures when they are asked a question. If they're asked about a subject, it's often pictured in the mind's eye. This causes a subject to look upwards in search of the answer. When a subject lies, there is no picture in the mind's eye, so they will look down or slightly to the left or right.

When we lie, our subconscious is put under enormous pressure. An attempt to relieve this pressure will result in a small movement of an arm or a leg, or the tapping of a foot or hand. This is known as non-verbal leakage. Another example of this is when a suspect shuffles about in his or her chair. Subconsciously, he or she is attempting to stand up and leave the room. Another technique that the RUC taught me involved using short but intense periods of questioning to gradually break down a suspect's resistance.

I began the interviews with Mason talking about his family and his job. This was designed to relax him. Then I changed tack slightly. 'You're very popular at the club,' I suggested. Mason looked pleased with himself. 'Particularly with the female members,' I added. I then mentioned the complainant and encouraged Mason to talk about her. Seventeen minutes later, his air of confidence started to slip. At first, he admitted tickling her. Then he confessed that he'd also touched her breasts. I pressed on, using the tactic of placing Mason under pressure and then stopping the interview to leave him alone. Throughout, I used intense unbroken eye contact to increase the strain on him. The short interviews meant I couldn't be accused of questioning him under duress.

Less than an hour after we'd started, Mason capitulated, confessing to a series of indecent assaults. However, he would not admit having sexual intercourse. We searched Mason's van and found a plastic box containing condoms and a tube of KY Jelly. Mason maintained that he used the condoms in his work as an electrician. 'And the KY lubricant?' I asked him. He was stumped.

I charged Mason with offences of indecent assault and unlawful sexual intercourse with a mental defective. The penalty at that time for unlawful sexual intercourse with a mental defective was a maximum of two years' imprisonment. Fortunately, the maximum penalty for indecent assault on a female was ten years.

Mason appeared before the Birmingham Crown Court, where he pleaded guilty. He was sentenced to just two years' probation. I couldn't believe it. It's no wonder that many people don't bother to report offences against them. Amongst officers, sexual offence inquiries are seen as ten times the work for half the glory.

After the Mason case, another investigation found its way onto my desk. A man in his early 20s had come into the police station and made a complaint of being sexually abused. I received the crime report with the witness statement pinned to the back. The more I read, the more horrified I became. The young man lived in a three-bedroom house in Bromford Lane in Erdington. It was a privately owned house, surrounded by council properties.

The victim lived with his mother and three younger sisters. The father had left the family years before. Across the road from the family home was a pub where the mother drank. She enjoyed darts and was friendly with members of the pub team. One man called John Sullivan took a particular interest in her. They became friends, which developed into a relationship.

Sullivan was a large man in his early 50s with a ruddy complexion. The mother was a small, timid woman, who had 'victim' written all over her. Sullivan moved into the family home. He had a dominant personality and quickly took over the running of the house. He took the opportunity to sexually abuse the young girls, who were aged between ten and thirteen. He eventually began having intercourse with them.

Sullivan then forced the brother to have sexual intercourse with his sisters so the older man could watch. Not satisfied with this, Sullivan then coerced the mother to have sexual intercourse with her son, again in Sullivan's presence. On many occasions, Sullivan also committed buggery on the son.

This went on for seven years, as the children went through puberty and entered adulthood. By that point, the son thought what had happened to his family was normal behaviour. However, the psychological damage to him and his sisters led to him contemplating suicide. In desperation, he came to the police.

My initial reaction was to go to Erdington and beat seven kinds of shit out of Sullivan. Then I came up with a more constructive game plan. The first thing was to get statements from the three sisters confirming the brother's story. This would be difficult, as we would have to intercept them without Sullivan's knowledge. He had a Svengali-like influence over them all. Fortunately, two of the sisters had left the family home, so I arranged for them to be interviewed by a policewoman. Their statements confirmed what the older brother was alleging.

The next step was to arrest Sullivan and the mother. Although the mother had clearly been under Sullivan's influence, she had still committed acts of incest with her son and would have to be prosecuted. After she'd been prosecuted, it would be possible to use her as a witness against Sullivan.

There was one further witness in the house: the sister who had not yet been interviewed. At 8 a.m. on a Monday, I arrived at the house on Bromford Lane. I knocked on the door with the customary policeman's knock – three hard bangs. After a few moments, the door was opened by a girl in her teens. 'Police,' I told her, flashing my ID. 'Is John Sullivan at home?'

'Yes, he's upstairs,' said the timid teenager.

The house was a tiny three-bedroom property. The living room was two rooms knocked into one and was crammed with furniture. None of the windows were open, and there was an overwhelming smell of body odour. In the kitchen, I saw the mother. I directed my partner to arrest her. 'I'm going after Sullivan,' I told him.

Upstairs, my prey was halfway through shaving. 'Are you John Sullivan?' I demanded.

'Yes, I am,' he replied, with white foam all over his face.

'I am from Queens Road CID. I am arresting you for having unlawful sexual intercourse.'

'You what?' he asked indignantly.

Sullivan dressed and was driven to the station. I kept the mother at the house to separate her from her partner and his influence. I needed a confession from her to break Sullivan. He was not going to admit to anything without a fight.

The remaining daughter was left in the care of a policewoman. The daughter confirmed that she'd had sex with Sullivan but refused to make a written statement. This was a blow.

After half an hour, the mother was taken to the police station, by which time Sullivan was safely locked away in a cell. I decided the sympathy route was the best way to proceed with her. I told her that I knew she'd been abused by a man whom she had trusted and that all the terrible things that had taken place were because of Sullivan's bullying influence. This quickly reduced her to tears. I sat in the interview as she admitted to having had sex with her son and described how Sullivan had committed buggery on the boy. She said that she knew Sullivan had been having sex with her daughters but was powerless to stop him.

Sullivan elected to have a solicitor in the interview room with him when I questioned him, which was his right. For over an hour, he sat there in total denial. His answer to each allegation was the same: 'No, didn't happen, never happened.' It didn't matter. I had enough evidence from the other witnesses to convict him.

I charged Sullivan with unlawful sexual intercourse and buggery. The mother was charged with incest. The case appeared at the Crown court, and all the family members attended. The daughter who refused to make a statement sat alone. The mother was placed on probation. John Sullivan was sentenced to six years' imprisonment – a ridiculously light sentence considering he had systematically raped three young girls and destroyed a young man's life.

eleven

THE UNTOUCHABLES

'I want you to clean up Coventry,' the superintendent said. 'Do whatever it takes.'

I'd just been given undercover approval to kick every criminal in the city into touch. I'd also been told that I had complete back-up from the divisional crime-support units and no restrictions on my budget. I left the super's office with my brain in overdrive.

Once again, Dagenham was my only choice as a partner. First in our sights was a villain called Brian Craven, a well-known fence. The way I saw it, if there was nobody around to shift the loot, there would be no thieves.

Craven was moving gear for a burglar called Billy Manise. The department were about to close in on Manise. 'We're going to nick him tomorrow,' said the officer in charge of the investigation.

'Have you got enough to charge him?' I asked.

'Not really,' came the answer.

'Right,' I said. 'Here's the plan. Arrest Manise and bang him up. Then send a couple of uniforms to nick me and put me in the same cell. I'll get him to reference me to all the other crooks in Hillfields.'

'Done,' said the officer, who was bemused but impressed at the simplicity of the idea.

The following morning, I was sitting in plain clothes in the car park of the Holyhead pub in Coventry. I was approached by two uniformed officers and arrested. They didn't tell me what I was being arrested for, because I suspect they didn't know themselves.

I was taken to Stoney Stanton Road Police Station, where, to achieve the full effect, I demanded a phone call to my solicitor. I telephoned Dagenham, and we had a carefully scripted conversation with him pretending to be my brief. I was then placed in a cell with Billy Manise. For the first 20 minutes, we sat in silence. I wasn't going to start the conversation. It would look too pushy. Eventually, Manise started to eye up my copy of *The Sun*. 'You finished with that?' he asked.

'Help yourself,' I said, foolishly handing him the paper. Instead of this being a conversation opener, Manise spent the next two hours with his head in the paper without saying a word.

I was bored off my bollocks, lying there with nothing to read. Manise finally handed back the paper and broke the silence. 'What you in for?' he asked.

'I got collared with a telly in the back of my mate's car,' I lied. 'It's not my car, and I don't know anything about a telly.'

'Stick to your story and they can't touch you,' he advised.

'What about you?' I probed.

'Burglary,' said Manise, 'but they can't prove anything. I'll just keep my mouth shut, and I'll be out of here in no time.'

'If you ever need anything moving, or whatever,' I offered helpfully, 'I know a few people who can shift things.'

'I've got some electrical gear that needs a home,' Manise said. 'Computers, that sort of stuff.'

'I know someone who might be interested,' I told him.

'Come and see me when you get out,' came the reply.

Two hours later, Manise was removed from the cell for interview. I was free to go. Now it was time to set up Brian Craven. Mark Sutton was the undercover officer whose job it was to befriend the target. Sutton was affectionately known as the Boy Scout because he was just five feet eight inches tall. He was the best dummy the department had. Dummy was the term for the first person into an operation who smoothed the way for introductions to other undercover officers. Sutton struck up a relationship with Craven, whom we nickamed Rodney because he looked remarkably like Rodney Trotter from *Only Fools and Horses*. Sutton then introduced Craven to me and Dagenham.

We said we had plenty of cash and were always looking for a deal on dodgy gear.

A couple of nights later, Craven called me. 'I've got something you might be interested in,' he whispered down the phone.

'What's that?'

'Twelve chequebooks and cards. All brand new.'

'Can we have a look?'

'Come over in an hour.'

That afternoon, Dagenham and I went to Craven's sparsely furnished council flat in the Wood End district of Coventry. Wood End was a run-down area that had been built in the 1960s. The district was a hotbed of crime, and the people who lived there were tough as they came. Even the dogs carried flick knives.

Craven showed us the stolen chequebooks. 'I've got the cards, too,' he added. 'I'm after 50 quid a book.'

'I'll take the lot, and I'll give you 20 quid a book.'

'How about 40?' Craven haggled.

'Twenty's all they're worth to me,' I said, shrugging.

'I'm selling them for someone else. Any lower and I don't make anything for myself.'

'Think about it and get back to us. Fancy a drink?'

We walked through the housing estate to a small pub and sat at an outside table. As I supped my beer, I started to probe Craven. 'Do you get any bigger gear? White goods? Computers? That sort of thing.'

'Sometimes. If I hear of anything, I'll let you know.'

A Land Rover pulled into the pub car park. A fat bloke wearing a padded shirt, which made him look twice his size, climbed out. He came marching across to where we were sitting. 'How's tricks, then?' Fatty said, drawing deeply on his cigarette.

'Not bad,' replied Craven, introducing us. 'These are a couple of mates down from Brum for a bit of business.'

'What sort of business?' enquired Fatty.

'The usual.'

'Would they be interested in a generator? Brand new. Someone left it lying about on the site I've been working on, so I had it away.'

'Not my scene, really,' I said. 'I'm not into plant. I might know someone who is.'

I had a plan to get Fatty and his stolen generator nicked. I knew a young undercover detective from Coventry who was trying to make a name for himself. His name was Martin. I knew him affectionately as Big Nose. I went inside the pub and made a couple of discreet phone calls. Then I returned to the table.

'Any luck?' Fatty asked.

'Might have a taker. He said he'd call me back.'

Two minutes later my phone rang. 'All right, Big Nose. Yeah, he's here. I'll put you on to him and you can sort it out yourself.' I handed Fatty my mobile phone.

'Crawley services in about an hour? I'll see you then,' agreed Fatty, who handed the phone back. 'Thanks for that, mate. I owe you one.'

'No problem. If it works out, give Brian here a drink.'

Dagenham and I finished our drinks and said our goodbyes. As we left, I made a note of the Land Rover's registration. On the way back to our car, I telephoned Martin with the details. 'OK, mate. Get the traffic cops to stop the Land Rover and breathalyse the driver. He's had a couple, so he'll be over the limit. You'll find the generator in the back of the Land Rover.'

Several hours later, I received a telephone call that everything had gone to plan and the £7,000 stolen generator had been recovered. Not bad for half an hour's work over a lunchtime pint. As for Craven, the plan was to send over a squad to do a drugs bust. The search would uncover the stolen chequebooks without Craven suspecting any link to us.

The chequebooks were recovered, along with a gram of speed from inside a vase in the living room. They made a right mess of his place: doors smashed off, furniture ripped apart. Luckily, it wasn't that pretty a place to begin with.

Craven didn't suspect a thing. He was soon back in touch offering to offload some computers. It was the link we needed to nail Manise. 'They've got 128 meg of RAM, CD-ROMs, monitors and printers,' babbled Craven.

Dagenham and I knew more about dismantling nuclear weapons

than we did about computers, but nevertheless we struck a deal with Craven. 'They want two hundred quid for each computer,' he said.

'I could go out and buy them new for that. Tell them we'll give them eighty quid.'

When buying stolen goods, a good rule of thumb is never to pay more than a third of the asking price of any item. Drugs, on the other hand, were a different matter.

'Can you get one for us to have a look at?' I asked.

Craven trooped off to his supplier and returned with one of the computers. 'They'll take eighty, but the deal has got to be done today,' he said. 'They've got another buyer interested in this stuff.'

'We'll have to go back to Birmingham to get the money,' I replied. 'Let's meet somewhere halfway to do the deal. You know the Malt Shovel? We'll be in the car park in one hour.'

The Malt Shovel was a pub on the A45, the main road between Birmingham and Coventry. There was only one way into the car park and one way out. Perfect for monitoring and controlling a developing situation. But we didn't actually need to do a full-scale bust. As ever, I had a simpler plan.

'I'll see you there in an hour,' confirmed Craven.

'So I know it's you, what will you be driving?' I asked.

'A black Hillman Avenger,' Craven replied. This was perfect: a distinctive 25-year-old car that was easily identifiable. It would be simple for a traffic patrol car to intercept it en route to the pub and nick them with all the gear before they even got there. The problem was, our commanding officer wanted some of the glory for herself. 'I want you to go through with the meeting as planned,' came the order. I couldn't quite see the point of getting all those people to make the bust when we could have them nicked with a minimum of fuss by two people in a marked police car.

Our other problem was getting hold of cash – flash money – so we looked like we genuinely meant to do business. The operational commander decided it wasn't necessary. 'You'll have to manage without it,' was the directive. We could improvise, but the risk was that it might cost us the bust. Some criminals won't let you get a sniff of the goods until you've shown them the colour of your money.

I parked up outside the Malt Shovel. Craven wasn't there, so I went in. Inside, I bumped straight into the operational commander but deliberately didn't acknowledge her. What the fuck was she doing? All those involved in the bust were tucked away out of sight. She'd come to gawp. Had anyone recognised her, it could have compromised the whole operation.

I went back outside and saw Craven pull into the car park. His Hillman Avenger was crammed to the roof with computer equipment. He pulled up, wound down the window, grinned and gave me the thumbs-up. A true plonker.

I leaned towards him and whispered, 'Money's in the car. Wait here.' I walked off and opened the boot of the car. As on previous operations, that was the signal for the bust to begin and for me to disappear.

Craven was arrested and computer equipment valued at £50,000 recovered. He squealed like a baby, and suddenly we had the evidence we needed to pin Manise. Job done.

At the debrief, I told the operational commander what I thought of her antics. She rounded on me, saying that she had been speaking to colleagues about me at a police function and they'd noted my attitude had changed since I'd been carrying out undercover work. I thanked her for discussing a secret operation at a police function and said that I would be duty bound to report her to the head of CID. She was eventually replaced, and Dagenham and I continued on our Coventry clean-up campaign without her. I would like to say it made our lives easier, but the crime rates in Coventry were reaching epidemic proportions.

We quickly infiltrated the activities of another fence called Willie Highfield. He was into selling everything, including drugs. Every time we went round to see him, his wife would have to drag him out of his bed after his previous evening's excesses with drink and drugs. He would crawl into the living room, where he would immediately roll a spliff before speaking to us.

Willie lived in a house with orange-box furniture. It was a right state. When he wasn't out thieving, I suspected he amused himself sitting at home watching the rats throwing themselves on the traps. It was that grim.

Willie eventually introduced us to two villains called Chas and Lou who dealt in counterfeit clothing. Chas was a heavily built man in his 30s. Lou was younger and more wiry in appearance, with a mouth full of gold teeth. He was fascinated by the gold crown, fashioned into the Adidas motif, that clipped over my front tooth. It had been specially made for me by my dentist, and I wore it on undercover occasions to make me seem a bit flash.

Chas and Lou seemed a bit more heavyweight than Willie when I first met them at his house. They'd filled his front room with samples of counterfeit clothing – known as snide gear – and stolen video recorders. I decided to test them out. 'Not really our scene,' I said, eyeing up their gear. 'What else've you got?'

They offered us a parcel of poor-quality forged notes, which I immediately knocked back. 'I couldn't shift this at a car-boot sale, mate. I need something a bit more meaty.'

'Well, there might be some blow on its way.'

'Resin or bush?'

'Resin. Two and a half grand a kilo.' We parted, promising to do business. Meanwhile, we remained in touch with Willie.

One morning, I turned up at Willie's home. There was a brand-new Volkswagen parked outside the house. It was a G60 Polo with a supercharged engine and clearly didn't belong to Willie. Unless he'd nicked it.

His wife answered the door. 'If you want Willie, he's not here. I've kicked him out. I've had enough of him. But come in. I've got somebody here who you might want to talk to.' She led me into the kitchen, where there was an attractive blonde smoking a spliff. She introduced herself as Diane. We began chatting, and it turned out she knew Chas and Lou. 'I do business with them,' she revealed.

'They want to do a deal with me for some weed, but they want too much money.'

'What they asking?'

'Two and a half grand a kilo.'

'The greedy bastards. They're getting it off me for less than two.'

'Perhaps we can do business directly,' I suggested. We exchanged numbers and agreed to make contact when the next consignment arrived. This was an important development. I was getting closer to the source of supply. People like Willie were small fry in comparison.

As I left the house, I made a careful note of the registration of Diane's car. When I then returned to headquarters, I passed on the intelligence, but I was ordered by a senior officer not to contact Diane again. 'Why not?' I asked.

'Because I'm ordering you not to,' was the response.

I began to make my own enquiries. I found out that Diane was the girlfriend of Mick Loughlin, one of the main drug dealers in Coventry and someone regarded as being 'untouchable'. Untouchables were supposed to be criminals so high up the food chain that it was difficult to pin anything on them. I had arrested plenty of untouchables in the past. A lot of their reputation turned out to be pure myth. Loughlin was only an untouchable because no one had actually sat down and thought of a plan to arrest him. Either that or someone was in his pocket.

I discovered that he was having an affair with a policewoman posted to the Regional Crime Squad. When I reported this, senior management became concerned that the operation would be compromised. Rather than use it to our advantage, they had the operation terminated. I made it clear to those above me that I was not happy and that this was still worth pursuing. Once again, my protests fell on deaf ears.

To finalise the paperwork, I went to Coventry to meet the operational commander who had to sign our pocket books and expenses. We were in the process of going through the paperwork when my pager bleeped and showed a message: 'Ring Willie.'

'What do you want me to do?' I asked the operational commander.

'See what he wants,' he replied.

I rang Willie, who was very excited. 'I can get you the dope as soon as you want it,' he ranted. 'I've also got a load of American Express travellers cheques.'

'I'll call you back in an hour,' I told him. The operational commander said that I should arrange a meeting with Willie. Meanwhile, he would seek advice as to whether we could continue the operation.

I met Willie that afternoon. He was in a very buoyant mood. His wife had let him back in the house, and he'd got his hands on a stash of good gear. He produced a stolen American Express travellers cheque, which I pocketed. 'I'll have that as a sample,' I said.

'I can show you the dope at my mate's place,' added Willie, who took me to a flat off the Holyhead Road. There were five or six other people sitting around smoking a joint. The smell of dope was thick in the air. Willie introduced me to his friend, who quickly ushered everyone out of the flat. From inside a magazine rack, he produced a kilo of cannabis resin. 'It's red wrap,' he announced. 'Nice and soft. Good gear.' Red wrap is the name given to cannabis resin that is wrapped in red cellophane, denoting high quality.

'You want a smoke?' asked Willie.

'No, just burn the end of it and let's see what it smells like.' Willie removed the cellophane and burned a corner of the slab with his cigarette lighter. A thick unmistakable waft of cannabis rose into the air. I examined the kilo block, which was of good quality. 'How much have you got?' I asked.

'How much do you want?'

'Twenty kilos.'

'You can have it for two and a half grand a kilo.'

'Behave!' I said, laughing. 'Do me twenty at two grand a kilo and we can talk proper business.'

'It's not up to me to negotiate,' he said. 'I'll have a word with my supplier and get back to you.'

Willie and I left the flat, and he launched into me about a deal on the travellers cheques. 'I've got a hundred grand's worth,' he said excitedly.

'Let's sort the dope out first. If I get the right deal for that, I'll take the American Express off you at the same time,' I assured him.

'What we looking at?' asked Willie.

'Ten per cent of face value,' I said, quoting him the market rate for stolen travellers cheques.

'Brilliant,' he enthused. 'That'll be brilliant.'

'It all depends on you sorting this dope deal out,' I reiterated. 'No dope deal, no cheque deal.'

I left Willie and returned to HQ, where I was told that the operation was now back on.

The following day, I met Willie. 'Have you sorted the price out yet?' I asked.

'I can get the 20 kilos, and I'll get the price as low as I can,' Willie assured me.

'When can you get it?'

'Couple of days.'

'If you get me the right price for the dope, I'll do a deal with the cheques at the same time.'

Willie's eyes lit up. To keep him keen, I took him for a drink at a pub called the Tow Rope, another establishment on the A45 Coventry to Birmingham road. While we were there, I suggested it would be a good location to hand over the gear.

Willie phoned the next day to say the deal was on. 'They're digging their heels in about the money,' he warned me. 'And they're sending somebody with me to mind the gear.'

'That's no problem,' I assured him. 'Don't forget the cheques.'

By that stage, I really didn't care if he turned up with the Nolan Sisters in tow, as long as they came carrying 20 kilos of blow and a fistful of American Express. 'I'll see you in the Tow Rope car park at one o'clock tomorrow,' I told him.

The following morning, Dagenham and I attended the operational briefing. We were introduced to the arrest and surveillance teams so that everyone would know who the real villains were. This would prevent anyone wasting their time giving chase to us if we had to leave the scene in a hurry. Dagenham would be carrying the flash money in a separate car to me. Hopefully, it wouldn't even get that far.

As I had done before, I suggested a traffic cop stop Willie before he got to the meeting. This would have been a lot quicker, but once more I was told to continue the operation as planned.

I called Willie who, to my surprise, was out of bed and sounding quite alert. 'You still on for one o'clock?' I asked.

'I'll be there,' Willie replied.

'Have you got the gear now?'

'I've got five kilos and all the American Express.'

I tore into him: 'Look, you wanker, I told you 20 kilos. I've got people waiting . . .'

'That's all I can get for the first deal,' he whimpered. 'They said if this goes all right, I can have as much as I like.'

'Well, you better pull it all together for the other 15 kilos pretty quick,' I said.

'I'm sorry, I'm sorry, but it's not my gear, that's why,' apologised Willie. As we spoke, the surveillance team were already sitting outside his house waiting to follow him to the rendezvous point.

At midday, Dagenham and I left HQ in separate cars to make the journey to Coventry. Dagenham parked on the forecourt of a hotel opposite the Tow Rope with the flash money. As I approached a roundabout near the pub, I stopped in a line of traffic. I looked to my right and saw a brown Ford Granada containing Willie and another man drive onto the roundabout in front of me. I allowed the Granada to clear the roundabout and then drove off in the opposite direction, much to the confusion of the surveillance team monitoring my movements. I drove on for several miles and then pulled over into a lay-by. A member of the surveillance team pulled in behind me. I explained that I wanted Willie to arrive at the car park a few minutes before me to give the arrest team time to take up their respective positions.

I remained where I was until the surveillance officer confirmed that Willie had arrived at the pub. I drove over and found a space at the opposite end of the car park to Willie. I didn't want to be too close to him when I called the strike.

I got out and walked towards the brown Ford Granada. The driver was a short, stocky man in his 40s wearing a tan sheepskin coat. He was the minder they'd sent to look after the gear. Willie was sitting in the front passenger seat. As I approached, the Sheepskin reached over and opened the rear door. I said nothing and got into the back of the Granada. 'It's all here,' said Willie.

'No it fucking isn't,' I snapped. 'I wanted 20 kilos. Now I've got to go knock a load of people back. How do you think that makes me look?' My tactic was to look like I could pull out of the deal at any moment. Often, undercover officers are so keen to get the deal sealed and the bust over that they blow it at the crucial moment.

My rant also had the desired effect on the Sheepskin, whose tough-guy act suddenly vanished. He began to apologise on Willie's behalf. 'Look, I'm sorry, but we don't know you. Once we've done a deal, there won't be a problem. There's plenty of gear where this came from.'

'Who the fuck are you?' I spat. 'I've been dealing with Willie here, and he knows I'm good for the money.'

Willie tried to calm me down by handing me a large parcel wrapped in Christmas paper. 'Here's the first lot,' he said. 'I promise you we'll sort you out with the rest.' I ripped open the parcel. It contained five kilos of red-wrap cannabis resin. Then Willie handed me a bundle of American Express travellers cheques, which I began to count. Willie was trembling. The Sheepskin got out of the car and started pacing up and down, smoking nervously. I could make them feel worse by haggling the price, but I'd already made my mind up to call the strike.

I handed the dope back to Willie. 'Hold on to this,' I told him. 'I'm going to get the money.' As I got out of the car, the Sheepskin began to apologise again. I looked at him and said, 'Shut up and get back in the car or the whole fucking deal is off.'

I then began the long walk to my car. It was the longest 30 yards on earth. I was so pumped up by what was about to happen that I had to stop myself from doing somersaults.

I was often described as brave to get involved in undercover operations. I always considered the officers reacting to my strike signal to be the brave ones. Once, during a Metropolitan Police undercover operation, a strike was called and the arresting officers descended on the criminal, who produced a firearm and shot one of them in the chest.

I reached my car and opened the boot – my signal for the strike to begin – and stood back. I looked left and saw the Granada. I looked right: no strike team. I remained where I was for what seemed like a lifetime. I looked across the road and could see the whiteness of

Dagenham's teeth. He was laughing at the complete absence of an arrest team.

'Another fuck-up,' I grumbled to myself. I looked back at the Granada and saw the Sheepskin was out of the car looking over in my direction. Then Willie's head poked up out of the vehicle from behind the driver's door.

At that moment, three cars squealed into the car park. The next thing I saw was the car door being slammed on Willie's head and Sheepskin being dragged to the floor. I turned and walked off towards Dagenham's car.

We hadn't needed the flash money this time, which was always annoying. One of the worst tasks before the operation was having to photocopy each note beforehand. I remember during one operation we had £250,000 flash money that had been supplied direct from the bank in sealed bags. I sat for several hours checking the money but could not get the amounts to balance. We had asked for the money to be in £10 and £20 notes. After counting the money three times, it still would not add up – not until we found three stray £5 notes in it. You can't trust anyone these days, not even the bank.

Willie and his partner were charged with drug-trafficking offences and possession of the stolen American Express cheques. An operation that was deemed to be dead in the water had suddenly come good. We still hadn't nailed the big guys, though. And we'd never get the chance.

That night, Dagenham called to tell me to go and buy a copy of the *Coventry Evening Standard*. On page 25, I saw a large photograph of the operational commander with the cannabis and American Express cheques spread out on a table in front of him. He had given an interview outlining the success of an undercover police operation named Operation Alonzo, which had led to the recovery. This exposed the entire operation and blew my cover, as the criminals now knew I was a police officer. I would never be able to work in Coventry again.

twelve

BOTTLING IT

Back at Queens Road CID, I had a new commanding officer. Like his predecessors, he was irritated by the lack of control he had over my movements. This often meant me leaving the Midlands area altogether. Whenever I was involved in an undercover operation, I would receive spook telephone calls at home. When I picked up, there would be no one on the other end. This was my boss checking where I was. Then something happened that made him reassess his attitude towards me.

One afternoon, a traffic officer pulled over a car for speeding on the Birmingham ring road. Suspicious of the driver's behaviour, the officer searched the car. Beneath the front seat he found a loaded sawn-off shotgun. The driver was arrested but denied any knowledge of the firearm. The gun was fingerprinted and the driver's fingerprints were all over the weapon. There was also another unidentified fingerprint on the gun. It was imperative to trace who the fingerprint belonged to. They had either used the gun or supplied it and as such were to be considered dangerous. The driver said nothing, and the investigation drew a blank.

I offered to make my own enquiries, and I found out the identity of the man who had supplied the gun through one of my informants. I handed the information over to Miller. A search warrant was executed, which resulted in the recovery of the barrel that had been sawn from the weapon found in the car.

I was something of an expert when it came to guns. As part of my undercover training, I'd been instructed in the stripping, assembly and recognition of small arms by a member of 22nd Special Air Service Regiment. My instructor was a wiry, red-headed Yorkshireman, who was a member of the team of SAS troopers that carried out the rescue of hostages at the Iranian Embassy in London in 1981. The techniques were complex, but he made them look simple. As each component was removed from each weapon, it was placed in a line. You could literally go back up the line of components with your eyes closed to reassemble the weapon.

The poor care criminals take of their weapons make them unreliable; for example, leaving the magazine of a semi-automatic weapon fully loaded for any length of time. This increases the chances of it jamming, because it compresses the spring, leaving it too weak to push a round correctly into the firing chamber.

As part of another investigation into the sale of illegal firearms, I paid a return visit to the SAS. The weapon I was investigating was a Beretta hand gun, which had had its normal 9-mm slide replaced with a .22 slide. The smaller-calibre ammunition would then have some of the charge removed, so if a person was shot in a crowded area, the round would remain in the body and not injure innocent bystanders. This, I suspected, was the case with the round used to murder television presenter Jill Dando some years later. The cartridge case recovered at the murder scene bore small marks consistent with the head of the bullet being removed and replaced.

Most of this self-educating was done off my own bat. It made me better at my job, as I proved with the shotgun trace. And with my insider knowledge of the local villainy scene, my new commander suddenly realised I was actually a very valuable asset. I may have been forthright in my dealings with criminals and less committed police officers, but I was a first-class copper. Whether I was undercover or on normal duties, I got results. My boss's attitude was further softened when he was called upon to manage an undercover operation. After that, he realised the need for me to operate in complete secrecy.

My next operation was assisting my old friends at the Gloucestershire Constabulary over in Cheltenham. The op centred on a pub called the Hare and Hounds. Like the last time I had gone undercover in the town, the premises in question had a serious problem with drug dealing. Once again, my brief was to infiltrate the pub and identify the main dealers. However, the operation was to turn into something much bigger.

Despite my reputation, infiltration into the criminal fraternity wasn't that straightforward. Without the assistance of an informant to make an introduction, it was almost impossible. And the police in Cheltenham didn't seem to have any informants.

I asked for up-to-date intelligence on the premises and the local criminals, and I was given a book of photographs. Most were New Age travellers and gypsies. I was also provided with a snail of a saloon car, which the department had bought at auction. Les Sleek's friendly car dealer had by now been abandoned.

The Specialist Operations Department had covertly set up accounts with a number of car-hire firms. For security, they used special company bank accounts so they couldn't be traced back to the police. This arrangement was fine until one bright senior officer recklessly informed someone in senior management at the hire companies of the true identity of the department. On another occasion, an undercover officer left his notebook in a hire car. The book was recovered, but the rental company could never be used again.

Secrecy of the department's activities was paramount. All it needed was for someone to get loose-lipped after a couple of drinks and start gobbing off. The whole set-up could be compromised, as would the personal safety of any undercover officers involved.

I decided to take Dagenham to Cheltenham as my undercover partner. We spent the next two weeks hanging about the Hare and Hounds getting our faces known. Our cover story was that we dealt in stolen property. I was given a supply of counterfeit Nike T-shirts, which had been recovered during another operation.

Most of the customers in the Hare and Hounds were of the crusty variety, with the exception of a tidily dressed man in his late 40s. His name was Gerry. Gerry was a decent pool player and rarely off the table. This gave me ample opportunity to engage him in conversation.

Gerry turned out to be the main man in the Hare and Hounds when it came to stolen property. One night I tested the water. 'Know anyone who might be interested in some snide Nike T-shirts at a pound a pop?' I asked.

'I can get the real thing in here for the same price,' Gerry replied, laughing.

I tried again. 'I've got a parcel of fags you might be interested in.'

'How many you got?'

'Two hundred packets at a quid each.'

'Bring 'em round to mine and I'll have a look.' Great. All I needed now was 200 packets of cigarettes. Through a contact at Customs and Excise, we got hold of a consignment of confiscated duty-free.

Two nights later, I was in his kitchen with a bin bag full of fags. He lived in a tidy little cottage not far from the pub. After we did the deal for the cigarettes, Gerry produced a small black box with two wires protruding out of it. 'Know what this is?' he asked.

'Looks like a bomb,' I replied.

'It'll save you a bomb,' said Gerry. 'Clip it either side of your electric meter and you'll never get another nasty bill.'

'How much?' I asked.

'Tenner each.'

'How many you got?'

'A dozen.'

'I know someone who'll have these off you,' I said. 'Give me a couple of days.'

Later that evening, Gerry pulled another surprise from up his well-ironed sleeve. His brother was doing some work for the local rector, who had a houseful of antiques. He had access to a spare set of keys. Gerry wanted us to sneak into the rector's house and photograph the antiques. 'We could see which are the best bits and have them away,' Gerry rather candidly suggested. 'It would be a good earner for all of us.'

'I'm always looking to make a few quid,' I said, smiling.

When the operational commander heard our story, he had an attack of the vapours. The rector was one of the top Freemasons in the country. The detective chief inspector's career would be in ruins if the house was burgled. Hoskin told us to arrange immediate surveillance on the property. I believe he went on to personally advise the rector to change his locks, thereby ingratiating himself in the process.

The information regarding the black boxes was passed to the Midlands Electricity Board, and they offered to buy as many as I could get my hands on to get them out of circulation. 'Why don't we just locate the source?' I suggested. 'Then you'll have none left to worry about.'

We asked for far more than Gerry could supply, and he obligingly introduced us to the electrician who made them. I put in an order and had the sparky followed and arrested with a van full of the little black boxes. I then complained to Gerry that I'd been let down when his man failed to turn up with my order. This endeared me to him even more.

One night in the Hare and Hounds, Gerry introduced me to a very strange- looking couple who I'd never seen in the pub before. The man was short with wiry hair, squinting eyes and very uneven teeth. There was something very odd about him. His wife was quiet, chubby and wore a pair of very unflattering large-rimmed spectacles. These two were the frumpiest pair of people I'd ever set eyes on.

We shook hands, and they stood at the bar drinking without saying a word. Not even to each other. When they left, Gerry nudged me and whispered, 'If you want any porno films and stuff, those two will fix you up. They're a right dirty pair.' They looked like the last people on earth you would imagine having sex, let alone promoting it.

The next time I saw them was in the newspapers. Gerry had introduced me to Fred and Rose West. The bodies of 15 young women, including their own daughter, were found hidden in their house and buried in their garden. When police first went round to investigate, Fred West was still at work. Rose called him up to say that the police were searching the premises inside and out. Fred was more concerned with the garden being ruined than being found out as a mass murderer. He went on to confess to murdering more women and burying them in the surrounding countryside. He offered to reveal the details of where he buried them at a rate of one a year, but he hanged himself in prison, taking that information to his grave.

I've met some really nasty pieces of work in my job, and I've never lost sleep over any of them. In fact, there's probably plenty of criminals out there who have nightmares over the memory of bumping into me. But the memory of shaking hands with Fred West still sends a shiver up my back.

Back at the Hare and Hounds, Dagenham and I continued to integrate with the local criminal fraternity, who were becoming more and more open. One afternoon, one of the druggies known as Chemical Ken flashed me a bundle of stolen credit cards. 'I'm off to do the shopping for the week,' he said with a wink before hopping onto his bike and cycling out of the pub car park.

'No you're fucking not,' I thought to myself. I quietly contacted HQ, and Ken was intercepted on the way home with bags of groceries and a pocketful of stolen credit cards. The operational commander was happy that the operation had finally started to show results. Once I'd gathered enough intelligence on the local dealers, the next task was to organise a full-scale raid on the Hare and Hounds.

One evening, Handy Tony, who was an informant for Dagenham, arranged to meet us on a social basis in Cheltenham. Tony was a short stocky man who wore Dr Martens and always had his hair cropped. He was often mistaken for a police officer but had actually been an informant for 20 years. He was a premier-league shoplifter with a weakness for 17-year-old boys. When he grew tired of them, he would inform Dagenham of any criminal activities they were involved in. Dagenham got his arrest, and Handy Tony got his boyfriends off his back, so to speak.

Tony had been wandering around one of the local amusement arcades of Cheltenham – a favourite place to pick up young men – when he bumped into an old friend from prison who was running the place. His name was Murray.

I'd come across Murray some years before when he worked as a taxi driver in Birmingham. He was a huge man with a propensity for violence. He had escaped from prison in Ireland, where he'd been convicted of firing a shotgun at a policeman. Dagenham asked if Handy Tony could introduce us to Murray. 'He's bound to be up to something,' Dagenham reasoned.

Meanwhile, Gerry kept us busy as ever. 'I can fix you up with two hundred quid's worth of groceries for seventy quid,' he said. 'You can have it once a week if you want it.' I put in an order. At the same time, I arranged to have him put under surveillance. 'See me at my place on Friday evening at about six o'clock and I'll have the goodies,' he told me.

That Friday, surveillance saw Gerry pick up a man in his 70s who walked with the use of a stick. They drove to Wales and visited half a dozen large supermarkets, where the old man bought £200 of groceries with a stolen credit card. No one would suspect the old man because of his condition.

I managed to dissuade my superior from arresting Gerry at that stage. I had a hunch that we could bust him for something much bigger. The operational commander greeted this with enthusiasm. Little did he realise the monster he was about to create.

With Dagenham on a week's leave, Handy Tony took me on my own to the amusement arcade to meet Murray, introducing me as an old partner in crime. 'What are you into?' Murray asked.

'Plastic. Credit cards mainly. I could sort you out with a couple of hundred quid's worth of groceries for seventy quid,' I added, stealing Gerry's patter.

'I'm more interested in selling than buying,' replied Murray. 'I can get my hands on fifty grand's worth of electrical gear from a little warehouse I know. I'm looking to shift it for 36.'

'If I help move it, I'd be after 10 per cent,' I said.

'You get a buyer lined up, and I'll go and screw the place,' added Murray.

I didn't know which warehouse Murray intended to rip off, so the plan was that I would lure him to a prearranged location with the stolen electrical equipment. The operational commander was happy with this, until I mentioned that I'd need £36,000. In cash. 'What do you need the £36,000 for?' he asked.

'If I say to Murray, "Show me your gear," and he says, "Show me your money," what am I supposed to do? Show him a photograph?'

'This is getting out of hand,' said the operational commander nervously, adding that Gloucestershire were only a small force and couldn't get their hands on that sort of money. He sat there in the front seat of my car with beads of sweat running down his face. Then he looked down at his feet where there was a piece of steel tubing wrapped in masking tape. 'What's this for?' he asked, picking up the pipe.

'It's for loosening nuts,' I said, meaning wheel nuts on a car. The operational commander thought I meant something else. He dropped the pipe and got out of the car as fast as he could.

I called him a week later to tell him I was going to speak to Murray. He seemed a lot calmer than when we'd last spoken. I went to Cheltenham and called in at the amusement arcade. 'Any news on that electrical stuff?' I asked.

'It's gone quiet,' Murray explained, 'but I can get hold of a caravan if you know anyone who wants a twenty-grand, top-of-the-range camper for twelve hundred quid.'

'I'll ask around,' I told him, delivering my standard stalling reply.

I gave my operational commander the update and suggested we offer to buy the caravan. He said that he could organise the cash, but, in order to protect the money, he wanted to know exactly how the transaction would take place.

'I'll bring someone from Birmingham as a buyer,' I explained.

'Why can't we use someone local?' he asked.

'I'm posing as a criminal from Birmingham, so it would be sensible to bring a buyer from Birmingham,' I explained.

'I'm not happy with a criminal from Birmingham coming to Cheltenham to handle £1,200 of police money to buy a stolen caravan,' the operational commander replied.

'I think you've got the wrong end of the stick, sir. The buyer will be another undercover police officer posing as a criminal. Not an actual criminal.'

Two days later, Murray called to say he'd got the van and to ask whether I had a buyer. 'I've got someone. I'll come over on Friday,' I said.

I told the operational commander, who asked me to delay the deal till Tuesday, as he was due to go away over the bank holiday on a cricket tour. But I could still meet with Murray to discuss the details of the deal. So, on the Friday I went to his house. His garden was full of large stone ornaments. Dozens of them. 'Very nice,' I said, pointing at the statues on his lawn. 'You a collector?'

'They're souvenirs. Whenever we go looking for a caravan to nick from someone's front drive, we have something from the garden as well.'

'Nice one,' I replied, laughing. In reality, this was pretty dumb. The ornaments connected Murray to the theft of the caravans. How gutting would it be to be convicted in court on the evidence of a garden gnome or plaster-cast rabbit?

'We've got the van,' Murray went on. 'It's a twin axle with a shower and central heating.'

'My buyer is away in Newcastle this weekend.'

'Which Newcastle?'

'Newcastle upon Tyne.'

'That's no problem,' said Murray, who was clearly pumped up. 'It's only five hours away. We can tow it up there tomorrow and do a deal.'

'He won't have the money until Tuesday. It's the bank holiday.'

I made a Mickey Mouse telephone call to Peter Scrawley, another undercover police officer whom I had lined up previously. I allowed Murray to speak to Scrawley to arrange the deal for the Tuesday.

Scrawley was a member of the Darlaston Drug Squad. I once travelled to Bradford with him on an operation involving the prospective purchase of a parcel of heroin. I was the minder for the money on that occasion. He also had a policewoman with him who was acting as his accomplice. This policewoman had previously been involved in an undercover drug operation that had got a bit hairy. There were threats of violence and intimidation, and her bottle went completely. At one point, she was about to reveal her true identity. Fortunately for her, she didn't, as the consequences could have been far worse.

In those situations, I always found it best to go on the offensive. On the Bradford operation, Scrawley and I were mucked about all day by the criminals, who demanded to see the money before they'd do the deal. I caused a bit of an upset when I punched one of them who tried to touch the cash. In the end, the criminals failed to produce the drugs. When they finally told us that they didn't have the gear, Scrawley told them he wasn't very happy. Me? I went berserk and demanded money from them to cover my time and travelling expenses. Had I not snapped and snarled at them, they might have felt that it was within their power to walk off with the flash money.

When Murray got off the phone, I went over the arrangements. 'Have the caravan on the northbound Strensham Services on the M5 on Tuesday afternoon at 4 p.m. Me and the buyer will meet you there.' Dagenham was due to return from leave that weekend, so he'd be available for the operation on the Tuesday.

I contacted the operational commander on his cricket tour to fill him in. While I was in the middle of a dangerous operation, he was in the middle of tea and cucumber sandwiches.

On the Tuesday morning, I telephoned him, but he wasn't available. I was told by his secretary that he was in a meeting. I eventually tracked him down at 1.00 p.m. 'Superintendent Thomas wants to organise a meeting to discuss the operation with you,' he said.

'Sir, it's one o'clock. Murray is going to be at Strensham Services at four o'clock with a stolen caravan. Have you got him under surveillance?'

'No, we haven't. You'll have to contact Murray and put the deal off for 24 hours until you have briefed the superintendent. He wants to be in charge personally. And one other thing. We can't let you have the cash. It's too risky.'

I couldn't believe it. I'd been working my guts out for this. Frustrated, I rang Murray at his home. 'He's not here,' said the voice at the other end. 'He's over at Pollard's.'

'Have you got Pollard's number?'

I rang and asked for Murray. 'There's been a fuck-up,' I said. 'The buyer can't pull the money together until tomorrow.'

Murray wasn't too pleased. 'I thought we had a deal,' he said.

'We still have,' I assured him. 'But there's no point in trying to pull it together today, cos it just won't happen.'

'If you're pulling my dick, you'll fucking know about it,' Murray said, turning on the charm.

'I guarantee I'll be there with the money and the buyer tomorrow.' I put down the phone. My heart was racing – not through fear, but excitement. Murray was involved with Pollard, a notorious criminal who was behind most of the serious crime in Gloucestershire. Pollard had a reputation for violence, and he was regarded as untouchable. We now had the number-one criminal target in Cheltenham in the frame. It would be the perfect opportunity to nail him.

The plan was to follow Murray and Pollard until they picked up the caravan. As soon as they were in possession, we'd arrest them. That way there would be no need for me to actually meet them with the money.

The following day, I met up with Dagenham. Murray and Pollard were under surveillance. They were moving around Cheltenham, but, so far, there was no sign of any caravan. At 4 p.m., surveillance called to say that Murray and Pollard were sitting at Strensham Services in a green Range Rover but that there was still no sign of any caravan. I'd have to meet them after all.

A few moments later, my mobile phone rang – it was Murray asking where I was. There'd been an accident on the M42, and I told him I was stuck in traffic. 'Have you got the caravan?' I asked.

'No. It's on a site not far from the motorway. We'll take you there when you get here.'

This put Dagenham and me in a difficult position, as we had no flash money. We had no prearranged signals for a strike and no back-up plan if things went wrong. As a precaution, I'd brought along £500 in forged £20 notes that we'd confiscated from another operation. Anything else we would have to leave in the lap of the gods.

Dagenham and I made our way along the M5 to Strensham Services with an envelope full of funny money. As we arrived, I could see Murray's green Range Rover. I parked up 50 yards away and walked casually over to meet them. As I approached, Murray and Pollard stood beside the driver's door. Pollard was a small, stocky, pit bull of a man with an olive complexion and naturally greasy hair. Murray smiled and introduced Jimmy, who shook my hand. He was built as solid as they come, and had an air of pure menace.

'The van's not far. You ready?' Pollard asked.

'I'll go and tell my buyer what's happening,' I said.

'He can come if he wants.'

'I think he'd rather stay put. Frankly, you lot scare the shit out of him.'

Pollard laughed and shook his head. 'Long as he's got the money, he's got absolutely nothing to be scared about,' he said, smiling.

I told Dagenham to wait, returned to Murray's Range Rover and climbed into the back. As I got in, I looked into the foot well of the front passenger seat and saw the butt of a shotgun protruding from under a coat. Sticking out next to it was the head of a claw hammer.

We drove off from the services through the rear exit and onto country lanes, away from the motorway. As we went, I spotted the surveillance team's vehicles all the way. At one point, I saw the motorcyclist from the team, who was wearing a denim jacket with a sheepskin collar. He might as well have been wearing a flag on his helmet.

On surveillance, an unremarkable dress code is one of the most important factors. Never wear anything with a badge on it. Always wear plain-coloured clothes. Women must always wear a skirt. This is because men will always look at a woman's backside if they are wearing trousers. And if you saw the rear ends of most of the women I worked with, I guarantee you'd never forget them.

I sat myself square in front of Murray's rear-view mirror to reduce the chances of him clocking the surveillance bike. Pollard started talking about bare-knuckle fighting, of which he was both an advocate and willing participant. Coupled with the memory of Murray's violent, gun-toting past, my afternoon wasn't shaping up too nicely. I could handle myself in any situation, but when it came to having to fight these two I would prefer to leg it.

We passed a small country pub and then turned into a gateway that led to a paddock enclosed by tall poplar trees. The site was full of caravans, broken washing machines and crazy-looking dogs that were all cock and teeth. We were greeted by a huge bloke, who looked as if he was carved out of granite. A giant of a man, he was at least six feet six inches tall with a chin like a snow plough and a chest the size of a fridge freezer. He had dark eyes and an unsmiling face. Now I was seriously outnumbered. Instinctively, I began to look around the site for possible escape routes.

At one end of the paddock was the stolen caravan. Graniteman showed me around the inside. It was very plush. I began to look around it like a prospective buyer, opening and closing doors and bouncing up and down on the seats to see how comfortable they were. In my head, I was trying to work out what my next move would be. I was thinking, 'Evidence, evidence.'

After ten minutes of cupboard-door slamming, I stepped outside. 'It's a good 'un, all right,' I said to Murray. 'Let's go and get you some cash. Then we'll come back and collect the van.'

'We'll all go back,' said Pollard.

'Why don't you stop here? My buyer is really sweating on this. If anyone makes him twitchy, he'll bolt,' I said. Pollard reluctantly agreed, which meant I'd reduced the number of people I would have to fight with by 50 per cent.

Murray and I got into his Range Rover and drove back through the winding country roads, with surveillance once again on our tail. Ten minutes later, we arrived at the motorway services. 'Wait here,' I said to Murray. 'Let me talk to my buyer.'

I walked over to Dagenham, stuck my head in his window and filled him in on the situation. 'What do we do now?' I asked. 'He's going to want to see the cash.'

'Send him back to the camp,' suggested Dagenham. 'Tell him we'll follow on in five minutes with the money.' It was a risk, but we had no choice. I turned and gave Murray the thumbs-up. I then walked back and told him that we'd be a few minutes behind him. To my relief, he didn't even blink at the suggestion.

'See you there,' he said before pulling away.

I watched Murray leave the services and waited for a few moments to make sure he didn't return. Dagenham and I then drove onto the M5 and headed home. Murray and Pollard were arrested, and the stolen caravan was recovered.

The operational commander instructed us to come to Cheltenham to debrief him on the operation. We arrived just before lunch, and he treated us to anecdotes of his activities as a young detective sergeant in Cheltenham. After 20 minutes of this, I enquired about the investigation into Murray and Pollard. 'I've been thinking about this,' announced the operational commander. 'I've decided that if I was to prosecute Murray and Pollard, I would have to disclose the highly sensitive information of the surveillance activities of the Gloucestershire Police. So, in view of this, I have decided not to charge either of them.'

We sat in silence for a moment whilst we took all this in. Then I opened my big mouth. 'Well, that was a waste of everyone's fucking time,' I said. 'I put my arse on the line for you lot. I thought I was coming to Gloucestershire to assist the police battling serious crime, not to fanny around with a bunch of boy scouts.'

Dagenham and I drove back to Birmingham, stunned by such an outrageous operational decision. Even so, I returned to Cheltenham to finish what I'd started at the Hare and Hounds. A total of 45 people were arrested for drug dealing, burglary and theft-related offences.

I received a commendation from Ron Hadfield, the chief constable of West Midlands Police. The commendation read, 'For dedication and investigatory skills displayed in an operation against serious crime.'

It was a pity that some people in the higher ranks didn't have the bottle to follow through on the really serious criminals.

thirteen

MAKING A KILLING

'What the hell is that?'

'What does it look like?'

'It looks like a gun.'

It was a gun. And I'd just dropped it into the lap of my new commanding officer in the middle of McDonald's. For some reason, known only to himself, he had insisted on meeting me in the Merry Hill Shopping Centre, one of the largest and busiest shopping malls in the Midlands. Just the place for an undercover police officer to maintain a low profile.

My new operation was to involve me posing as a contract killer. The latest operational commander was an annoying bag of wind. I thought I'd wind him up a bit by introducing him to a 9-mm Browning high-powered semi-automatic pistol I'd borrowed from the Firearms and Explosives Department. He wasn't too happy. 'For God's sake, put it away,' he hissed, turning a lovely shade of beetroot. I thought he was going to have a heart attack. I slid the gun back into my jacket pocket and listened to the briefing.

Paddy Carolan was an Irish taxi driver who lived in Dudley. An informant told us that Carolan was looking for a hit man, someone to murder his son-in-law, who had been mistreating his daughter. He made various approaches to people to hire a contract killer. It was up to us to stop him before he succeeded.

Arrangements were made with the informant for me to meet Carolan.

I had a few days to prepare for the role of a contract killer. I did some investigation into a similar undercover operation that had taken place a few years before. The targets of the operation were a West Midlands police officer called Michael Ambrose and Mary Montague, the wife of a heavyweight Birmingham criminal. Ambrose, of Greek descent, was charming and well-liked throughout the force. Mary was the wife of local villain Sean Montague, who was under investigation for a large-scale mortgage fraud.

It was during investigations into Montague that Ambrose first got to know Mary. They soon struck up a relationship that was to be Ambrose's downfall. Mary confided in Ambrose that her husband was an animal who regularly beat her. He had also shot the family Labrador and beaten to death the children's pony in their presence.

Mary said that she would like to get rid of her husband and asked Ambrose for help. By that point, Ambrose was smitten, and his better judgement went straight down the pan. He approached a club owner named Stavros to enlist the services of a killer from the Greek community. But unknown to Ambrose, Stavros was a police informant.

Ambrose has always maintained that he intended to set up Mary. However, an undercover operation was mounted with officers posing as contract killers. A number of tape-recorded meetings with Ambrose contained sufficient evidence to arrest and charge him with conspiracy to murder. At trial, Mary Montague pleaded guilty and received a suspended sentence. Ambrose pleaded not guilty and was also convicted. He got seven years.

In a way, he was lucky. Jail was the safest place for him. Even though his life inside was made a living hell because he was a copper, it was not half as much hell as he would eventually have to suffer when he got out to face the very violent Mr Montague.

On the day I was to meet Paddy Carolan, I was told by the Force Technical Support Unit that a tape recorder I'd requested was not available. 'So what am I supposed to do?' I asked in frustration. 'Get him to speak into a loud hailer?'

The Force Technical Support Unit held all the equipment used by the Midlands forces. Some of the equipment was more suited to the

Antiques Roadshow than twentieth-century policing. Abuse from fellow officers was a regular occurrence, so they just shrugged an apologetic shrug and left me to rant to myself.

The tape recorders themselves weren't exactly worth writing home about. For a start, they were so sensitive that any background noise would be picked up instantly. This meant you always had to find somewhere quiet to record evidence. They could not be used in a car with the engine running, for example, as the engine noise would make anything else unintelligible. The other problem was that they were the size of a sandwich box and difficult to conceal. The usual method was to tape the recorder to the torso of the undercover officer. This was not only uncomfortable, it was dangerous, especially if you got patted down by a suspicious villain.

I was once introduced to a security company who manufactured recording devices for the SAS. I was shown a digital recorder and a transmitting device that was so small it would fit into an electronic key ring. Unfortunately, at £300 it didn't fit into the police budget. While the force would go to any lengths to save money, it seems they weren't prepared to pay out to protect an officer's life.

I met Carolan in the car park of an American-style diner on the site of an old mosaic factory near Dudley. I arrived to find him sitting in a battered old Mercedes with the taxi sign stuck to the roof. He was a small but stocky man with a shock of curly hair, like Bob Hoskins in a Scouser wig.

I signalled for him to come over. This was to get him used to being in my car, where I could record him. If I had a frigging tape recorder. 'I'm Ronnie,' I said, shaking his hand. 'That's all you need to know. I hear you need a hand with some pest control.'

'Yes, my gobshite son-in-law.'

'Now, who else knows about this?'

'My wife. That's it.'

'Right, here's how we play it. From now on, anything we talk about is between me and you. You tell no one, not even your missus.'

'Right.'

'And I will contact you. You cannot contact me. Got that?'

'Yes,' said Carolan.

'I've got to be happy with you, and you've to be happy with me, because if this goes tits up, we're both fucked, and I'll know who to blame.'

'OK.'

I kept the meeting short. Without the tape recorder, there was no point in getting too much information. To get him for conspiracy to murder, I would have to get him to spell out exactly what it was that he wanted.

We met again a few days later. I arrived at the car park and once again found Carolan waiting for me in his taxi. I waved him over to my car. Safely under the seat was the Nagra tape recorder I'd activated moments earlier. Carolan, breathless from the walk across the car park, sat down heavily in the front passenger seat.

'Right,' I barked. 'Let's get on with it.'

'OK . . .'

'Tell me what it is that you want me to do.'

'I want my son-in-law done,' said Carolan.

'Done?'

'I need you to get rid of him,' he said.

'How d'you mean?'

'I mean get rid of him for good. Kill him,' Carolan enunciated clearly, his eyes fixed on mine. 'I want that bastard dead.'

'Now we're getting somewhere,' I said coolly, slowly stretching out in my seat. 'Right, I need to know who this bloke is and what he looks like. I want the most recent photograph of Robbins you've got. I want to know where he lives, where he drinks and I want details of the car he drives. I need all this information by the next time I see you. Do you understand?'

'Yes,' Carolan replied.

I paused for a moment, looked out the window and then announced, 'It's going to cost you twenty grand. Cash. Half up front and the other half when the job's finished.'

Carolan fell silent for a moment. The cold reality of all this had left him deflated. 'It will take a bit of time to get the money,' he finally answered, his voice now almost a whisper.

'You've got two weeks,' I instructed him. 'You sure you want this? Because once you give me the nod, that's it. There's no going back.'

'Yes,' he said, nodding. 'I definitely want you to do this.'

'And another thing,' I added as he was about to get out of the car. 'I'm going to need £200 the next time we meet.'

'What for?'

'To pay for the gun.' If he couldn't come up with the cash for the hit, then the gun money would be enough to nail him.

Two weeks later, we met again. As Carolan got into my car, I noticed how tired he looked. 'Have you sorted the money out?' I asked.

'I've got the gun money,' he said, handing over an envelope full of tens, which I counted out.

'Good, because I've got the gun,' I said, opening the glove compartment and giving him a peek at the Browning pistol I'd shoved into my governor's lap. I explained that I'd have to get rid of it after, as it would have a signature. A signature is the term given to the unique marks left on a bullet head as it goes through the gun barrel. The bullet found at the scene of a crime can then be linked back to the gun.

'The big money's going to take a few more days,' said Carolan apologetically. 'My wife's sorting it out.'

'Your fucking wife?' I said, exasperated. 'I told you not to discuss this with anyone . . .'

'I'm sorry. The only way I can get the money for this is with a second mortgage. I need her to sign the documents,' Carolan explained.

I warned him that if anything should go wrong, I would come looking for him and his missus. 'She's not going to say a word,' insisted Carolan. 'She wants him dead, too.'

He then went on to explain exactly what a thoroughly nasty piece of work his son-in-law was. Carolan's daughter had met her future husband, a local tearaway, when she was training to be a nurse. Carolan had made clear his reservations about the relationship, but his daughter chose to ignore her father. The young couple eventually got married and had three children, a boy and two girls.

Everything seemed to be working out OK. Then one night, the eldest granddaughter turned up at Carolan's house hysterical. Her mother had been attacked by her father and had run off. When they found her, they discovered that she'd taken a severe beating. And it wasn't the first time. Carolan's daughter broke down and told him what a dreadful life she had with this animal. She was working, and he was taking all her money and not paying the mortgage.

Carolan put up the money for his daughter to get a divorce, and her solicitor got a court order to get his son-in-law out of the house, but legally he still had access to the kids. One morning, he took the youngest girl to Stratford, where he raped her and then frightened her into keeping quiet. She was ten years old. Twelve months later, he raped the eldest girl, who was fifteen, in her own bed. She told her mother, and Carolan's son-in-law was arrested and charged with two counts of rape. Despite very strong evidence, including semen found in the girl's bed, he somehow got off both charges.

Carolan talked without a break for over 35 minutes. Fortunately, the Nagra tape lasted for four hours. I sat there listening, my blood boiling. I suddenly felt a pang of sympathy for Carolan. This was no gangster. This was a man who had an awful lot on his mind. Unfortunately for him, what was on his mind was against the law. Off the record, I would have shot his son-in-law for nothing.

'Have you got all the info I asked you for?' He handed over the details on Robbins, written neatly in his own handwriting. More evidence. 'You won't see me again,' I added. 'Someone will contact you for the first payment and then again afterwards for the rest. Nothing will happen until you hand over the money.'

We parted company. As I drove from the car park, I saw Carolan was trying to follow me from a distance. I put my foot to the floor and used some defensive driving techniques to shake him off.

Carolan was arrested and charged with conspiracy to murder. He was given an interesting sentence of two years' imprisonment, suspended for life. I felt truly sorry for a man who was only trying to right the most dreadful of wrongs.

The really bad guys are often harder to catch. Like a hit man called Peter O'Toole, who was happy to carry out shootings for small amounts of cash, which led to him gaining the reputation that he did it for the enjoyment, not the money.

O'Toole was born in Birmingham into a well-known crime family. His uncle was shot dead in a city-centre pub in the mid-1990s, following a bungled importation of a large quantity of cannabis. He was killed because he was suspected of being a police informant. As a 17 year old, O'Toole was convicted of grievous bodily harm. He'd been caught shoplifting by a security officer, whom he went on to stab four times in the chest. At 20, he slashed the face of a 16 year old in a fish-and-chip shop because he was looking at O'Toole in a funny way. The lad needed 118 stitches to hold his face together. O'Toole appeared at court but astonishingly jumped over the dock, escaped in a waiting car and fled the country to Torremolinos in southern Spain. There, he quickly moved into the criminal scene, running errands for British gangsters in the area.

One night, O'Toole was drinking heavily in a Spanish bar called Loonies when he began to throw snooker balls. He was told to leave the premises by the bar owner. O'Toole returned with a gun and began spraying bullets around the bar, hitting a Liverpool holidaymaker in the head.

With the police after him, O'Toole returned to Birmingham and joined forces with lifelong friend Gary Morgan. The two began importing large consignments of cannabis.

In the course of their dealings, Anthony Morecroft, another criminal, crossed Morgan and O'Toole, so Morgan persuaded O'Toole to take him out. Morecroft was shot by O'Toole in a Birmingham tourist trap known as Brindley Place. Miraculously, he survived by diving into a canal to escape. The crime was investigated, but Morecroft refused to cooperate with the police, so they had no evidence with which to arrest O'Toole.

When Morgan refused to pay for the failed Morecroft hit, O'Toole was left fuming. Morgan also began to run up serious debts with his drug suppliers. Ironically, O'Toole was then handed £2,900 by a drug dealer for a hit on Morgan. O'Toole arranged a meeting in the car park of the Aston Hotel, just yards from Villa Park. They met and exchanged pleasantries before O'Toole shot Morgan twice in the head from point-blank range. Morgan's body, slumped at the wheel of his car, was not discovered for five hours, as passers-by thought he was sleeping. His mobile phone was recovered with 32 missed calls. O'Toole was convicted of murder and sentenced to 30 years in prison.

fourteen

THE LOWEST OF THE LOW

'Foxtrot One to Zulu One. Premises on fire. Reports of persons trapped on premises.' My radio blurted out the address. It wasn't my call, but I was in the area. Any help I could offer, I would. As I arrived, the Goons were smashing in the door. The Goons was a police nickname for the fire service. At the scene of a fire, they smashed everything that couldn't be flooded.

There was smoke pouring from the upstairs of the house. Through the front-room window, I noticed a man pacing up and down. He was tall with a beard and long dreadlocks, and he was carrying a walking stick in his hand. 'There's someone in the living room!' I yelled.

One of the Goons rushed into the room. As he came through the door, the Rastafarian started waving his stick about. Then I realised that it wasn't a walking stick but a machete. He thrashed it wildly at the fireman, who backed out of the room, slamming the door behind him. My brain immediately went into overdrive. I stormed into the house, completely ignoring the fact that the place was on fire. I kicked open the living-room door, picked up a wooden coffee table and ran at the Rasta, yelling. He stopped momentarily, wide-eyed at this maniac coming at him with a piece of furniture. I hit him with the table and sent us both crashing into the bay window.

The uniformed officers had arrived at that point. As the Rastafarian crashed through the window, they sprayed us both with CS gas, a

155

lungful of which is like inhaling bleach. I couldn't breathe, and my eyes felt like they were on fire.

I felt a hand grab me by the collar, and I was dragged out into the street. I spent five minutes coughing my guts up. Gradually, I began to regain my sight. The Rasta was handcuffed and lying face down in the front garden. He was shouting all sorts of strange patois. It was difficult to understand, but the odd bits I could make out were all about hellfire and damnation. He was either high as a kite or mad as a fish. He wouldn't shut up. Even as they manhandled him into the back of the police van, he continued to shout and wail.

The Goons brought the fire under control, and I began to get myself together. As I was sitting on the bonnet of my car still feeling the effects of the CS gas, the fire officer in charge came over. 'You better come and have a look at this,' he said. I followed him into the house to an upstairs bedroom. This was the source of the fire. On the bed was the body of a young black girl in her 20s. Her face was covered in blood.

'Right,' I declared. 'Don't touch anything. This is a crime scene now. Everybody out.' Everyone left the house, leaving me with the body. I radioed for an ambulance to remove it. The scenes of crime officers then arrived, along with Quincy, the Home Office pathologist. I went downstairs and left them to it.

As I stood at the front door of the house reflecting on what had happened, Quincy waddled down the stairs. 'All right, where are they then?' he asked.

'Where are what?' I replied.

'Her eyes. Somebody's whipped them out.'

Minutes later, one of the scenes of crime officers appeared with a plastic bag. Inside the bag was a spoon, covered in blood. I fought the urge to throw up. 'Murder weapon?' I said.

'I don't know about that,' Quincy replied. 'But you're going to have to come with me to the post-mortem, as you found the body.'

As the ambulance crew stretchered the body out of the house, the scenes of crime officer reappeared with another plastic bag. 'You'd better take these with you, too,' he said, offering the bag to Quincy. 'I found them down the back of the sofa.' It was the girl's eyes.

At the post-mortem, Quincy found a foreign object in the girl's vagina. It turned out to be a cactus. He couldn't establish whether this, or the removal of her eyes, had been carried out before or after she was killed.

The murder had all the hallmarks of a ritualistic killing. The Rasta was charged but never went to court. He was declared insane, unfit for trial, and was sent to Rampton mental institution for life.

There are some evil people in the world. Unfortunately, as a copper, you get to meet a lot of them. I once had to take a witness statement from a man who had just had the windows smashed in on his Mercedes. Someone had then thrown sulphuric acid into his eyes. It was a revenge attack, following an argument over a game of cards. Members of a Turkish card school had fallen out over money, and this was how it was resolved. Acid burns the skin on contact. The damage is devastating and irreparable. It's very disconcerting trying to interview someone when their face is melting in front of you.

A pair of burglars I once investigated showed no sign of remorse as I confronted them with details of their particularly nasty handiwork. They'd burgled a pub. When the publican had said that he couldn't open the safe, they had got hold of the family Labrador, threatening to kill it. The landlord had continued to insist that he couldn't open the safe. The burglars had then chopped the dog in half with a chainsaw. The reason the landlord couldn't open the safe was that it had a timelock device, which meant it couldn't be opened until the following morning. You cannot even begin to imagine the mess at the crime scene.

When I was offered the opportunity to go undercover to help trap a paedophile, I jumped at it. These bastards are the lowest of the low. The informant had known the target for some time and said he'd become aware of his interest in underage girls. The target had also demonstrated an enthusiasm for child pornography. The informant added that the target admitted to chatting to very young girls on the Internet and suspected that he stored indecent images on his computer.

'Why not get a search warrant and turn him over?' I asked.

'This is a sensitive inquiry,' the head of intelligence replied. 'We need it treated in a sensitive way.'

'Why do you want to be sensitive about a fucking paedophile?' I asked. This made everyone in the room twitch. Then came the revelation that the person I was investigating was a police officer. This put a completely different light on the job. If he was a paedophile, he deserved to be sent to prison. If he wasn't, the allegations could ruin his career. I made my mind up to do the job as straight as a die. If the guy was at it, I would make sure he burned in hell. Equally, if he wasn't, I would make sure whoever made the allegations got their comeuppance.

We code named the suspect Uncle. I asked to see a photograph of him, so I could make sure we hadn't crossed paths in the past. The informant then arranged for me to bump into the suspect over a pint. The rendezvous was at a pub in Worcester. I shook hands with the informant, and he bought me a drink. Uncle was standing nearby. The informant then introduced us, and by the end of the evening Uncle had ingratiated himself into our huddle.

He was full of questions, and I happily plied him with the usual Ronnie bullshit: I had a carpet-cleaning business, and I did a bit of buying and selling. (At that time, my brother had an upholstery-cleaning company, so I wasn't completely winging it.) I told him I spent a lot of time on the Internet tracking things down. In return, I purposely asked him no personal questions about himself whatsoever. I wanted him to open up to me, rather than me pumping him for information, which might have put him on his guard.

The following Friday, I met the informant again in the same pub. Uncle was there, and the evening ended with all three of us going for a curry. During the meal, Uncle mentioned that he was looking to sell some limited-edition models of cars he'd collected as an investment. 'EBay's your best bet,' I told him.

'I've never used it,' he admitted.

'It's easy. I buy and sell stuff on it all the time,' I added.

'It all sounds a bit complicated,' he said, laughing.

'It's a piece of piss. Trust me. You'll need photos to upload onto the website. I've got a digital camera you can borrow.'

The next day, I drove to Uncle's house to look at his models. They were still in their boxes, each with a numbered certificate. The house was in a modern development, and inside it was immaculate. Underneath the stairs was his computer terminal.

'Nice place. Is your missus out?'

'I'm divorced. There's a couple of women on the horizon, but nothing serious. I'm pretty friendly with one of my neighbours, which is handy, as she does my ironing.'

I took photos of the model cars and showed him how to upload them onto eBay. He left me for a moment to put the kettle on. Quickly, I clicked on the favourites button, which displayed a list of the websites that Uncle liked to visit. There were a lot of chat-room addresses, but I couldn't make a mental list of them all in the seconds I had.

As Uncle returned to the room, I swiftly hid the list. He sat down at the terminal and called up a photograph of an attractive blonde woman with two small girls. 'That's my obliging neighbour,' he said, 'and her two gorgeous daughters.' The girls couldn't have been more than five and seven years old. 'I do her a few favours. You know, pick the kids up from school and babysit occasionally.'

'Where's her husband?'

'She's separated. He doesn't tip up any money for the kids, so she's struggling a bit. I help out a bit, buying them bits and pieces.' This was a classic paedophile ploy: ingratiate yourself with a struggling parent, make them feel grateful in order to gain their trust and then get to work on their children.

I updated HQ on my findings, and I was told that my car had been checked on the police force's national computer. Uncle was having a sniff round. He would now have details of a bogus company to whom my vehicle was registered, but he would not have access to my personal details. It was time for some subterfuge. We placed false data on the intelligence system that said I was involved in handling stolen property. It also said that I was suspected of indecency with children, particularly young girls. The entry was backdated.

In order for him to access my personal details, he would need more information. To bait the trap a little further, I bought a pay-as-you-go mobile phone registered in my bogus name. If I gave Uncle my mobile number, he could check out certain details that would give him the necessary information to interrogate the intelligence system further. The head of the Paedophile Unit also supplied me with some seized contact magazines. They contained adverts for girls who looked to be no more than 14 or 15 years old.

One Friday, I rang Uncle on my mobile. I suggested that I could pick him up from his house before we went for a drink. That way we could check on the progress of the sale of his models on eBay. He sounded keen on the idea of him drinking and me driving.

I picked him up and drove into Worcester. On the way, I stopped at a service station for petrol. As I stood in the cashier's queue waiting to pay, I watched as he picked up the contact magazines I'd left in the passenger door and thumbed through them.

Later on in the pub, Uncle got drunk and invited me to a barbecue over at his place the following Sunday. As I dropped him off after closing, he repeated the invitation.

On the Sunday, I arrived at his house just before seven. He offered me a beer and asked me to sit down. 'The barbecue is at my girlfriend's across the road. There's something I need to talk to you about before we go.'

'Fire away.'

'I'm a policeman, and I have to be careful about who I'm associating with. I will come straight to the point. I've checked you out.'

'Checked me out? What d'you mean?'

'On the police computer.'

'What the fuck have you done that for?'

'I'm sorry, Ronnie. I have to be careful about who I'm associating with, that's all. You've got one conviction for handling stolen goods. So what?' I was waiting for him to say something about my fabricated interest in young girls, but he said nothing. He was being sly. 'Look, Ronnie, it's out in the open now. I trust you. Don't worry.'

In a flash, I devised a plan to get him into the net. 'All right, let's see how much you trust me,' I said. 'I need a favour.'

'If I can help, I will.'

'A friend of mine has had a car damaged in a hit and run. She got the number of the car but needs to find out who the owner is. Can you get it checked for me?'

'Get me the number, and I'll do it for you.'

He shook my hand. We left his house and went across the road to his neighbour's. There I was introduced to Barbara and her two young daughters, Emily and Jane. I chatted with Barbara whilst Uncle cooked the food in the garden. Barbara was very attractive and extremely flirty. The food was dreadful – economy beef burgers and cheap sausages that had about as much meat in them as a plank of wood.

As the evening progressed, Uncle became more and more drunk. As he did so, he became increasingly tactile with the children, particularly Emily, the older of the two.

At 10 p.m., I'd drunk as much as I dared, and I announced that I was leaving. Uncle said that he was going home too. As I left, Barbara kissed me full on the lips. Uncle kissed the two little girls, and I saw him squeeze Emily's bottom.

We left the house, and Uncle staggered back across the road. 'Care for a nightcap?' he slurred.

'Go on then.' I wanted to get a good look around his house. It would be easy with him in such a state. I said that I needed to use the toilet and went upstairs. I had a quick scan of all the bedrooms but saw nothing unusual. I flushed the toilet and came back downstairs. Uncle then put on a pornographic video and sat glued to the screen. A young girl of about ten or eleven was having sex with a fully grown man.

'What do you think of this, then?' leered my host.

'I can get this copied if you want,' I offered, avoiding the question and hoping to get hold of a video for evidence.

'No thanks. I'd better hang on to it.'

I'd had enough. 'I've got to go,' I said.

'Ring me with that car number you want checked,' he reminded me.

First thing on Monday morning, I gave HQ a detailed account of what had taken place at the barbecue. 'He's in possession of child pornography,' I concluded. 'I suggest we issue a search warrant on his home immediately.'

'He may have those tapes legitimately for an investigation,' said the commanding officer. 'We can't risk getting this wrong.'

'He's a fucking paedo. What we can risk is letting him get away with this,' I implored, but as before my appeal fell on deaf ears. After 20 minutes of hitting my head against a management brick wall, I gave in and agreed to gain further evidence.

The following day, I went on a tour of the scrapyards and got myself the registration number of a wrecked car. I telephoned Uncle to give him the number and asked him to let me know who the registered owner was.

That evening, he called to invite me over. 'I've got something for you,' he said. When I went over later on, Barbara was in the living room with the television on. Uncle ushered me into the kitchen and produced a computer printout of the vehicle details I'd given him. 'There's your hit-and-run driver,' he smiled, handing me the printout.

'Can I keep this?' I asked.

'Yeah, but destroy it when you've finished with it. And don't give it to anyone else.'

As I stood in the kitchen, I could see the television in a reflection in a glass cabinet. 'What's Barbara watching?'

'Another one of my exhibits.' I walked into the living room and Barbara stood up. She looked a little flushed and said hello. She kissed me on the cheek. On the screen behind her was a man having sex with a young girl. Barbara walked past me into the kitchen and told Uncle she was going home to feed her children. She said goodbye and asked him to call at her house later. After she'd left, Uncle went into the living room and turned off the television.

'Is she into this kiddie porn stuff?' I asked.

'She likes all sorts of things.'

'What about you?'

'We all have our little secrets, don't we, Ronnie?'

'I don't know what you mean.'

'What adults do in private is their own business, isn't it?' he replied. 'What are you into, Ronnie?'

'Bit of this, bit of that,' I replied noncommittally before changing the subject. 'That vehicle check you did. Do I owe you anything?'

'That's on the house, Ronnie. Consider it a favour.'

'Well, anything I can do in return, just let me know.'

The following morning, I went straight to the head of Proactive Complaints. I had witnessed the mother of two young girls watching paedophile porn, so there was a high chance that her children were at risk. 'We still need something more solid,' was the response.

'Perhaps we should wait until one of the girls is abused,' I suggested sarcastically. 'Would that be enough evidence?' I added that I was going to make a detailed note of our meeting. I didn't want to be blamed if the investigation went belly up. He said that he would arrange an urgent meeting with the head of social services.

I decided that I'd get Uncle drunk, so I took him to a lap-dancing club in Moseley. The guy who ran security was an ex-policeman whom I could trust, and he sorted me out with a private room. I ordered a bottle of champagne and paid one of the girls to dance for us. This got him ramped up, and he began to drink more heavily. Soon we were surrounded by more girls keen to take advantage of our relaxed state. By then, it was clear that the beer was in but the brains were out. I decided to go for it. I shooed the girls away, saying we wanted to talk in private. 'So, what's old Barbara like in the sack, then?' I asked.

'She's a real goer,' slurred Uncle, adding intimate details about her sexual performance.

'I was surprised to see her watching that kiddie porn,' I said.

'She's up for anything,' replied Uncle.

'Anything?' I said.

'Oh, yes. She likes the idea of her girls getting involved.'

I felt my temper rise. I calmed myself with the thought that any second he was going to say something that would bury him. I pushed on. 'Involved in what?'

'Photos would be enough to start with.'

'Who'd take the photographs?'

'You can if you want,' he said, smiling. 'I know all about you.'

'What do you mean?' I asked.

'I've seen your record. You're all over the database.'

'You've been checking up on me again?'

'Yes, you've got a very colourful background,' he replied, grinning.

'Well, me and you both.'

'I'm pretty certain that Barbara will let me have the oldest girl whenever I am ready. She's ready, believe me.'

'How do you know?'

'I've been working on her for quite a while now,' he said. I interpreted this as the advanced stage of grooming. Paedophiles are cunning. They can spend months, sometimes years, building up a relationship with their victims.

'So what's the next move?' I asked.

'I'll see the eldest daughter on her own and try her out. Then we'll know for sure.'

I continued to push champagne into Uncle until he could hardly speak. At 2 a.m., I poured him into the car and drove him home to Worcester, where I left him staggering up his driveway. On my way back to Birmingham, I called the head of Proactive Complaints. 'There's been a serious development,' I said. 'I'm on my way to HQ. I'll meet you there in an hour.'

'Have you any idea what the time is?' asked the superintendent.

'I know exactly what the time is. HQ, one hour.' I put down the phone.

At 5.30 a.m., the head of Proactive Complaints came into the reception of HQ, and I was taken to his office on the third floor. I ran through my disturbing conversation in the lapdancing club. 'I believe he's going to rape his girlfriend's little girl,' I said.

'Where's this going to take place?' asked the superintendent.

'I don't bloody know! He didn't give me a fucking itinerary! I've done my bit. It's in your hands now,' I said and left the superintendent's office.

The wheels of the organisation then began slowly to turn. I completed my statement of evidence and handed it over to the head of Proactive Complaints. It was at that point that I divulged that Uncle had checked a vehicle for me on the police national computer. I handed over the computer printout I'd been given by him. No one at that time realised the relevance of this.

Uncle was nicked and charged with conspiring with Barbara to have unlawful sexual intercourse with a girl under 13 years old and possession of indecent images of children. The case went to court and was thrown out because the images that had been taken from his computer had been sent to him by the Proactive Complaints department. That was like posting a kilo of cannabis through someone's door before kicking it in and expecting to get a result. I had done my part in the operation only to have it destroyed by amateurish behaviour from above.

Uncle appeared before a police disciplinary hearing charged with improper use of the police national computer and improper disclosure of information. He was sacked. I heard some time later that he had applied for a position with the prison service. If the inmates ever found out about his past, he'd have been torn to shreds.

fifteen

THE A TEAM

Gaining promotion was a slow process. Not because I wasn't good enough, but because of the amount of time I spent away from conventional police duties in my undercover role. The Career Development department had never heard of Specialist Operations, so the chief superintendent at the station where I carried out my regular duties submitted a report supporting my application for promotion.

Sadly, the same man who was so supportive was arrested shortly after his retirement for a large-scale fraud involving holiday homes in northern France. During the course of the inquiry, his strange lifestyle was uncovered. He had served time in Northern Ireland. Since his return, he'd been forever looking over his shoulder, convinced that he was being pursued by the IRA. For this reason, he always carried a loaded revolver, but he didn't have a licence for it. At his trial, he claimed that his service in Northern Ireland had affected him so badly that the balance of his mind had been disturbed. (Although not so disturbed that he didn't have the presence of mind to carry out a complicated property deception.)

I was granted a promotion interview, which was chaired by a Superintendent Bob Morris. Our paths had crossed many times during our careers. The first occasion was when he came to visit me at my home when I applied to join the police service, the second was at Steelhouse Lane when a squad was formed to combat vehicle crime in the centre of Birmingham. The detection rate for vehicle crime when the squad was formed was 7 per cent. After six weeks, I had improved it to 57 per cent.

I got the job and was posted to my old stomping ground at Steelhouse Lane. On my first day in the role of sergeant, I found myself dealing with a siege situation. A domestic dispute had taken place between a young couple that had got quite heated. The woman had run off, and the man had grabbed a knife, locking himself in the house. As I stared at him through the letterbox, I could see him sitting on the stairs with a large carving knife poised over his stomach. 'If you come any closer, I'll stab myself!' he screamed. I said nothing, which only made him shout louder, presumably because he thought I hadn't heard him. With the noise he was making, most of Birmingham would have had an earful by then. And it was starting to get on my nerves.

Officers arrived carrying the 'Number One Public Order Kit', which basically consisted of helmets and riot shields. This was an improvement on the dustbin lids we'd been issued with when I first joined the police force. I donned the kit and prepared to do battle.

It was suggested that we batter the door down and then rush the bloke. 'By the time we get through, he'll have kebabed himself,' I said. 'I've got a better idea.'

I got another officer to start talking to the man through the letterbox: 'Just take it easy, mate. Everything's going to be all right. Just don't do anything stupid, now. OK?'

'I'll fucking kill myself. I will. I'll fucking do it!'

'I'll fucking kill you myself if you don't shut up,' I thought as I clambered up onto the porch and forced entrance via an upstairs window. I crawled through the bedroom and peeked over the top of the stairs. Through the steam on my visor I could see the crown of the man's head as he continued to scream.

'Just fuck off and leave me alone! I'll fucking do it. I fucking will!'

I had a problem. There were 15 steps between me and the man. Could I get down them before he skewered himself or worse skewered me? I was fit, and I was fast, but I wasn't stupid. Get it wrong and there'd be claret everywhere.

The therapy session at the bottom of the stairs continued. 'Let's just take it easy, yeah?' said the voice through the letterbox. 'Let's just keep it nice and calm.'

'Fuck off, copper! Just fuck off!'

The siege was going nowhere, so I took my helmet off and, drawing on my experience playing American football, threw it as hard as I could. With a sharp crack, it caught the man squarely on top of his head, pitching him forward off the step. As he fell onto his knees, I flew down the stairs. With my shield, I knocked the carving knife from his hand, and with my free hand I neutralised him with a hook to the jaw, which sent him sprawling through a fish tank in the hallway. This was hardly the practice of a trained negotiator, but it did the job. The other officers rammed the door and arrived to find me standing over the man with his face in the carpet, covered in goldfish. 'Lock him up,' I ordered, 'before he does any more damage.'

I quickly adjusted to my new role and gained the respect of most of the shift, as I could always be relied upon to make a decision. I began to streamline procedures that I felt were inefficient. For example, there was a protracted procedure for night-duty officers handing over persons arrested during the night to the early-turn officers to fill in the necessary paperwork. This was slow and seriously depleted the number of officers actually on the streets. To speed things up, I posted another officer to work with me on the handover, leaving the rest of the shift free to go on patrol. One morning, we dealt with six different arrests before breakfast, which was unheard of.

I went through a period of several months without contact with Specialist Operations. I was having too good a time in uniform.

A short time after my promotion, my old friend David Donovan arrived at Steelhouse Lane as the new chief inspector. Despite his rise through the ranks, Donovan remained the same affable bloke that he had always been. He'd been told that a spell in uniform away from CID would enhance his promotion prospects. And he fell for it.

I began a short attachment with a newly created department known as the Crime Bureau. This was staffed mainly by civilians or the lame, the sick and the dying from uniformed staff. Their function was to take reports of crime over the telephone, complete reports and maintain computer records. Attached to the Crime Bureau was an intelligence cell that contained a number of detectives who didn't seem to have a clue what they were supposed to be doing, so I was asked to breathe some life into the place.

Dave Donovan then approached me to set up a Robbery Squad. In a previous attempt to reduce robberies, management at Steelhouse Lane had increased uniform presence in what were now called robbery 'hot spots', as the phrase 'black spot' was no longer politically correct. This was at a time when police officers were being made to wear yellow reflective jackets and walk around looking like lollipop ladies. The idea was that they would be more visible and therefore more of a deterrent. The initiative had resulted in an increase in robberies of 14 per cent.

Donovan now wanted a proactive crackdown. Another approach was called for. I jumped at the chance, setting up Operation Reverse 22, which consisted of me, two detectives and twelve uniformed constables, who I insisted worked in plain clothes. I was given a tiny overtime budget, covert radio sets and an office the size of a shoebox. On the upside, we were provided with two leased luxury cars to roar about Birmingham in.

I told my team that I would adopt the same policy as the legendary football manager Brian Clough. If they didn't produce results, they'd be off the team. This wasn't particularly in keeping with the police-training ethos, which said that if someone was crap, you had to look for something that they did well to provide a balanced approach. The way I saw it, being crap didn't help catch criminals.

With this in mind, I enlisted an officer whom I'd worked with in the past. He was a giant of a man called Harvey, and he was an exceptional policeman in every respect. Physically, he resembled Desperate Dan, with a stubbly chin and a chest the size of Norfolk. Before joining the police force, he'd been in the army. He joined at 16 and was posted to St George Barracks in Sutton Coldfield. At that time, he was six feet four inches tall and fifteen stone but still just a boy. The other soldiers bullied him incessantly, until one day in the mess a body-building soldier punched him square in the face. Harvey rose to his feet and tore the body builder apart. He was dragged away and ordered to see the commanding officer, fully expecting to be disciplined for handing out a beating. Instead, the commanding officer shook his hand and told him he would now represent the regiment at boxing. He went on to become the British Army heavyweight champion.

He later joined the police but resigned to support his wife, who was suffering from post-natal depression. Within a month, he realised that he had made a mistake, so he applied to rejoin and was readmitted. It was then that I grabbed him to spend time with me in the Robbery Squad.

Like me, Harvey liked to work hard and train hard. He was in peak physical condition. One day, he was training in the police-station gym. Another policeman, who was a black belt in some martial art or other, was pummelling the heavy bag. There was a new inspector at the station, and he came into the gym for a look around the facilities.

'Fancy doing a spot of sparring?' asked Black Belt, keen to show off his fighting prowess.

'All right,' Harvey said, 'but I promise I won't hit you too hard.' Black Belt's eyes flickered in annoyance as he took up his best kung-fu stance. BANG. Harvey knocked him out with a short left hook to the chin. Game over.

As impressive as he was, I was wise enough to know that there couldn't be all arse kickers like Harvey in the team. There also needed to be some solid back-up. If I'm honest, I'd always had something of a sexist attitude towards women. Until I met Cheryl Moorstock, who weighed in at 15 stone and could drink all the other officers in the squad under the table. She was a ruthless interviewer and could scare the hell out of the cockiest of villains. She was also an excellent detective. I suggested to the chief constable that if we had 12 policewomen like Cheryl, we would be able to get rid of the rest of the females in the force.

One of the other women on the Reverse 22 team was called Debbie Brew, but she was nicknamed Heineken because she refreshed the parts of anyone who came into contact with her. She flirted shamelessly with the male officers in the group. Her skirts were always short, her blouses tight. She was the life and soul of the set-up and very, very sexy. She was also very, very gay. Everybody knew it, but it still didn't stop the male officers thinking that they could seduce her into switching sides. Her speciality was bedding straight women. She had more success than most of the males in the squad put together.

Then there was Carol Stewart, a mixed-race girl with a body made in heaven but mood swings that would try the patience of a saint. For this, she earned herself the title of 'GW', which we told her stood for 'Girly Woman', because she always looked younger than her age. In fact, it actually stood for 'God's Witch', because she could be charming one moment and a mentalist the next. But she was one of the hardest workers I ever met, and that was vitally important to me.

The male contingent included the Gimp, who had a fascination for pornographic films. The Gimp had been part of a police static-observation team, which had involved sitting still for long periods. He could be given one of the most tedious tasks to perform, which he would complete without a complaint. If I'd given him a handful of salt and asked him to count the grains, he'd have done it unquestioningly.

At the opposite end of the scale, there was Indiana Jones, who was something of a loner. Indy had served with the SAS, spending six weeks behind enemy lines in the Gulf War. He was an odd fish but ruthlessly efficient. He always referred to criminals as 'the enemy', which was something I really liked about him.

When my squad started work, street robberies were being reported at a rate of ten a day. I decided that the only thing that was preventing arrests from being made was the paperwork that kept officers off the street, so I took responsibility for the preparation of all files of evidence, which freed up my officers to be out on the streets. And the fact that they weren't in uniform gave them an element of surprise.

I came up with a couple of other working practices to increase the number of arrests. The first was that we would get a detailed description from the victim of the clothing worn by the offender – it's often easier for people to recall garments than it is faces. Clothing would then be the first thing that we recovered from suspects' homes after they were arrested. This had a surprising but useful psychological effect. Many offenders would assume that the clothing we'd bagged was strong enough evidence to identify them, so they would end up confessing to their crime.

The second practice I implemented was that when a person reported a robbery, they would be taken back to the area where the offence had taken place. Most offenders operate within a distinct territory – they tend not to stray too far. If the first sweep failed, we would repeat the exercise a week later. It was incredible the number of offenders we picked up simply walking along the street.

In five months, we arrested over two hundred and fifty people. Management thought that this was a stroke of genius. It even made it into the newspapers. To me, it was just what basic policing was all about: using your brain. Many policemen I served with never seemed to fully engage that most powerful organ in the human body.

The newly installed CCTV in the city centre also made an excellent weapon in the fight against street crime. It was controlled by civilian operators, one of whom was an absolute genius at recognising offenders *before* they committed robberies. He had a knack for spotting shifty-looking people purely by their body language. This would give officers the opportunity to take up positions where they could arrest the offenders in the act.

We confiscated knives, axes and razors. And it wasn't just street robberies we tackled. The squad found themselves investigating armed robberies at banks and building societies, none of which was in the operation's remit. At one stage, a city-centre building society was robbed twice in three weeks. Both robberies took place on a Thursday afternoon. Indiana was convinced that this was a pattern and went to stake out the premises. I only found out because he failed to show up for a departmental meeting. 'Where's Indy?' I asked.

'He's surrounding the building society,' Heineken said.

'On his own?'

'Yes, sir.'

I quickly dispatched officers to the scene. This wasn't to protect Indy but to safeguard the robbers, who might have ended up having their throats slit with cheese wire had they turned up.

The squad became so successful that it was responsible for the detection of 33 per cent of the robberies committed in the West Midlands area. Other divisions would come to see us to copy the formula. The instances of street robbery in our area went from ten a day down to two.

One of the crimes we successfully targeted was called 'jacking'. Many female commuters would leave their handbags on show on the front or back seats of their cars when driving home. Robbers would hang about in slow-moving traffic, and when a car stopped they would break the window or force the door and grab the bag. A favourite jacking spot was Bristol Street, as there was always a heavy build-up of traffic there during rush hour. So, I sent my team over to stake it out.

One evening, a man was spotted walking along a line of cars, peering in. The officers moved in just as the robber broke the window of a car and seized a handbag. The man then legged it faster than Linford Christie on a pint of cappuccino. Most of the officers struggled to keep up. One officer, however, stuck with him all the way. Unfortunately for the jacker, that officer was Harvey.

As the robber ran into a multi-storey car park, he finally found himself cornered. He turned and faced his pursuer. The jacker then tried to head-butt Harvey, who simply stepped neatly out of range. He then gave the runner a lesson in reasonable force to effect an arrest. I interviewed the man the following day. He had a broken nose and was covered in bruises. 'The officer beat me with an iron bar,' he complained.

'That wasn't an iron bar, that was the new extendable police baton,' I explained. 'We're all carrying them now.'

'That's lethal, man.'

'They are. So make sure you tell all your thieving friends.'

The department was featured in a television documentary. My tough approach was likened to that of Superintendent Ray Mallon from Cleveland, whose zero-tolerance policies destroyed the criminal population of Middlesbrough. Mallon earned himself the title of 'Robocop'. Sadly, the police organisation went on to destroy him. He was the subject of a corruption investigation by senior officers that cost Cleveland council-tax payers £7 million. The witch hunt, named Operation Lancet, was primarily motivated by petty jealousies over Mallon's success.

Perhaps this was something I should have taken more notice of myself. Jealousy was something I had become very familiar with, and it would eventually lead to some very uncomfortable moments in my career.

The postscript to the Mallon affair had a couple of interesting twists. Two of the senior officers responsible for the investigation left the force. Robert Turnbull, who was an assistant chief constable at the time, received a £180,000 golden handshake – plus £50,000 a year pension – and took a job as police commissioner to the Turks and Caicos Islands in the Caribbean. Calls for Turnbull to return to explain why so much public money had been wasted were ignored, even though the £40,000-a-year, tax-free job he had landed also included free flights home to England whenever he wanted.

Another officer, Kevin Pitt, left under slightly less glamorous circumstances. At the time of Operation Lancet, he was district commander. He went on to be promoted to chief superintendent. On a visit to Lithuania to advise on the training of anti-corruption officers, Pitt was caught on CCTV having a late-night slash against the Lithuanian presidential palace. He was arrested and charged with violating public order. He received a fine of 200 litai, about £35. He returned to Cleveland and resigned in shame, 30 years' police service literally pissed up the wall.

Despite the success of Operation Reverse 22, one aspect saddened me. We would regularly be accused of being racists. Only 5 per cent of the people arrested by Reverse 22 were white, the remainder being predominantly black. It was never the intention to target the black community, many of whom I regarded as true friends. But the unfortunate truth was that they were responsible for most of the robberies on our patch.

In the course of Operation Reverse 22, I used a regular informer. His code name was Trick Rick, and I'd arrested him for the theft of a wallet and chequebook. Trick Rick admitted the robbery, and I offered to go easy if he agreed to turn informer. The Lord Chief Justice had ruled that any criminal who supplied reliable information that led to arrest and prosecution would be entitled to a substantial reduction in sentence. A confidential letter would be supplied to the trial judge, who would take this into account when passing sentence. This usually meant a suspended sentence rather than a term of imprisonment.

The amount of money paid to informants has always been a sensitive subject. In drug cases, informants were usually rewarded with 10 per cent of the value of the drugs recovered. I paid the informant on Operation Longline, which led to the recovery of a Transit van full of cannabis, £15,000. On another occasion, I paid an informant £100 for information that led to the arrest and conviction of a man for murder. It was very inconsistent, but it was also invaluable in helping to solve crime.

I paid Trick Rick £50 for each piece of successful information that he supplied. We nipped a spate of early morning robberies in the bud using information supplied by him. Trick Rick identified the culprit, who was followed and arrested in the act of snatching a handbag from a commuter. He also identified a thief who stalked multi-storey car parks stealing cars as the owners were about to get in. One evening, a woman returning to her brand-new Ford Probe was dragged from the car and the vehicle was stolen. Within hours, Trick Rick was on the phone to tell me where the stolen car was parked. He said that the robber was called Lionel Parsons and that he knew when he would be returning to the vehicle.

As Parsons went back for the vehicle, we were waiting for him in unmarked cars. He tried to ram his way out of the car park, injuring one officer quite badly. He was then arrested, charged and sent to a young offenders' remand centre. After several weeks, a kind-hearted magistrate released him from custody on bail. Within a week, Parsons attacked another female motorist in the same multi-storey car park. On this occasion, the woman was brutally raped. In the early hours of the following morning, I arrested him. His clothing was seized, and he was picked out in an ID parade. He was interviewed and denied the offence.

At that time, DNA testing was in its infancy. Semen samples taken from the victim were compared with a sample from Parsons. He had a remarkably low sperm count, and the sample taken from the victim could not be matched accurately enough. He could not be charged and walked free. I was gutted.

sixteen

PURE ECSTASY PART I:
THE SET-UP

Late one summer, Billy The Truth found himself before Birmingham Crown Court charged with burglary. For many years, I'd managed to keep him out of jail. His valuable assistance as an informer had led to more quality arrests than I cared to remember. As a result, the court had always gone lightly on him. On this occasion, his luck ran out. He was found guilty and sentenced to three years' imprisonment. In real terms, he would serve a year.

Around that time, the Home Office introduced new regulations to assist the police in boosting detection rates. One of these was the provision for offences to be written off. A person serving a custodial sentence would be given the opportunity to admit other offences in the knowledge that they would not be prosecuted. These offences would be written off without burdening the courts. At the same time, they also provided a lift to the crime-detection rate.

Billy The Truth was a one-man crime wave. He had committed more burglaries than Judith Chalmers has had free holidays. He could always tell you how many weeks it was until the clocks were put back, thus making it dark enough in the evenings so he could go out plying his trade.

As a treat, I decided to get him out of jail for three days so he could help boost detection figures. I submitted the relevant paperwork and went to Stafford Prison to collect him. I took with me a young inexperienced detective, who could not believe what he was hearing. As we travelled back to Birmingham, Billy spent the entire journey pointing to various roads where he had done burglaries. 'I've done three down that road and five down that one,' he confessed. 'And I've done at least a dozen down that road . . .' Like I said, the trouble with Billy The Truth was that once he started, you would have to shoot him to stop him talking.

On Billy's arrival at the police station, his details were recorded by the custody officer. I told the officer I would be taking Billy out to show me the locations where he had committed offences. We left the station and went straight to Billy's home address. To the horror of the young detective, I then left Billy on his own. I gave him instructions not to go out, or answer the front door or telephone. I trusted him, and he trusted me. I knew he would not let me down.

Every evening, I collected him from home and took him back to the police station, where his wife would come and visit him so as not to arouse suspicion. After three days, Billy had admitted to 300 burglaries, which were all written off. I then took him back to Stafford Prison. Back at the station, the police detection-rate files were bulging.

Things were starting to look busy on the undercover front, too. I was summoned to discuss an out-of-town drug operation under the supervision of the Regional Drug Squad. The target was an Ecstasy dealer called Nigel Patrick, who lived in Middlesbrough. The information was being supplied by his estranged wife, who lived in Wolverhampton. The wife's motive for becoming a police informer was to gain custody of their child. To me, this made the quality of the information being supplied unreliable. How wrong I was.

Ecstasy was fast taking a grip on the club scene. Its correct name is MDMA, short for methylenedioxymethamphetamine. You'd have to be off your tits to even contemplate trying to pronounce that. MDMA was first produced in 1912 to help stem bleeding. It was issued to German troops in the First World War as a stimulant and an appetite suppressant but was abandoned after it made the soldiers less aggressive. It surfaced again in the late 1970s when a group of American therapists used the relaxing nature of the drug to supplement psychotherapy sessions.

Illicit use of MDMA started in the 1980s and was instrumental in the development of the '90s rave culture.

Patrick ran a rave club, where he also supplied Ecstasy. I thought about the potential difficulties of the operation. The first was my age. I was 33. If I went to a club, I would stick out like a racing dog's bollocks. I remembered going to clubs in my early 20s and seeing men in their 30s. I used to think: what are these wrinklies doing in here? What I needed was a younger woman with me to help my cover.

Sadly, the females on the books of Specialist Operations weren't that attractive. In fact, you couldn't have punched clay uglier. However, I had a regular policewoman in mind called Diane Saunders. She wasn't trained in undercover techniques, but it was her ability to mix with other people that I was after. She was black, she was attractive and she was a little bit cocky, which I liked. I ran it past the operational commander, who OK'd the idea.

I approached Diane, who jumped at the chance of a night out paid for by the police. Her role would be to assist with the initial introduction to Patrick. Once I'd established contact, Diane would step back, leaving me to continue the operation.

Patrick's wife made arrangements for a chance meeting in a pub called The Crossways in Middlesbrough the following Friday. On the Friday afternoon, I had a meeting with Diane and spent two hours briefing her. My cover story was that I was involved in organising doormen on the club scene in Birmingham. She'd first met me five years ago at a place called the Q Club. I was known as a bit of a gangster, but I'd never been to prison.

In undercover operations, I regularly found myself coming out with all sorts of fairy stories. But I always remained fully aware of the lies I could never spin. To tell another criminal that you'd been to prison was extremely risky, especially if they'd been through the system themselves. You could easily be caught out if they started talking about procedures inside that you knew nothing about.

Using Diane was also something of a gamble. I made it clear to her how important it was that she understood when to back off and let me take control.

After the briefing, I rolled two joints. I gave one to Diane and kept the other. She was astonished at the skill I displayed in building the spliffs, a technique I had learned during my wilder days on the council estate. 'You're a bit handy,' she said, laughing while she put the joint into her handbag.

'Relax,' I told her. 'They're just tobacco.'

Later that evening, I picked up Diane from her home. I was met at the door by a white woman, whom Diane introduced as her mother. She was an adopted child, which was something I didn't know. This was a great failing in my personality. I rarely paid attention to other people's personal lives. I was totally focused on my own performance. Self-centred is the best description I can think of. Obsessed was how others might have viewed me. I would never ask personal questions of people I met or colleagues from the force, unless it was something to do with work. A means to an end. I spent my time getting to know the lives of criminals inside out, because I needed to achieve results. Those closer to home didn't receive such attention. It made me good at my job but bad at relationships.

I remember being asked on an interview board what I thought my strong point was, to which I replied being ruthless. I was then asked what I considered to be a weak point. I said that I *liked* being ruthless.

We arrived in Middlesbrough at about 9.30 p.m. It was a cold and wintry evening. Even so, the place was jumping with people. We found our way to The Crossways pub, but there was no sign of the informant, Patrick's wife. For a rare moment, I relaxed. I was out having a drink paid for by the firm accompanied by a nice-looking girl. After about 45 minutes, the informant arrived on her own. I went to the bar and left the girls to fine-tune their cover stories. Diane was posing as an old friend of the wife's from college. I was the boyfriend.

When I returned from the bar, the girls had been joined by a short, stocky bloke in his late 20s: the target, Nigel Patrick. I handed the girls their drinks but said nothing to Patrick until the informant introduced me. We shook hands and eyed each other up like gunslingers. The girls continued to chatter like old friends, which forced me and Patrick into some small talk. 'So what do you do?' asked Patrick.

'I'm in the security game,' I replied. 'I sort out doormen for clubs and bars.'

'I bet you make a nice few quid out of that.'

'It's not bad,' I said noncommittally. 'What about you?'

'I buy and sell cars. I also run a club. I'm off there after the pub. You should come. It's very lively.'

'I'll see what the missus says,' I said, smiling and motioning towards Diane. 'I've promised to take her out for a meal.'

'Come afterwards,' enthused Patrick. 'It doesn't really get going till well after midnight.'

'We'll see how the evening pans out.'

After a couple more rounds, Patrick sloped off, repeating the invitation to visit his club. He seemed very keen, which was a good sign that he was intrigued by me.

Diane and I left the informant and went to a nearby Balti restaurant. It was full of the usual after-pub brigade, drinking cans of warm Cobra followed by a curry chaser. An hour later, we made our way to Velvets. The bouncer on the door searched us and found the dummy joint in Diane's cigarette packet. She was told she could not come into the club unless the joint was confiscated. This provided a nice bit of credibility for our cover.

I was about to pay the £15 entrance fee when Patrick showed his face. 'Put your money away,' he said, waving us through. 'You're my personal guests.' He then introduced me to all the doormen as though I was Mr Group Four Security.

The chill-out room, full of saucer-eyed people lounging around on the soft furnishings chatting for England, was on the ground floor. The main dance area was upstairs, and the bar was doing a roaring trade in bottled water at £2 a pop. The room was a sweat box. Many clubbers were stripped to the waist, clearly out of their trees. Everyone was bouncing up and down, blowing whistles. Diane joined in. I gave it my best shot, but Frank Bruno had more rhythm than I did, and I shuffled around like a vicar at a disco.

The bass from the music was so heavy that it was beginning to hurt my chest, so I headed back downstairs. As I reached the ground floor,

I met Patrick, who was in a bit of a panic. 'Someone's collapsed,' he said. 'I think it's a dodgy E. They're in a pretty bad way.'

By the door, I saw the body of a young man lying on his back with blood pouring from his mouth. He was as stiff as a poker and surrounded by doormen who were looking on helplessly. I pushed between them and rolled the casualty on to his side into the recovery position. I tried to put my fingers in his mouth, to make sure his airway was clear, but he had his tongue between his teeth. I squeezed his jaw but couldn't get him to open his mouth. He was having some sort of fit and had bitten his tongue with such force it had split open. 'He needs to go to hospital,' I said.

'I can't risk an ambulance,' said Patrick. 'The old Bill will be all over us. There's a cottage hospital just outside the town. I'll drive him there in my car.'

We carried the man to Patrick's Jeep and sped off out of town. At the hospital, we told them that we'd found the bloke collapsed in the street. They hooked him up to a monitor, which showed he had an irregular heartbeat. 'We think he might have taken an E,' added Diane, making sure that they had the necessary information to apply suitable treatment.

We decided it would be better if we didn't hang around, so we sneaked off to smoke the Mickey Mouse joint I'd hidden in my sock. 'Thanks for helping out,' said Patrick. 'That could have got really nasty. This is good shit,' he added, drawing on pure tobacco. 'If you ever need any E, let me know.'

'Tonight wasn't exactly a good advert,' I said, smiling.

'I was thinking more that you might like to make some money from it,' Patrick replied, laughing. 'And there's plenty of money to be made with the punters. I can get as many Es as you want. So if you want me to turn you on, just ask.'

Patrick was fishing to see how straight I was. In many clubs, it was the bouncers who controlled the drugs. They knew who the dealers were, and it was up to them who they let in. The dealers they let in then had to pay the bouncers a commission. Sometimes payment was in cash. Sometimes drugs. It could be very lucrative indeed.

As ever, I didn't want to appear too keen. I wanted to let him do the running, to make it seem like it was his idea. 'I'm more into coke,' I replied.

'I can always get my hands on some decent coke,' said Patrick, handing me his mobile number. 'Just let me know.'

In return, I gave him a pager number that was registered to one of our hookey companies, so there was no way it could be linked to me.

It was now 5 a.m. Patrick returned to the club, but Diane and I still had the long journey back to Birmingham. 'What next?' she asked.

'Now it's just me and Patrick,' I told her. 'Thanks for your help, but I won't be needing you any more.' It was a shame, really, as she was very good company. But this was work. I was confident that I'd initiated a successful relationship with the target, and that Patrick's wife was now sufficiently protected for the operation to proceed.

Four days later, I received a message from Patrick asking me to call him. I did so from a public telephone box in Stratford-upon-Avon, just to add a bit of confusion if the target was expecting me to call from a Birmingham number.

'I'm going to be in Coventry tomorrow. Any chance of a meet?' he asked.

I wasn't safe in Coventry after my undercover status had been compromised there. The phone I'd been using for that operation had been passed on to a member of the Met, who had continued to receive calls, all threatening extreme violence. I steered Patrick towards TGI Friday's on the A45 Birmingham to Coventry road, well out of the city. 'What's the occasion?' I asked.

'Just a bit of business you might be interested in.'

The following day, I breezed into TGI's. Patrick greeted me with a relaxed smile, and we shook hands. I ordered a drink and sat down at the bar. 'I've got something coming up,' said Patrick cryptically. 'And I need a reliable partner.'

'Partner? For what?'

'I've got a load of Ecstasy powder on order from the States. I've got to go there to finalise the deal. Basically, I need some back-up. These are heavy people, you know.'

Ecstasy powder was a far better commodity than tablets. If it was pure, it could be diluted many times before being compressed into tablets. This would massively increase the profit margins.

'Let's start a bit slower, eh?' I suggested. 'Get to know each other, yeah? Then we can talk bigger business.'

'Sure,' said Patrick, slightly deflated.

'Now, what about that bit of coke we talked about?'

'I can arrange a couple of grams for you straight away,' he replied, visibly perking up.

'Give me a call when it's sorted.'

Four days later, I received a message from Patrick asking me to call him. 'I've got what you want,' he said.

'Go to a landline and page me with the number,' I said abruptly. 'I don't want to talk on a mobile.'

Mobiles are famously unsafe, as they're easy to listen in on with a radio scanner. In slack periods of Drug Squad work, we would often switch on a radio scanner in the office and listen to all the drug deals and other impropriety being discussed on the airwaves. The scanner would home in on the strongest radio signal at any given time, which caused it to hop from one phone to another.

It is also possible to obtain what is known as a cell site, which can pinpoint the exact location of a mobile phone at any particular time. Osama Bin Laden was being tracked in Afghanistan using cell-site technology. That was until someone decided to publish the fact in the media. Bin Laden turned his phone off, and the trail went cold.

Cell-site technology was also used in a high-profile murder inquiry in Birmingham when two sisters were shot dead on New Year's Eve. They were caught up in an act of retaliation in a gang war. The brother of one of the girls was tracked by his phone and charged with her murder.

Patrick paged me his home telephone number, and I called him back on his landline. 'I've got two grams of coke for you,' he said. 'It's really good stuff.'

'When can I get it?' I asked.

'Whenever you want. If you don't mind coming up to Middlesbrough.'

'Birmingham would suit me better.'

'I just feel a bit safer up here. I know everyone,' he replied. This was the first sign of caution that he'd shown. I didn't want him backing off, so I told him I was due to go up north the following week and would stop in Middlesbrough to pick up the gear.

I gave it a week and then called him, suggesting that we meet outside The Crossways the following day. I then made arrangements to get hold of the money to pay for the cocaine. I decided that £160 would be more than enough, but I wanted £400 to look a bit flash.

The process to get the money was long-winded. A written report from me to the operational commander detailing the reason for the request and the amount was then endorsed by the operational commander before being forwarded to the head of CID for his authorisation. Then I had to go to the Finance Department at HQ to collect the cash.

The following day, I set off on my journey to Middlesbrough. I had commandeered an Audi, which was the best car the department owned. I used it so often that other members of the department sarcastically referred to it as 'Ronnie's Car'.

My head was so full of the operation, I didn't see the patrol car behind me as I belted along in the fast lane of the motorway. Suddenly, blue lights appeared in the rear-view mirror and a pair of headlights flashed, indicating that I was to pull over. I made my way onto the hard shoulder, where I was instructed to get out of my vehicle and into the rear of the police car.

'Is this your car, sir?' enquired one of the police officers.

'No, it's my firm's,' I replied.

'Do you have your driving licence or any other identity documents with you?' the officer asked.

'No, I'm sorry, I haven't,' I said apologetically.

'Do you mind turning out your pockets, sir?'

I pulled out the £400 cash, together with a hookey letter from the Inland Revenue. It related to an imaginary investigation being conducted into my affairs. This had been supplied by a friendly member of the Inland Revenue fraud investigation team in order to help with my cover. The letter was closely scrutinised by one of the police officers. 'Is this your name and address on this letter from the tax man?' asked the officer.

'Yes, that's me.'

'Well, there's something wrong with this. It looks like there's a mistake in the address.'

Things weren't helped by my reluctance to answer questions regarding the £400 in cash. 'I am arresting you under section 25 of the Police and Criminal Evidence Act,' said the officer. 'I am not convinced about your means of identity.'

I was carted off to Derby Police Station. When I was asked whom I would like to be informed of my arrest, I requested to see the local detective inspector. I was then placed in a cell, where I waited for an hour. Eventually, the door was opened by a grey-haired man in a suit. He said that he was a detective inspector. I demanded to see his warrant card, which he produced. I then had no choice but to tell him that I was an undercover police officer. I then gave him a telephone number to call to verify my story.

I was then left alone in the cell for another 20 minutes, until the detective inspector returned with a smile on his face and a cup of tea in his hand. I sat and drank the tea whilst he tried to quiz me – until I reminded him politely that I was involved in a secret operation. He then invited me into the CID office as though I was some sort of celebrity. I said it would not be appropriate but thanked him for his hospitality.

The two motorway officers returned me to my car, which was still on the hard shoulder where I'd left it. They lectured me about observing the speed limit and using my rear-view mirror. I didn't know what they had been told about me, so I stayed quiet and nodded like a good citizen. But I was back in my car and breaking the speed limit again as soon as I could, trying to make up for lost time. I did use my mirror, though.

I arrived in Middlesbrough late. Patrick was standing outside the front of the pub. As I stopped, he pointed to the car park across the road where his Jeep was parked. He gestured for me to follow him and then walked to his car and got in. I followed him as he drove out of Middlesbrough and into the countryside for five or six miles. Then we came to a halt. We both left our vehicles and Patrick pointed to a Coca-Cola can in the middle of a grass verge. 'That's where your gear is.' I walked to the can and picked it up. Inside was a plastic bag containing white powder. 'I don't want any money,' said Patrick. 'Just take it. It's a gift. If you like it, I can get you more.'

Back in Birmingham, I examined the packet. Along with the coke, there was also an Ecstasy tablet, which had obviously been left as a taster. The drugs were sent to the Forensic Science Lab for testing. The cocaine was 82 per cent pure, which is almost as good as it gets. The Ecstasy tablet was also good quality.

A few days later, I got a message from Patrick that he was in the Midlands. Once again, we met at TGI Friday's. 'That coke was good gear,' I said. 'We can set that up again as soon as you like.'

'Ecstasy is where the money is,' said Patrick. 'If you can help me sort out this American deal, you can have a cut. And it won't cost you anything.' Without drawing breath, he continued, 'I'm going to arrange an importation of a kilo of MDMA powder. Have you any idea how many tablets we can make out of that? Thousands. The pills are selling in the clubs for twenty-five quid a time. It'll be like winning the lottery.'

'What do you want me to do?' I asked.

'I need someone to come out there with me to watch my back. A minder.'

'We hardly know each other but you're willing to involve me in a deal like this?' I said. 'What's the catch?'

'There is no catch,' replied Patrick. 'You're in the security business. And I need some security. I just feel I can trust you.' This was a laugh, as the security business is mostly run by criminals who would run you over as soon as look at you.

'How do you propose to get the gear back from America?' I asked.

'A few years ago, I was living in Goa in India,' explained Patrick. 'While I was there, I worked in a factory where I learned how to build a suitcase. I can build one around a parcel of gear, and Customs won't have any idea it's there. You can look at the bag from any angle, and it looks straight. I've also got somebody who's agreed to carry it back through Customs. The only problem I've got is finding someone to turn it into tablets.'

As quick as a flash, I said, 'That's not a problem. I've got a mate who is in the sports supplement business. He would make the pills for the right money.'

Patrick nearly fell off his chair when I said this. 'That's fantastic,' he said, smiling. 'Can I meet this bloke so we can sort out a deal?'

'Wind your neck in a minute,' I cut in. 'Sorting out an importation of a suitcase full of Ecstasy powder is one thing. Now you want me to sort out getting the stuff turned into pills – that's different. You're a stranger. He doesn't know you. I'll sort the deal out with the pill maker when the gear arrives. We don't want to be telling anybody anything until we've got the gear.'

'OK,' agreed Patrick, slightly taken aback.

'Whereabouts in the States is this gear coming from?' I asked.

'I've got a contact in LA. He's a lawyer who can put a deal together.'

'And exactly what do you want me to do?'

'I just want you to back me up and look menacing,' he said.

'If I do go, I want to travel separately,' I suggested.

'Not a problem,' said Patrick. 'But I want to get out there by the end of the month.'

'I'll have to check my commitments and get back to you. In the meantime, I'll show you the factory where the body-building stuff is made.'

We left the restaurant and drove to an industrial unit in Stirchley owned by a company called Turbopower. The company had nothing to do with drugs but the rear of the premises resembled a factory. 'When we go inside, keep your mouth shut,' I said firmly. 'Don't mention anything about any deals or whatever.'

The front of the premises was a shop. Inside, the staff knew me by sight, as I had regularly bought body-building supplements from them, and they greeted me as a friend. The boss then came out into the shop, and we shook hands. They were big lads, all into the body-building game. Patrick stood there saying nothing but looking excited. As we left, my credibility went through the roof. I thought Patrick was going to kiss my feet.

'What sort of logo shall we get put on the back of the tablets?' he asked.

'AVFC,' I fired back.

'What does that mean?'

'Aston Villa Football Club, you muppet.'

Back at the undercover HQ, a meeting was held to decide on the best way forward. I really fancied a trip to America but had to clear it with my superiors. I ran through all the aspects of what had been happening, and it was agreed that I should go with Patrick to LA. The appropriate authorities would be made aware of what was going on. This meant liaising with Customs and Excise in the UK and the Drug Enforcement Agency (DEA) in America.

Contacting the DEA meant a trip to the American Embassy in London. It was an impressive building with enormous twin eagles over the entrance. Once there, I was introduced to three special agents. I ran through what had taken place in the operation, and I was told that I would be able to continue without interference. I would be supplied with contact numbers should I get into difficulties. It would be my responsibility to keep the DEA informed of any developments for my own safety. I was then given four telephone numbers and a contact password, 'Nemesis', which would make me instantly identifiable to whoever took my call.

After the briefing, we adjourned to a nearby pub, where we swapped our antecedents. The agents turned out to be a former ice-cream salesman, an insurance broker and a police officer with less than two years' experience. It was much like our Special Branch, which was full of people who didn't quite make the grade elsewhere.

The following day, I was contacted by Patrick, who asked if I could come to Middlesbrough for a boys' day out. 'There's something going on you might be interested in,' he added cryptically.

I made the arduous trip up the motorway and made my way straight into The Crossways, where I found Patrick with a group of other men. They all looked like gypsies. We had a quick drink, then got into Patrick's Jeep, leaving my Audi in the car park.

'Where are we off to?' I enquired as we sped off into the countryside.

'Don't worry. It's just a bit of fun. I think you'll enjoy this,' he said, grinning, clearly in his element.

After about 15 minutes, we came to a farm at the end of a long driveway, well away from the road. We pulled up outside a large barn. Inside there were bales of hay arranged into a ring with large wooden boards around the perimeter. Standing above this ring were about 50 other men. The air was heavy with cigarette smoke. I looked around and could see two men were taking cash from people in the crowd. I realised that they were bookmakers. Everyone closed in around the edge of the ring as the biggest pit bull I had ever seen was led into the arena like a heavyweight boxer. The dog was extremely agitated. Its stump of a tail was wagging furiously as it strutted around.

The excitement of the crowd increased as a second dog came into the ring with its handler. The first dog stiffened and lunged towards the second animal. Both dog handlers pulled at their leads, their biceps bulging to restrain their animals. A referee shouted out details of each dog's history. As the dogs' muzzles were removed, they snapped and snarled at one another, their eyes bulging and teeth dripping with saliva. They had become monsters, driven into a frenzy by the baying of the crowd.

The referee stood to one side with his arm raised. He then dropped his arm, and the dogs were released. They flew at one another, biting and howling insanely. As they tore into one another, blood and saliva pebble-dashed the sandy ring. They rolled over and over, tearing at one another like a pair of crocodiles. They just kept at each other, biting and snarling and snapping with such violence that it was truly shocking.

Then, one of the dogs got a grip with its jaws on the snout of its opponent. I could hear the crunch of bone as the dog started to rip the face from its opponent. The animal's snout began to split apart as it screamed in pain. Still they continued to thrash at one another, until, finally, the handlers began to beat them with short batons. This caused a break between the animals. Snaffles were placed around their heads, so they could be dragged apart. Both were seriously damaged. One dog's head was devastated. The crowd was stoked.

I'd lost sight of Patrick in the throng. Eventually, he reappeared looking wild-eyed and flushed. He was clearly excited by all the brutality. 'What do you think? What do you think?' he gushed.

'I'll be honest,' I said. 'I was expecting a couple of strippers.'

'It isn't over yet. There'll be some more in a few minutes.'

'Look, we need to go somewhere to have a talk.'

With a disappointed look on his face, we left the arena, and I made Patrick drive me back to Mansfield, where we went to The Crossways for a drink. 'I'm on for coming to America,' I said. 'But I want to know what I'm getting out of all this.'

'I'll give you three ounces of powder.'

'I want five ounces. Take it or leave it,' I said quickly. 'If things get out of hand in the States, it will be me who'll be sorting out the villains.'

'OK,' said Patrick. 'Five ounces.'

'And if you want me to organise the pills, I'll want another five ounces.'

Patrick went quiet. This was a real test of his control over the situation. To his credit, he didn't cave in. 'One thing at a time, eh?' he said calmly. 'Let's get the stuff back here first. Then we can talk more business.'

We then made the final arrangements. I would fly out on the last Friday of the month and meet him at a hotel in LA on the following Monday. Patrick had already sorted out a courier who would meet us in LA. He suggested we stay at the Holiday Inn in Santa Monica.

I went back to the office and presented my superior with the facts. The flight was paid for on one of our bogus company credit cards. It included a two-day stopover in Chicago. This would add a bit of subterfuge to my story when I arrived in Los Angeles.

seventeen

PURE ECSTASY PART II: THE DEAL

A week later, I was on the plane across the Atlantic. I landed in Chicago, which was freezing cold and thick with fog. That night, I watched the Chicago Bears beat up the Miami Dolphins and spent the rest of the evening in a bar with a number of the Bears players. One in particular, William 'the Refrigerator' Perry, was an absolute giant. Despite his size, he performed one of the most amazing feats I had ever seen by a 25-stone man. He jumped up on to a table and down again 20 times without stopping. The bar shook in its foundations.

On the Monday morning, I limped into the airport to catch my internal flight to Los Angeles. As I entered the aircraft, the stewardess smiled and informed me that newspapers were available and there was a complimentary bar. At that moment, I would have drunk a glass of stagnant ditch water rather than face more alcohol.

The flight was fairly short. I arrived at Los Angeles Airport, where I was met by Patrick – he was difficult to miss. He was wearing a Hawaiian shirt, baggy board shorts, a back-to-front baseball cap and was jumping up and down as I came into the arrivals lounge. 'Don't draw attention to yourself,' I thought.

He rushed towards me and shook my hand. 'All right, mate. Am I glad to see you. The hotel's great. It's got a pool and everything.'

'Just remember, we're here to do business,' I reminded him, pissing somewhat on his fireworks. 'We're not on our holidays.'

We walked out of the airport to the car park. Patrick's hire car was the size of a pencil sharpener. It had tourist written all over it. As we set off on the journey to Santa Monica, he filled me in on the plan. 'My contact here is a lawyer. He's the one who's going to put the deal together. The courier is also here. She's English, and her name is Rebecca.'

We arrived at the hotel. I put my bag in my room and went for a walk down to Santa Monica Beach. On the pier, there was a stall selling knives. I didn't have my usual knife with me, so I bought a tasty-looking flick knife as a bit of insurance.

I went back to the hotel where I had a shower and dozed off. I was woken by the telephone. It was Patrick. 'Come down to the bar. I've got somebody I want you to meet.'

Patrick was at the bar with a middle-aged hippy smoking a roll-up. She looked like she'd got lost on her way home from Glastonbury. 'Ronnie, this is Rebecca.'

She shook hands like a man and handed me a bottle of beer. We then got stuck into the bar, drinking beer with Jack Daniel's chasers. The conversation was relaxed, and we were laughing and joking. At one point, Patrick and Rebecca went off to the bathroom. Rebecca left her handbag behind, which was unusual for a woman. I seized the opportunity to rifle through her bag and found a driving licence. I made a mental note of the details and put everything back as I had found it.

Leaving a jacket unattended was always a good ploy when engaged in an operation. I seldom carried identity documents, but I did if I intended to leave them strategically to be found. You could guarantee that if you left your coat somewhere, the villains would always go through the pockets.

When Patrick and Rebecca returned, I finished my drink and went to bed, leaving them both at the bar. I got up at 6 a.m. and put on my running kit. I took some change from my wallet and ran along the seafront for a couple of miles until I saw some isolated telephone boxes. I called one of the numbers the DEA had given me. It rang several times before it was answered. I gave my password, along with details of the hotel I was staying at. I also mentioned that I had identified the courier for the drugs. I was not interrogated in any way. It was just like talking to someone in a call centre who noted what I had to say and thanked me for calling.

I returned to the hotel and went to my room to watch CNN. At about 9.30 a.m., I went down to breakfast. I was joined 15 minutes later by Patrick, who was sporting a hangover. 'What time did you get to bed?' I asked.

'We finished at about 2 a.m.'

'Where do you know her from?'

'She was in Goa when I was there. She's a bit of an old hippy, but she's completely trustworthy.'

'I don't think it's a good idea to spend too much time with her until we've got the gear. We don't want to be linked with her in any way once she picks the gear up. Now, what's happening with this lawyer bloke?'

'He's a shrewd cookie. He will never have his hands directly on the gear. He just does the talking. Chill out and enjoy the surroundings.'

'Look, I am here to do business. I'm not on a jolly,' I hissed. 'Get on the phone and get a meeting organised.' Patrick got up from the table and slunk away to make the necessary calls.

I decided to take Patrick's advice and enjoy the surroundings, so I took a cab and went for a look around LA. Later that day, I wandered back to the hotel and stopped for a drink. I found myself chatting up the girl behind the bar. Her name was Olinda, and she was a dab hand at mixing cocktails. I made the mistake of asking her if she knew how to mix a Long Island Iced Tea. A Long Island Iced Tea consists of tequila, triple sec, vodka, gin, white rum and Coca-Cola. It looks and tastes like iced tea but is absolute rocket fuel. Apart from the cola, it's 12 ounces of pure alcohol.

Olinda took delight in mixing me two cocktails, which I downed one after another. I then meandered out into Santa Monica. The effect of the booze was staggering. My speech had gone, but I was bolt upright, stiff as a poker. I remember seeing a band playing Beatles songs, which I tried to sing along to. I eventually made my way back to the hotel bar and asked Olinda if there was an antidote. She helpfully mixed me an Absolut Vodka martini. I drank it and then crawled to bed.

I awoke in the morning and peeled my tongue from the pillow. I drank every drop of liquid I could find, put on my sunglasses and went down for breakfast. Patrick was already there. 'I've contacted The Lawyer,' he told me. 'We've got a meeting this afternoon at the Chateau Marmont.'

The Chateau Marmont is a copy of an eighteenth-century French chateau. It sits above Sunset Boulevard and has a colourful history, having seen every kind of scandal imaginable. It was there that John Belushi died of a cocaine and heroin overdose in 1982.

We arrived at the Marmont in the pencil sharpener and were met by a member of the staff in a smart uniform. Patrick wound down the window and stuck his head out. 'Where can I park?' he asked.

'It's valet parking, you twat,' I whispered to him as I got out of the car. 'They park the car for you.'

I was wearing a close-fitting black T-shirt and black trousers. Patrick was dressed in baggy shorts, another Hawaiian shirt and the mandatory back-to-front baseball cap. 'It might be a good idea if you took your cap off,' I suggested.

'What do you mean?'

'This is a top-dollar hotel. It's probably full of film stars. You're not doing yourself any favours looking like a novelty act off Blackpool beach.' Like a scolded schoolboy, Patrick reluctantly took off his cap.

We walked into the hotel and entered the bar, where a middle-aged man in a sharp suit was sitting on a leather settee. Patrick nodded and made a beeline for him. As he closed in, an enormous black man moved from the bar and put his hand on Patrick's chest, stopping him dead in his tracks. I grabbed the man's wrist and stared him full in the face. He stiffened but didn't back down.

The middle-aged man sitting at the table interrupted our little dance. 'It's all right. These are my guests.' The minder pulled his wrist away, and I stepped forward to usher Patrick towards the sofa.

'Sit down, sit down,' said the man in the suit, but I remained standing, eyeballing his minder, who backed away to the bar. The Lawyer got up and offered me his hand. 'Nigel and I already know each other.'

The Lawyer was overweight, with the grey pallor of a man with a heart condition. He told his minder to get us some drinks. Patrick ordered a beer, but I had nothing, as I wanted to stay alert.

'I apologise for that a moment ago,' offered The Lawyer. 'A poor introduction.' I said nothing, instead freezing him with my best stare. 'How are you enjoying your time in Los Angeles?' he continued.

'I've been to Disney World and Universal Studios,' blabbed Patrick. 'I'm having a great time.' Again, I said nothing.

'What's wrong?' asked The Lawyer. 'Cat got your tongue?'

'I'm here to do business,' I finally piped up. 'So why don't we just get on with it?'

'There's no need to be frosty. We should get to know each other.'

'I thought you two already knew one another.'

'That's true, but any friend of Nigel's is welcome in my company.'

'If that's the case, get rid of your gorilla at the bar and maybe we can talk a bit of business.'

The Lawyer gestured to his minder, who walked out of the bar mumbling. Holman followed him, said a few words and then returned to the table smiling. 'I understand you are in Los Angeles looking for a parcel,' he began. 'I can put together a kilo of powder whenever you want it.'

'As long as we all know what we're talking about,' I clarified.

'Why are you so aggressive?' he asked.

'I wasn't aware that I was being aggressive,' I answered.

'Right,' he continued. 'In all conversation from now on, we should refer to the drugs as a wedding present.'

The Lawyer used two forms of terminology I had heard many times before. A 'parcel' is a term for a commodity used by London villains. And Asian heroin dealers often used the term 'getting married' in telephone conversations when referring to dates when drugs would arrive.

Patrick finally entered the negotiations: 'Is the price as we have discussed?'

'I want £25,000, which is to be paid into the First National Bank in London the day before the drugs are handed over.'

'I want to see the gear before we hand over any money,' I insisted.

'If you wish,' conceded The Lawyer. 'I'll need a couple of days to put it all together.' Amazingly, he then gave me a business card, and we parted company.

'I'm going to organise the money transfer,' said Patrick in the car on the way back to Santa Monica. 'I've done this before, and I trust him.'

Back at the hotel, I went to my room and changed into my running kit. Armed with The Lawyer's business card, I set off for my phone box so that I could update the DEA on Holman's involvement. When I'd finished, I jogged back to the hotel and went in search of Patrick.

'Come and see the suitcase,' he said, ushering me into his room. He then showed me a brown vanity case made of leather and talked me through exactly what he was going to do with the drugs. 'I'll take the case apart and put the gear around the frame. Then I'll glue it all back together. It's a small bag, so it can stay as hand luggage. It's less likely to get searched,' Patrick added.

'How long will that take you?' I asked.

'The bag takes a couple of hours to pull apart and rebuild. Then we'll have to wait overnight for the glue to set hard.'

I spent the following morning by the hotel pool. After lunch, I went for a wander around Santa Monica Beach to watch the young ladies roller skating along the seafront in their thongs. I returned to the hotel later that evening and caught up with Patrick. 'Have you heard anything yet?' I enquired.

'No, nothing.'

'Let's get on his case. Tell him we want to see that sample now.'

'It's too late to phone him. I'll do it first thing in the morning.'

The following morning, I was straight onto Patrick and told him to phone The Lawyer, which he did. 'We've to go to the car park by the Los Angeles Memorial Coliseum at midday,' said Patrick excitedly. 'Someone will meet us there with a sample.'

It was already 11 a.m. We had an hour to find the place, so we set off in the pencil sharpener clutching a map. Forty minutes later, we rocked up in the enormous car park next to the magnificent Coliseum stadium. After a few minutes, a police car drove into the parking lot and began circling us like a shark. Patrick started to get nervous.

'Just act like a couple of stupid English tourists,' I said. 'If anyone asks, we've come here to gawp.'

The police car crawled alongside our car and stopped. I could sense the increase in Patrick's heart rate as his breathing quickened. The policeman signalled for us to wind down the window, which I did. I was just about to say something when the cop threw a small packet onto my lap and then drove off. I waited till the police car had left the parking lot and opened the packet. It was the sample. How much more corrupt could this transaction be?

'Do you feel happier now we've got a sample? Do you feel you can trust the deal now?' Patrick asked.

'It makes me more nervous,' I said, earnestly getting into character. 'Think about it. All they have to do is wait for the money to be transferred and then nick us in possession. The Lawyer gets his twenty-five grand, and the bent coppers get their hands on the drugs to sell again.' This quietened Patrick down.

I needed to speak to the DEA quickly in case we got caught up in something we couldn't control. Once we were back at the hotel, it was on with the running kit and off to the phone box. When I got through, I demanded to speak to someone with some rank and was transferred to a Lieutenant John Cheney. I told him the situation, and he said he would make enquiries to ensure an operation wasn't being staged to lock us up. I said I needed an answer quickly and would ring back in two hours.

I went back to the hotel and made my way to Patrick's room. 'Have you tested the gear yet?' I asked.

'I'm not sure how to,' he said, shrugging.

'You'll have to try it,' I said. Patrick dabbed a little on his finger and put it on his tongue. He said that it tasted very bitter, similar to an Ecstasy tablet. 'Have some more, just to be sure,' I said, egging him on. Patrick dabbed another fingerful onto his tongue.

'D'you want to have a go?' he asked, offering me the packet.

'You must be joking,' I told him. 'I'm not touching that shit.'

After 15 minutes, a satisfied grin started to work its way across his face. He said he could feel a warm glow coming up through his body. After another 15 minutes, his eyes started to roll a little. The grin got bigger. His jaw started to chew a little. His head started to rock back and forth. 'Yep, it's good gear all right,' he said, grinning and nodding like a seafront donkey. 'Excellent gear.'

I decided to leave him to it. I didn't want to have to sit there all night while he talked his head off. I walked out of the hotel to find a telephone. I rang the DEA number and asked to speak to Lieutenant Cheney. 'Any news?'

'There are no large-scale Ecstasy jobs in progress in LA at this time,' he told me. 'It looks like a corrupt cop, which we'll look into.'

'And what about me?' I asked. 'Any chance of some back-up?'

'I'll organise someone to keep an eye on you,' he assured me. 'Just in case it gets nasty.'

The following morning, I met Patrick at breakfast. He'd been up most of the night partying on his own. Just him and MTV. 'You look like shit,' I told him. His pupils were still as wide as Frisbees, his skin pale and sweaty.

'It's very good gear,' he said with a grin and his eyes all over the place. 'I had some more just to make sure.'

'Great. Now lay off it. I don't want you off your rocker and cocking everything up.'

'Relax,' said Patrick as he smiled and put his arm around my shoulder like a friendly uncle. 'Everything's going to be fine. Trust me.'

Patrick went off to call The Lawyer to find out when we could pick up the rest of the parcel. An hour later, he rang me on the hotel phone. Before he could say anything, I stopped him short and told him to come to my room. I didn't trust hotel phones. I remembered an assignment called Operation Pillow Talk. A criminal called Tommy Stewart went to a hotel to set up a large-scale cannabis deal. He sat in his room chatting about it with his girlfriend. The room's intercom was accidentally left on, and the conversation was transmitted to the reception. The manager called the police, and Stewart was arrested. He later fled to Spain's Costa del Crime.

Patrick came into my room. 'The deal is on for tomorrow. I have arranged for the cash to be wired to the First National Bank this afternoon.'

'If you're happy to pay up before you've had the merchandise.'

'I'm happy I can trust The Lawyer. We've got a meeting with him this afternoon at a tennis club to finalise everything.'

The tennis club was a ten-minute drive from the hotel. It was a huge complex with sumptuous facilities and a car park littered with Porsches and Ferraris. The whole place smelled of money. Most of the clients were middle-aged men with mahogany tans and top-dollar tennis gear. Everyone was drinking carrot juice.

The Lawyer was sitting near the juice bar with a fantastic-looking blonde. As we approached, he said something to her and she left the table. We sat down, and The Lawyer asked us if we wanted a drink. 'Anything as long as it hasn't got a carrot in it,' I answered.

'Water please,' said Patrick, still feeling the effects of the previous night's drug testing.

It was then down to business with everyone talking in code. 'I am pleased with the arrangements for the wedding and look forward to receiving the gift,' said The Lawyer.

'I have arranged for the gift to be delivered this afternoon,' said Patrick. 'When will I get my invitation?'

'Tomorrow. I will have it delivered to your hotel.'

'I want the invitation to be handed over personally,' I interrupted bluntly. 'Otherwise I might have to fuck up your reception party.'

'I give you my word that I'll see to it personally,' answered The Lawyer. 'I'd like to think we have a long and happy relationship ahead of us.'

'So, you'll be handing over the invitation yourself?' I asked.

'That's out of the question,' he replied.

'OK. I'll meet you while my partner collects the invitation. You can stay with me until it's done.'

'I'll meet you in the bar of the Holiday Inn at midday,' he replied. 'I'll tell you then where to collect the parcel.'

Later that day, we met with Rebecca on Santa Monica Pier for something to eat. She looked more like Joan Baez than ever before.

After she'd left us, I asked Patrick what he was paying her for doing this. 'Five grand, but she'd probably be happy with a free flight to London.'

'What are the chances of her ripping us off?'

'No chance of that. We've known each other for years. I trust her completely.'

I went back into planning mode. As a precaution, I decided we would check out of the Holiday Inn after the deal was done. I told Patrick to book two rooms in the nearby Best Western Hotel. It was a strange situation, and I was becoming anxious about the deal. In less than a week, I'd be locking my partners up in jail.

That evening, Patrick insisted on buying bottles of champagne. 'We're going to be rich!' he said. I didn't share his optimism, but I did share his champagne. After four glasses, I told Patrick I was off to bed. In fact, I went for a walk to find a telephone kiosk to update the DEA.

After a restless night's sleep, I went down for breakfast. There was no sign of Patrick until I'd almost finished. He came limping into the breakfast room, very hung-over. 'You better sort yourself out. The Lawyer will be here in an hour.'

Patrick took a couple of Panadols and downed a large orange juice. 'I'll be all right,' he said.

I went out for a run to focus myself. I returned, showered, dressed and slipped my flick knife into my pocket. Old habits die hard. I wandered around the hotel pool area and finally headed into the bar at about 11.50 a.m. Patrick joined me and began drinking. 'Take it easy on the booze,' I advised. 'We don't know how far you've got to drive.'

At midday, The Lawyer and his minder from the Chateau Marmont came into the bar. The Lawyer was smiling. His minder was trying his best to look menacing. 'Why've you got security with you? Do you feel threatened?' I enquired.

'I'll send him away if he causes you a problem.'

'Oh, he won't cause me a problem,' I said, smiling.

The Lawyer instructed his minder to wait in the car and then told us where to pick up the gear. 'If you drive out of Santa Monica towards the city, you will come to a Wendy's diner. If you go inside and get a coffee, you will be met with the parcel.'

I saw The Lawyer had a mobile phone. I asked him for the number. 'Why do you want that?' he asked.

'When he's got the parcel, he can call us. You're not leaving my side until we get that call.'

Before he left, I pulled Patrick to one side. I told him to drive out of the hotel to the nearest car park and then take a taxi to the restaurant. This was a spot of dry cleaning – a criminal term for an anti-surveillance tactic.

The Lawyer and I sat together for nearly an hour. He tried to engage me in pleasant conversation. I grunted back one-word answers until his mobile phone rang. It was Patrick, who said that he had the wedding invitation and was on the way back. The Lawyer shook hands with me and said he looked forward to meeting again. Then he left the bar.

Half an hour later, Patrick came into the bar carrying a sports bag. He was flushed and excited. 'Get your stuff and check out,' I told him. 'I'll meet you in the Best Western Hotel.'

eighteen

PURE ECSTASY PART III: THE BUST

I made my way to the Best Western on foot, making sure I wasn't being followed. I threw my things on the bed and went down to see Patrick. He was in his room with six packets of white powder. I then watched with fascination as he dismantled the leather case along the seams with a modelling knife. He slipped each of the white packages into the sides of the bag and then secured each seam with epoxy resin until it was reassembled. When he'd finished, it looked like an empty leather vanity case. It was brilliant. He placed the bag in the wardrobe.

'I need a drink,' said Patrick.

'I'll see you in the bar.'

I went to my room and booked a club-class seat on the same flight as Patrick and Rebecca. I deserved it. Let them fly cattle class. I then went down to the public telephone in the lobby to call the DEA. I told them we were in possession of the merchandise and would be leaving the country the following evening.

Down in the bar, Patrick was wading into the champagne. 'Take it easy,' I said. 'It would be a shame to let ourselves down now so close to the finish line.'

I woke early the following morning with lots on my mind. As usual, there was no one to talk to. I went out for a run to clear my head before breakfast. I returned to find Patrick in his usual hung-over state. 'Tell Rebecca to meet us in the hotel at 3 p.m.,' I said. 'And dump the hire car so we can take a taxi to the airport.'

It was now a case of killing time. In Specialist Operations, it was a tradition to buy the tackiest gift to take back to the office. The Best Western Hotel had a fake Mexican band that played each evening at dinner, so I bought a cassette of their music to play in the office.

At 3 p.m., Rebecca arrived at the hotel and went straight to Patrick's room. This time, she looked like Hot Lips Houlihan from Mash. Once again, I barked out instructions: 'We'll travel to the airport together and separate at the terminal. When we get to Gatwick, Rebecca, you take the train into London and check into the Bloomsbury Crest at Russell Square. Stay in your room with the bag until we contact you. The following day, you are to travel to Birmingham by coach from Victoria. Nigel will pick you up from the coach station. Got that?' I made her repeat her instructions so that I knew she understood.

Rebecca was remarkably relaxed considering she was about to smuggle a bag load of class A drugs into the United Kingdom. During the taxi journey, I turned to her and said, 'We'll be watching you.'

'What do you mean?' she asked.

'Don't get any silly ideas, that's all.'

At the taxi drop-off, we parted company. I watched Rebecca and Patrick head for a long wait in the economy-class queue. I was whisked through club-class check-in and made myself comfortable in the club-class lounge.

Take-off was at 6 p.m. I sank into my club-class seat and slept until the early hours, when the plane slipped into Gatwick Airport. At the baggage collection, I saw Patrick with Rebecca a few paces behind. The place was buzzing with armed police, sniffer dogs and Customs officers. My bottle started to twitch. This wouldn't have been the first time Customs and Excise had come steaming through a police operation. They had access to our intelligence, but we did not have access to theirs.

Customs officers lined everyone up from the Los Angeles flight and asked them to produce their passports. I saw Rebecca and Patrick in front of me in the line. Suddenly, the Customs officers descended on an Afro-Caribbean passenger, whom they dragged into a mirror-windowed office. The remainder of the passengers, including Rebecca and Patrick, were allowed through the green channel.

I later discovered that the Afro-Caribbean bloke had half a kilo of cocaine hidden in his underpants. The sniffer dog had been put on the plane and had gone straight to his seat, which had led to the arrest. This had got us off the hook.

This is a trick often used by drug smugglers in Holland. A number of lorries cross the Channel from Holland to the UK carrying drugs. Someone will tip off Customs, and one of the vehicles carrying drugs will be intercepted. This allows several other lorries, also carrying drugs, to go through unchecked.

In the arrivals lounge, I collared Patrick. 'What's the matter with you?' I asked. 'Why did you walk through Customs with Rebecca? Do you like playing Russian roulette? That's the whole point of having a courier. They take all the risks. Where is she now?'

'She's gone to get her train.'

'I hope she sticks to the script.'

We caught our train for the usual miserable journey to Birmingham, stopping at virtually every station on the way. The food on board was up to the usual standard – an individual fruit pie and a can of Tartan bitter. Available nowhere else on earth.

As we parted company at New Street Station, I clocked the surveillance team who'd been on the train with us. I made my way to the office for a quick debrief. I was unshaven, and my mouth tasted like the crotch of a tramp's pants. I went home to sleep and was back in the office for 7 a.m. I'd kept detailed notes of everything that had taken place, and it was now my job to write it all up. I scribbled away for five hours.

At midday, I telephoned Patrick. It wasn't good news. 'I can't find Rebecca,' he said in a panic. 'She didn't stay at the Bloomsbury Crest.'

'Well, you'd better fucking find her,' I shouted, 'or I'll be dancing on your fucking head until you do.'

'I'm going to London to look for her.'

London? To look for her? Where do you start? I would have laughed at such a ridiculous idea, but my mind was fuzzy with frustration and jetlag. After everything I'd gone through, I was about to be shown up by some airy-fairy hippy. I was angry. I was upset. I was also in deep shit if the gear had gone missing. The operation had not been cheap. To screw it up at the last hurdle would have been expensive, not to mention professionally humiliating.

I phoned my contact in the Metropolitan Police in London. Half an hour later, I got a call back to say that Met surveillance had followed Rebecca from the airport. She'd spent the night in a hostel, obviously so she could pocket the cash that she'd been given for the Bloomsbury Crest.

There was now a possibility that she'd get busted in London and the Met would get the credit. But the really frustrating thing was that I couldn't tell Patrick where she was without blowing my cover. So, I had to wait.

At 5 p.m., I received a telephone call from Patrick. I already knew where he was because I had surveillance on him. 'I've found her. We're on a coach. We'll be in Birmingham in a couple of hours.'

'What happened?' I asked, already knowing the answer.

'I'll explain later,' said Patrick.

'Where can we meet?' I asked.

'We're going to stay at a friend's flat over in Moseley.' He gave me the address and we arranged to meet the following morning. The surveillance team followed them back to Birmingham and put them to bed in a flat in Trafalgar Road, Moseley, so I knew he wasn't lying.

We couldn't bust them that night, because we needed confirmation that they had the drugs on them. It was up to me to find out. I had to go to the flat the following morning and clock the drugs. Then I would give the signal by mobile telephone to Dagenham, and the arrest teams would arrive.

At 9.30 a.m. the next day, I phoned and woke Patrick from his sleep. 'Is everything all right? Is Rebecca still with you? She nearly gave me a fucking heart attack.'

'She's here. She just didn't fancy the Bloomsbury Crest.'

'She's got the bag with her, right?'

'Yeah. It's all here.'

'I'll be over in an hour. Then we can go and see the pill man.'

I told my superior that the gear was in the flat and he could go and bust the place. He said we had to stick to the original plan: I was to go to the flat, confirm that the gear was there and then give the signal.

At 10.30 a.m., I arrived in Trafalgar Road and parked up outside a large Victorian house that had been converted into flats. I purposely left my mobile phone in the car and went into the building. It was tatty, with worn carpets, and had a damp, musty smell. I made my way up the stairs, and I felt my mouth begin to go dry.

Patrick greeted me at the door and showed me through to the kitchen, where Rebecca was sitting supping a cup of herbal tea that smelled worse than she did. 'Fancy a cup?' she asked.

'No, you're all right,' I said. 'I've just had one.'

We went into the lounge. There on the sofa was the leather vanity case. 'Now, what about my ten ounces?'

'Do you want them now?'

'Yes. I want it all separated before we see the pill man.'

'All right, but I haven't got any powder scales here.'

'Open the case up, and let's make sure everything is still there.' Patrick disappeared off to the kitchen. 'Get us a cup of proper tea while you are there,' I shouted. 'None of that hippy piss.' He returned with two cups of tea and a knife. The tea tasted like it had six sugars in, but it moistened my mouth.

He expertly slit open the bag and removed a packet of white powder. I examined the packet and then put it down on the coffee table. 'I'll give the pill man a ring,' I said, feeling my pockets for my phone. 'Bollocks! I've left my mobile in the car.'

'Use mine,' offered Patrick.

'If he doesn't recognise the number, he won't answer. It won't take a minute.'

It was only a minute, but everything was in slow motion. I wandered down the stairs feeling even more nervous than before. All I could hear was the sound of my own heartbeat in my ears. This was it. Weeks of planning, acting and playing the big man was all designed for this moment. The bust. It always had the same effect on me. It was like stage fright. I reached the car, composed myself and made the call. 'Game on,' I said to Dagenham. Then I drove down the road and waited for the cavalry to pile in.

I watched as the house was hit. Three Drug Squad officers smashed in the front door. Round the back there'd be another half-dozen officers doing the same. Nothing changes. I left them to it and drove quietly back to the Specialist Operations office to finish some nice, sedate paperwork.

Patrick and Rebecca were arrested, and we recovered a kilo and a half of pure MDMA powder. The potential for production of Ecstasy tablets from this was colossal. The tablets were on sale in night clubs at anything up to £25. This recovery was, therefore, the largest in the world at that time, with a street value of over £46 million.

nineteen

THE SHIT BENEATH MY SHOES

'Tea?'

'Yes, please.'

'Biscuit?'

'No, thanks.'

It was all very pleasant. I was in the assistant chief constable's office on the seventh floor of Midland Police HQ, with a lovely view over downtown Birmingham. On a clear day you could see the arse end of Aston. Fortunately for me, it was overcast.

'I'll come straight to the point,' said the assistant chief constable, grabbing himself a custard cream. 'An undercover operation of a very serious nature has come up. I've examined the profiles of all the officers in Specialist Operations, and you're the best suited to this job.'

This sounded familiar. When I was a young detective, I was often hauled into the office of a senior officer and told that I was the best one for the job. What it really meant was no one else wanted to do it.

'That's very flattering, sir,' I replied, trying my best to look flattered. 'What is it?'

'It's a paedophile investigation,' he said solemnly.

'What's the angle?'

'We have information from a reliable source that two paedophiles who are about to be released from prison are planning to commit further offences when they get out. We are in the process of making arrangements for you to be put in prison with them.'

'I haven't said I'll do the job yet,' I replied.

'Well, if you don't think you're up to it . . .'

That was one sure way of getting me to sign up: to suggest I couldn't do the job. It was like a red rag to a bull. 'I'm up to it, sir. When do we start?'

'Right away, I'm afraid.'

The paedophiles were being held in Stafford Prison. They were due for release in just over a week. I would spend one night in Winson Green Prison, and then I'd be transferred, alone, to Stafford. Sex offenders are placed in solitary confinement to prevent them being harmed by other inmates.

I was supplied with the intelligence on the two targets, Michael O'Neill and Paul Grosvenor, including photographs to identify them. The two of them had been overheard discussing a plan to kidnap and sexually abuse young girls. The informant was serving a prison sentence, so there was a chance that this could just be a scam to get him more privileges. If it wasn't a scam, then we needed to move very quickly indeed.

A day later, I was off to prison. I was given a set of prison clothes to wear and a sports holdall containing some of my own clothes. It was important to ensure that no clothing or belongings could lead back to the police. I remembered hearing stories of undercover soldiers in Northern Ireland being rumbled by terrorists because they were wearing army-issue socks or watch straps.

I was hidden under a blanket in the back of a car and driven to Winson Green Prison. We entered the jail without the vehicle being searched, which I found remarkable. Once inside, I was whisked out of the car, through a door, up a long staircase and onto a landing. I was then put into a cell on my own. The door slammed shut behind me.

The cell was tiny with just two bunk beds, a chair, a table and a washbasin. There was no toilet, just a bucket. A small window overlooked another wing of the prison. The place was incredibly warm and noisy. A four-inch pipe ran along the wall of the cell and was scalding hot to the touch. The constant noise was that of other prisoners shouting and doors being slammed shut.

The cell was painted a dull grey, with only one or two etchings on the wall. This was a bit of a disappointment, as I'd thought that if I had become bored I could at least have read the walls. Somebody had scratched 'Jesus saves' on the wall. Beneath it, someone else had scribbled 'But Beckham scores on the rebound'.

'If that's the level of wit, then get me out of here quick,' I thought to myself.

It was late afternoon. I had eaten everything I could throughout the day, because I didn't want to dine with the inmates. I'd heard plenty of stories of nonces having their food spiked with anything from cleaning fluid to human turds.

I was only due to stay for one night, and I'd made it clear in the briefing that I didn't want to come out of my cell until I left the place. Paedophiles were always a target for other prisoners, and I didn't want anything going wrong before the operation had even begun. So much for promises. At 6 p.m., my cell door was opened, and I was marched down to the canteen, where I was served some slop and a cup of tea. Everyone went quiet and stared at me, and I felt like a gunslinger walking into a saloon. I picked at the food and took a couple of sips of tea. Then I told the screw that I wanted to return to my cell. I was led back in silence. I lay on one of the bunks and drifted into an uneasy sleep, still dressed in my clothes.

I was woken in the morning by the clanking of keys in the cell door. I was taken down into the courtyard, where a prison van was waiting. The journey to Stafford Prison took 40 minutes. Inside the van, it was hot and airless.

Once inside Stafford, I was strip-searched and every orifice was examined in front of a group of prison officers and prison orderlies – low-risk inmates who are given various menial tasks throughout the prison. I was then handcuffed and taken to the lifers' wing, which was separate from the main prison. There I was treated to an interview with the screw in charge. He read me the riot act about being found in possession of alcohol and drugs.

The first day was a long one. They say that if you can't do the time, don't do the crime. Even after a few hours, I knew there was no way I could spend any serious stretch of time inside a prison.

I took advantage of a walk around the yard to enjoy some fresh air after the stale atmosphere inside, and that evening I sat with a few of the other inmates watching television. I recognised the targets, O'Neill and Grosvenor, but didn't speak to them. They were both nonces – you could see it right away. O'Neill was unkempt and greasy-looking, with fingernails chewed to the quick. Grosvenor wore bottle-thick glasses that magnified his eyes, and he shuffled about in an irritatingly fidgety way.

I ended up having a conversation with a little old bloke called Mickey, who was very upfront with his line of questioning. 'Why are you here, son?' he enquired.

'I gave my missus a slap,' I lied.

'Me too!' Mickey replied, patting my back. 'I caught my wife in bed with another man, so I gave it to them both with a hatchet.'

'You killed them?'

'No, just a few cuts and bruises. My brief said that if I pleaded guilty, I might get five years.'

'What happened?'

'I got 20.'

'You should have twatted your brief with the hatchet.'

I had to wait till lunchtime the following day before I made contact with O'Neill and Grosvenor. As always, I let the targets approach me. 'Where're you from?' O'Neill asked.

'Birmingham,' I said.

'Me and my mate are from Wolverhampton,' added O'Neill, introducing Grosvenor, the quieter of the two.

'What brings you here?' asked Grosvenor.

'You what?' I asked.

'What he's asking is, what are you in here for?' explained O'Neill.

'What the fuck is it to you?' I snapped.

'Hey, just asking. There's no secrets round here, mate. We're all friends, if you know what I mean.'

'No, I don't fucking know what you mean.'

'You told Mickey that you were in for knocking your wife about.'

'That's right.'

'We heard it was something else,' said O'Neill.

'Oh, yeah,' I replied. 'What have you heard?'

'Look, it doesn't matter what we heard,' said O'Neill calmly.

'All you need to know is that you and us, we're not too dissimilar, you know?' chipped in Grosvenor. 'We need to stick with our own kind.'

My cover story was that I had sexually abused my daughter. This information had been quietly slipped onto the prison grapevine the day I arrived. 'What are you on about?' I asked, still playing dumb.

'We're in here for the same reason you are,' levelled O'Neill.

'Kids, huh?' said Grosvenor. 'They make up stories and everyone believes them . . .'

'We need to be able to trust each other,' continued O'Neill with a whisper. 'Who knows, we might become friends.'

Now that we all knew we were sex offenders, the conversation calmed down. This was classic paedophile behaviour: always trying to establish a little network. The operation had begun.

For the next week, I had to endure O'Neill and Grosvenor buzzing around me, their new-found friend. Nothing was too much trouble for them. I tried to mix with the other inmates, but everywhere I turned my two new buddies appeared. They never missed an opportunity to engage me in conversation. There was no escape. At lunchtime, they always insisted on sitting with me.

'What you are going to do when you get out on Monday?' enquired O'Neill over a bowl of slop.

'Is there anything you don't know about me?' I asked.

'There's a list of names on the board with all the release dates. We're on it, and so are you,' explained Grosvenor.

'We've got a flat in West Bromwich, if you need anywhere to crash,' said O'Neill.

'I'm going to stay with my old lady until I can sort out somewhere to live,' I replied.

'When you're settled, you'll have to come round for a drink,' O'Neill suggested, scribbling down the address.

At 6 a.m. on the Monday, I was woken by the screws. After a shower,

I signed for my belongings, received £18 in cash and was pushed into the outside world. I arrived home just after 9 a.m. My message pager was in the kitchen, and at 9.30 it began bleeping for me to contact the office. I called and was asked what time I was coming in. Bollocks to that. I told them that I was taking the rest of the day off. It would take that long to scrub off the smell of stale cigarettes. A week behind bars had been hard work.

The following morning, I arrived at Specialist Operations HQ for a debrief. The head of the Paedophile Unit said that she was disappointed I'd not phoned in during the week I was inside with an update. I just shook my head and sighed, which said everything. I then requested the use of a car, preferably an old knacker. Specialist Operations still had an old maroon Rover 3500, which was ideal.

At the end of the week, I took the car to West Bromwich to call in on O'Neill and Grosvenor. The address was in Beeches Road, where the once-posh Victorian houses had all been broken up into bedsits. The door was opened by Grosvenor, who was pleased to see me. 'Hello, mate. This is a nice surprise,' he said, ushering me inside.

The place was a large room with two beds, a settee and a kitchen. There were empty cans everywhere. It stank of cigarettes, beer and dirty socks.

O'Neill was in a lively mood. 'I'm going to chase up a few of my old contacts,' he said, grinning. 'I used to be friendly with one of my neighbour's kids before I got done. She was a little darling, dead friendly. She'd do anything.'

'How old is she?' I asked.

'She'll be 15 now,' said O'Neill. 'I hope I can find her. I haven't had my leg over for five years.'

'Is that what you're into?' I asked.

'I prefer them a lot younger. Some of them are grateful. You know, buy them a few things, give them a few quid.' Simple maths showed that if what he was saying was true, he'd been having sex with a ten year old. 'We should get together and see if we can do something which would be for all our benefit. We could go and have a drive around a few schools for some likely victims.'

'What do you mean?'

'You know, the old puppy dog and bag of sweets routine.'

'Think about what you're suggesting,' I said.

'What's to think about?' replied O'Neill.

'We've just got out of prison. I don't want to be going straight back.'

O'Neill was suggesting child abduction. Kidnap. I needed a way to record this evidence properly. I wanted the case to be watertight, but it was going to be another nightmare. The tape recorders I'd used on the contract-killer case were too bulky. Technology had moved on, but the police force hadn't. The equipment supplied by the Technical Support Unit was out of the ark. All the gear used by the department had to have Home Office approval and be Home Office tested. But by the time the equipment had been tested and approved, it was usually obsolete.

I made some enquiries with West Midlands Police. They had a T-shirt camera and a baseball-cap camera, both of which had the ability to record audio evidence. But I'd never used any of it, and I needed kit that was totally reliable. Any cock-ups risked the targets walking free.

I contacted a mate from the SAS. He put me in touch with a captain from 14 Intelligence Company, who were deployed almost exclusively in Northern Ireland. Their role was surveillance of terrorists and infiltration into the paramilitary organisations. The captain supplied me with body microphones and recording equipment that was the smallest I had ever seen. The recording was digital, so the reproduction was first class. This was an unofficial loan, which was always the case with anything I did with special forces. I was able to go to them because there was a brown envelope attached to my personal file that could only be opened by an officer of the rank of chief superintendent. Inside was a report detailing my involvement and training with UK special forces.

Back at HQ, I requested a surveillance team so that they could corroborate my evidence in the form of photographs as we moved from location to location. I also got my hands on a mobile telephone from Specialist Operations. I'd decided I would encourage O'Neill and Grosvenor to use mobiles, too. That way we could use cell-site technology to track their position at any given time.

The next time I met the targets, I was fully wired up. We went to a pub in West Bromwich High Street for a drink. As the alcohol began to take effect, more of their heinous plan began to unfold. O'Neill continued to steer the proceedings. He was clearly the brighter of the two. 'I've got eight schools all over the Midlands that we can go and have a look at.'

'Draw me a list,' I suggested, 'then I'll get the map out and find the best routes to and from them.' I was the only one who had a car. They couldn't get to any of these schools without me driving them. It was a very important safety net.

O'Neill drew up a list with names of schools in Nottingham, Leicester and Solihull. I then got them to tell me what they knew about the schools and repeat what they had planned. 'You want us to kidnap one of these kids?' I reiterated for the benefit of the tape recorder. 'That's some serious shit.'

'That's why we've got to be careful.'

The longer I spent with O'Neill and Grosvenor, the more aggressive I felt towards them. I had to get these two locked up. And fast. If I didn't, I might have been tempted to deal with them myself in a Ronnie Howard hands-on manner. It might not have been legal, but it would have been very satisfying.

Transcribing the tapes of our conversations took for ever. Recordings were supposed to speed up the process of collecting evidence. In fact, they slowed them down. But I couldn't afford to slip up.

Our next meeting involved checking out the schools on O'Neill's list. This time, I had surveillance in tow. When I arrived at the flat, O'Neill and Grosvenor already had their coats on and were ready to go. 'Where first?' I asked.

'Staffordshire,' instructed O'Neill. 'Head for a place called Leek. There's a couple of schools there. They'll be turning out by the time we get there.'

'We aren't going to do anything today, are we?' I asked.

'No, I just want to see if we spot any potential victims,' said O'Neill. 'We can pick one off when we're ready.'

We travelled up the M6 and left the motorway at a place called Stone. We arrived in Leek at 3.15 p.m. and parked up near a school. Fifteen minutes later, the pupils came pouring out. I stayed in the car while O'Neill and Grosvenor went out on foot to survey the scene. I knew that surveillance were getting good footage.

'There's one or two that might be OK for our purposes,' noted O'Neill on the return journey to West Bromwich.

'What exactly are we thinking of doing?' I asked, once again playing dumb for the benefit of my concealed tape recorder.

'I've got a dog lead. We'll say we're looking for a lost dog and get the girls to come with us,' suggested Grosvenor.

'We'll grab them and then shag them as many times as we can before we get caught,' announced O'Neill. This was a strange comment, because of all the criminals I had ever dealt with, none were of the opinion that they would ever be caught. It meant that O'Neill and Grosvenor were prepared to take huge risks to get what they wanted. This made them doubly dangerous.

'Where are we going to do this?' I persisted. 'We can't take them back to the flat.'

'I want to buy a van,' revealed O'Neill. 'We can take it in turns to shag them in the back. We can fit it out with carpet on the floor and egg boxes on the wall to soundproof it. We'll ply them with alcopops and then take it in turns to video them as we're having sex with them.' The more I heard, the more I hated them. But worse was to come.

I dropped them back at the bedsit and arranged to go to a car auction with them later in the week. In the meantime, I met with my superiors to discuss the developments in the operation. My main concern was how far we were going to let it run. I proposed that we should let them purchase the van, but I would have to stay close to them so that they didn't go off and do anything without me. This was a little like playing Russian roulette. I had secured enough evidence to prove a conspiracy, but we needed to screw the lid on with these two.

The car auctions were held on a Thursday evening over at nearby Oldbury. I arranged with O'Neill to meet him and Grosvenor in the afternoon, as they wanted to check out some more schools before going to buy the van. This time we went to Solihull, where we went through the same routine. Once again, surveillance were in tow, gathering vital video and photographic evidence.

We returned to the bedsit to wait till the auction began and opened a few cans of supermarket lager. O'Neill then put on a pornographic video. They were on the bone of their arses, but they had a huge colour television and a video recorder. I remember when I was a probationary policeman going into some of the poorest houses in the most run-down areas, they'd have no sheets on the bed and no carpets on the floor, but they all seemed to have a state-of-the-art, 26-inch colour television.

The video featured young teenagers having sex. It showed everything from oral sex to buggery. O'Neill then produced an Ordnance Survey map, which he spread out on the floor. He'd highlighted the schools from his list, along with the local parks and scrubland. Bizarrely, he'd even made a note of the names of the headmasters of each school.

Paedophiles are meticulous planners. They can spend months, even years, working on ensnaring a victim. I'd studied profiles as part of my training. Of all the criminals I ever dealt with, these were the most cunning.

'All we need now is the van,' declared O'Neill through a mouthful of corned beef and beans. 'I've got £500. You reckon that should be enough for what we need?'

'Should be plenty,' I said. 'We're not looking for a racing car, are we?'

'We should get a van with a sliding side door. It'll be quicker to drag them in if we pull up alongside them.'

'If they make any sort of noise, I'll superglue their lips together,' said O'Neill, laughing. 'That'll shut them up.' The sick thing was that I believed he actually meant it.

As we were about to leave for the auction, he produced a carrier bag containing three black hoods and several rolls of gaffer tape, none of which needed explanation. It was increasingly obvious that they were determined to carry out what they'd been threatening. I'd already made it clear to my superiors what I would do if they tried to abduct a child in my presence. 'Neither of the targets will remain in any physical condition to run away,' was my firm response.

I once went to a Turkish bath with my younger brother, who was 13 at the time. While I was out of the room, my brother was approached by a middle-aged man who invited him to his house. When I found this out, I walked calmly over to the man, who was sitting in the hottest room in the house, and gave him a swift kick in the throat. 'Proposition my brother again,' I told him as he cowered on the floor, 'and I'll pull your head out through your arse.'

At the auction, O'Neill found one van in the price bracket he could afford. It was an ex-motorway maintenance van. It was bright yellow with an orange light on the roof – subtle as a firework in your face. The surveillance team weren't going to lose that in a hurry.

O'Neill handed over the cash, but the auctioneers wouldn't release the van until they were shown proof of insurance. This was good for me, because it meant the van would be out of action for a couple of days until Grosvenor received his next dole cheque. He would use the cash to obtain a cover note.

As I dropped them off back at the bedsit, O'Neill pulled me to one side. 'You around tomorrow? I've got something important to show you.'

'Yes. What is it?'

'I'll show you tomorrow.'

After an early morning briefing at HQ, I arrived at the bedsit at 10 a.m. O'Neill was on his own. Grosvenor had gone to investigate the insurance for the van. I was told we were going to Worcester. O'Neill and I got into my car and headed for the M5. 'Why are we going to Worcester?' I asked.

'I want to go to Malvern to check something out,' said O'Neill.

'Check what out?'

'Just wait and see.'

Talking to O'Neill was like pulling teeth out of a dead donkey. He directed me to a spot called Eastnor Castle at the foot of the large range of hills that traverse Malvern. I parked the car and walked with O'Neill into the hills until we reached a crop of rocks. In the middle, there was a large cave with sheer sides, almost like a well cut into the rock. O'Neill threw a stone into the cave, which bounced off the walls and finally splashed into water at the bottom. It took several seconds before it hit the bottom. It was very, very deep.

'This is where we can dispose of the girls when we've finished with them,' O'Neill announced. 'We can throw them down there. The fall will probably kill them. No one will ever find them. We can't get caught if they're never found.'

This was a new development. We were now going to commit murder. 'When did you dream this up?' I asked.

'I've always thought we should do this,' was his matter-of-fact reply. 'It's the only way to stay out of jail. We have to learn to kidnap and murder them.'

I got him to repeat this several times so that there would be no argument that what he intended was completely premeditated. Then I asked, 'Is Paul up for this with you?'

'Paul is with me on this. We've been talking about this all the time we were inside.'

I looked around the hills and hoped the surveillance team were covering us. In rural surroundings, they would be using crops officers, who were specially trained for this sort of terrain.

I had O'Neill's confession. All I needed now was the same from his partner. Back in West Bromwich I got straight onto Grosvenor. 'Michael's just shown me the cave you're going to throw these girls into,' I told him. 'He says you're OK with this. I need to know from you that you are. We're talking kidnap, rape and murder here. I'm not getting involved with anyone who's going to wobble.'

'Me and Michael have known each other a long time. We decided all this a long time ago. I'm with him all the way.'

I reported this update back to HQ. It was time to nail these two. On the Monday morning, I took O'Neill and Grosvenor to pick up the van. It was driven back to West Bromwich and parked in a garage behind the bedsit. I left the pair of them drawing up a shopping list of all the gear they'd need to kit the van out with. As I left the flat, I picked up the keys to the van. I didn't want them doing anything in my absence.

I made my way to Specialist Operations and contacted the cavalry. At 5 a.m. the following morning, the flat was raided and O'Neill and Grosvenor were arrested. Vital evidence, such as the list of schools, maps, the dog lead, alcopops, superglue, rolls of gaffer tape and the hoods, was recovered.

O'Neill and Grosvenor appeared at the Crown court, and I gave evidence for three days from behind a screen to protect my identity. The tapes I had made were replayed, amounting to over 100 hours of recordings. They were convicted and sentenced to life imprisonment. I was commended by the trial judge.

After the trial, there was the usual backslapping, and I was told that I was to be recommended for the Queen's Police Medal. The award ended up going to a chief superintendent who had come up with a blueprint for community policing, which involved officers playing table tennis with the bone idle. I wasn't that bothered. The award would have had to be given in secret, so no one would have even known that I'd got it. I'd received all sorts of commendations throughout my career and still hadn't found anywhere I could spend them.

twenty

THE STITCH-UP PART II

It was 12.50 p.m. as I turned onto the Washwood Heath Road on a hot balmy afternoon in July. An unmistakable air of frustration surrounded me as I sped past the chaos of the Asian shops. Ahead of me was the Fox and Dogs pub. Two doors down the road was Khan's Café, where I knew I'd find Janay, the heroin dealer who'd organised the baseball-bat reception party. This time, I wasn't alone.

I eased off the gas. As I parked the car, the anger I had felt during the previous night's ambush returned. Khan's was a small, smoky establishment full of men playing cards, shooting pool and scratching their arses. As Dagenham and I entered, it was like walking into a Wild West saloon. Everyone in the room froze. Standing beside the pool table was Janay. He looked very surprised to see me. I grabbed him by the collar and dragged him out of the door. 'You fucking set me up,' I hissed as I yanked him onto the street.

As we reached the pavement, Janay suddenly blurted out, 'I know who you are. I know who you are.' I pulled him up to my face by his lapels. 'You're old Bill,' he squeaked.

'I'll fucking old Bill you if you don't shut your mouth right now.'

By then, Janay was up on his tiptoes, desperately trying to suck in air as I almost lifted him off his feet. Before I could inflict any permanent damage, Dagenham extracted him from my grip and bundled him into our unmarked car.

As we drove off, Janay continued his rant: 'I'm an informer. I know you're coppers. I'm an informer. I want protection.' He then revealed the name of the officer he said he was informing for. I hadn't worked with him, but I knew him. His nickname was Kit Kat, so called because he always seemed to be on his break, and Dagenham and I had crossed paths with him before. A year or so previously, we'd had a tip-off about a scrapyard owner who was ringing cars. This was a scam in which stolen vehicles had their plates and engine numbers swapped for cars that had already been scrapped. The newly christened cars could then be resold or shipped abroad. The vehicles we were interested in were suspected of being used for drug smuggling.

One night, Dagenham and I paid the yard an unofficial visit to check for evidence. 'If we get nicked, I'll say we were looking for our football,' said Dagenham as we climbed over the chain-link fencing.

'If we get nicked, I won't be saying anything,' I replied.

We slipped past the Portakabin office and began examining the vehicles and engines around the premises. It was littered with the carcasses of dozens of high-performance cars. We noted the chassis and engine numbers and nipped back over the fence. Back at the station, a dozen of them checked out as being stolen. We passed the intelligence on to Kit Kat, whose patch the scrapyard was on. A few weeks later, we contacted him for an update. 'We turned the yard over,' said Kit Kat. 'It was as clean as a whistle. Your informant wants shooting.' In fact, it was Kit Kat who needed shooting, as we were about to find out.

As we made our way back along the Washwood Heath Road, Janay went on to reveal something else. Not only was he Kit Kat's informant, he was also the cousin of the man who owned the scrapyard suspected of car ringing. This explained why it was never busted. Janay also told us that when I first arranged – undercover – to set up the heroin deal, he went to Kit Kat for advice. Janay gave Kit Kat my description and told him that I'd be driving a grey Saab Turbo. The day before the deal, I'd parked the Saab at the station where Kit Kat was working. Kit

Kat realised that Janay was about to be busted. Rather than tip me off and steer Janay away from the deal, Kit Kat chose to blow my cover. This was tantamount to signing an undercover officer's death warrant.

Over the course of my career, I'd witnessed first hand what criminals do to people who cross them. In Liverpool, I was taken to a flat to watch a man being tortured by a gang of drug dealers. He was beaten black and blue, burned with candles, had boiling water poured over his legs and had one of his toes cut off. And he wasn't even the man who'd ripped them off. They couldn't get hold of him, so they'd tortured his brother instead.

A Midlands drug dealer called Errol Hoskins was caught stitching up his suppliers. As punishment, he was shot through both knees, both elbows and finished off with a bullet in the throat. Miraculously, he survived. As he lay unconscious, his head tipped to one side and closed the wound in his neck, stopping him from bleeding to death.

Several months later, after he was discharged from hospital, Dagenham and I visited Hoskins to see if he would turn informer. As we hammered on his door, we heard screams coming from inside the house. We forced our way in and found an empty wheelchair sitting in the hallway. A search of the house revealed that it was empty. We eventually found Hoskins behind a pile of junk in the shed, sobbing his heart out. He thought we were his tormentors coming back to finish him off. Sheer fear had given him the strength to fling himself out of the wheelchair and drag himself and his crippled body out of the back door and up the garden.

Errol was one of the lucky ones. Lucky he didn't end up shot through the back of the head. Or pushed off the 20th-floor balcony of a tower block. Or chopped to pieces and stuffed into a suitcase. He was lucky he wasn't a copper. And I was lucky I hadn't ended up with my skull smashed in by a baseball bat.

With my cover blown, I arrested Janay and took him back to the station. I was all for protecting informants. I'd done it with Billy The Truth enough times. I'd even done it for informants of other officers. A few months before, an informant of a fellow officer had tipped him off about a supplier who was driving back to London with a car load of drugs. I was immediately put in charge of the operation. Surveillance picked up the car on its way out of Birmingham, heading towards Coventry. We followed it for five miles, then I radioed the officers in the traffic patrol car, who pulled the target over.

Twenty kilos of cannabis were recovered. The driver was arrested and taken to Little Park Street Police Station in Coventry. There were nineteen kilo-blocks of cannabis wrapped in clingfilm and one more of the same weight in a white polythene bag.

As we were recording the exhibits, I received a telephone call: 'The blow in the white bag has been in the informant's possession. His fingerprints will be all over it. Get rid of the bag.' I removed the gear from the plastic bag and replaced the cannabis back on the pile. As the drugs were counted again, one of the traffic officers asked where the drugs in the white polythene bag had gone.

'They're here,' I said, pointing to the stash I'd placed back on the pile. 'The bag is of no evidential value.'

Then I realised why I had been told to handle the operation: if any jiggery-pokery was required, I'd be the one to have to do it. I would also have the pleasure of preparing the papers for Crown court. The driver was charged with possession of controlled drugs with intent to supply. The informant was safe.

Janay was another matter. Informer or not, he'd thrown me to the lions. We raided his house and found three kilos of heroin. Janay went to court and was released on bail. He immediately fled to Pakistan.

I complained to management about Kit Kat, who came looking for me. He greeted me with a poke in the chest. 'You're trying to ruin me, you bastard,' he growled.

'I think you'll find it's you who's trying to ruin me,' I replied. I took hold of his finger and twisted his hand back into a wrist lock. I offered to continue the discussion out in the street. Kit Kat declined.

His actions were reported to the Complaints and Discipline Department. The matter was investigated and came to nothing. Kit Kat was eventually promoted.

For the first time during my career as a police officer, I seriously thought about packing it in. If the force wouldn't back me up on a matter as important as this, what was the point in taking those risks? I was the one they relied on. The one who put his neck on the line. The one who got results. There was an old saying in the police force: 'Big jobs cause big problems; no jobs cause no problems.'

I once again asked a superintendent on one occasion how many officers worked at a particular police station, to which he replied, 'About half of them.' And it was true. I'd often worked alongside incompetence, laziness and corruption. I'd ruined a marriage, sacrificed a lifetime of normality, driven myself to the limit. The moment I asked for support, a bit of personal welfare assurance, it was nowhere to be found.

As Kit Kat's career strolled happily up the corridor, mine was about to be rocked to its very foundations. Six weeks after the failed heroin bust, I was called into the detective superintendent's office. 'I'm afraid I have some bad news,' he said, ashen faced.

'And what is that?' I enquired.

'Someone has reported you for stealing a quantity of drugs.'

'Is this a joke?' I asked, not believing what I was hearing.

'No, it's not.'

'And who's making these allegations?'

'You'll find out soon enough,' he said. 'In the meantime, you're not to leave the office.'

I returned to my desk and phoned Dagenham. 'Someone's fitting me up,' I said.

'Then they'd better hope they've made a good job of it,' replied Dagenham, 'cos I wouldn't like to be in their shoes when you come out of it the other end smelling of Brut.'

At 7 p.m., I made my way to police HQ to be interviewed by the Complaints and Discipline Department. The allegation was that whilst on a drugs-bust operation I had removed a small quantity of cannabis and put it in my pocket. My home was searched, as was my desk, but nothing was found. This was hardly surprising, because there was nothing to find.

I needed a lawyer but couldn't afford to pay lawyer prices. My legal representative was supplied by the Police Federation. This representation was paid for from contributions deducted from my wages each month.

The person interviewing me turned out to be Superintendent Ernie Doyle, the man who'd been in charge of Operation Siberia. This was an inquiry into Drug Squad corruption and had cost the taxpayer £2 million, although it came up with nothing. I began to wonder whether I was being used as a scapegoat, a trophy head to justify wasting all that public money.

During my interview, I told Doyle exactly what had happened. The house we raided was in Moseley. We sledgehammered the door and found five people in the front room in a haze of ganja smoke. They were arrested and the house was searched. Upstairs, we found hydroponics equipment. This was used to grow marijuana plants at a rapid rate using water and heat lamps. (I once did a surveillance run in a helicopter over a premises suspected of growing marijuana. Through the thermal imaging camera, the heat created by the lamps made it look like the roof was on fire.)

During our search, one of the officers also found several bags of weed in the fridge. In amongst this was a smaller bag containing a dark green substance. 'What's this?' asked the officer.

I took some out of the bag, rolled it between my fingers and sniffed it. 'Smells like skunk,' I said, dropping it back into the bag. (Skunk is a super-strength strain of marijuana containing up to seven times more hallucinogenic – or THC – than a normal plant.) The evidence was taken back to the station. We had recovered £3,000 worth of cannabis that morning.

It turned out that the allegation against me was that I had pocketed the skunk. It was made by the officer who'd found the drugs in the fridge. The amount I was accused of stealing was the size of a fingernail. There were no other witnesses to the incident, so it was his word against mine.

I finished the interview feeling confident, until I was told that the deputy chief constable had decided I was to be suspended from duty. I handed in my warrant card and headed home. I was inundated with phone calls from colleagues, shocked at what was going on. I was like a caged animal, prowling the house. I decided that the best way to get rid of my aggression was to go to the gym and lift some weights. I'd also always found running a great form of relaxation, so I set about pounding the streets, jogging ten or twelve miles a day. During my years in the police force, fear was a sensation that I always managed to suppress. Now, a trumped-up allegation of theft of a tiny piece of cannabis was making my stomach churn.

The papers on the investigation were sent to the director of public prosecutions. I asked Dagenham to look over the file of evidence against me. 'Most of the evidence is hearsay. The rest is uncorroborated,' was his verdict. Then Dagenham spotted a huge flaw in the evidence. The witness had told the investigators he had not discussed the allegation with anyone. However, when one of his colleagues was interviewed, he said that the witness had been discussing it with other officers for a week before he filed the complaint. The officer had therefore made a false claim in his statement of evidence. In other words, I could prove he was a liar.

One morning, as I was climbing the walls at home, I got a call from a friend who worked in the security services. Over a beer, I told him what was happening. He asked me if I might be interested in coming to work with him. I'd made a decision many years before that I would never carry a gun for the police. They don't pay you any more money, and if you shoot somebody, the first thing they do is lock you up. One of my mates in the SAS had been interviewed six times under caution for murder.

Despite my reluctance to use firearms, it was still a very tempting offer. But rather than resign, what I wanted to do was clear my name. I said that I'd think about the offer and let him know.

In the meantime, I received a letter saying that I was needed in court to give evidence regarding the 20 kilos of cannabis we'd seized from the car boot. I was still able to give evidence to support a case I'd worked on prior to my suspension. Anything to get out of the house.

Arrangements were made for me to be picked up in Birmingham and taken to the Crown court in Coventry. On the morning of the trial, I put on a suit and travelled into Birmingham city centre by train. I arrived at 9.30 a.m. It was bucketing down. An hour later, my lift hadn't arrived. I suddenly took stock of what was going on. Here I was, standing in the pissing rain. I was expected to go to court and lie, under oath, about the kilo of cannabis in the white plastic bag. Back at HQ, my name was being dragged through the mud. I jumped in a cab and headed home. I spent the rest of the day in the gym taking out my frustration on a punchbag.

My suspension lasted five months. The papers were returned from the director of public prosecutions, who ruled that there was no evidence to support a criminal prosecution. I was innocent. Game over. Except that it wasn't. The Police Complaints Authority ruled that although there was no criminal case to answer, there was disciplinary action to be taken for 'misappropriating a small quantity of cannabis'. This was not stealing cannabis but taking it and not putting it where it was supposed to go.

The charge was bullshit. But, again, I was confident of beating the allegation. The disciplinary hearing lasted two days, during which I had to endure a former colleague lying through his teeth about me. I then gave my account of what had taken place. For some reason, my lawyer chose not to use the trump card that the witness statement was flawed.

At the end of the hearing, a queue of senior officers testified to the quality and commitment of my performance throughout my career. The chief constable then spent two hours deliberating on the evidence. I returned to the conference room to be told that I wasn't going to be disciplined. I was elated. But then came the bombshell. 'I'm going to recommend that you resign,' he said.

'Resign? For what?' I exploded. 'I haven't done anything illegal. So why the fuck should I resign?' What about all the other officers I'd worked with who'd been found guilty of misconduct? The ones who had been shunted off quietly to other parts of the force? Why hadn't they been forced to resign?

I was in such a rage, I couldn't bear to listen to any more. All I could hear was the sound of my own heart beating so loudly that I thought my chest was going to explode. I walked out of the hearing and was met by friends and colleagues who were waiting to find out the verdict. When I told them, there was a collective, stunned silence. I was offered lifts home and invitations to go for a drink, but I refused. Instead, I went home and ignored the telephone for a couple of days. The answer machine was full of colleagues calling to share their disbelief and support. I was reminded about the only piece of Latin I knew. *Illegitimi non carborundum* – Don't let the bastards grind you down.

I called Dagenham and went for a much-needed drink. We went over it all again. And it still didn't make sense. We discussed all the ways I could fight the decision. Then Dagenham looked up at me and asked, 'Do you really want to go through it all again?'

I looked at him and sensed a weariness. Like me, he'd given his all to the police force. Like me, he'd seen the way that it had chewed people up and spat them out. But the problem was that I never knew when to give up. I once got called to a house where a seven-year-old boy had collapsed. I arrived before the ambulance to find the parents distraught. The child wasn't breathing. I massaged his heart and started mouth-to-mouth resuscitation. 'Come on, come on,' I whispered, half to the child and half to myself. I drew back momentarily to check for a pulse. As I did so, the boy's body heaved and a projectile of his vomit hit me in the face. A sign of life. I wiped my cheek and piled on. My clothes were dripping with sweat. On and on I went.

After what seemed like an eternity, the ambulance arrived, and I had to be dragged off. As the paramedics took over, I collapsed in the hall. The ambulance crew applied oxygen and checked for a pulse. Nothing. The parents were hysterical. 'One more time,' I urged the paramedic. 'One more.' He gave another kiss of life then stopped. The look in his eyes told me the boy was dead. As the child's body was taken away on a stretcher, I sobbed my heart out. The post-mortem later revealed the boy had been suffering from septicaemia. The vomiting was caused by trapped air in his stomach. He was already dead. Nothing I could have done would have saved him.

Dagenham's words continued to ricochet around my head. Was it finally time to let go? I'd been a copper for 23 years. My own life had always taken second place, and now I was accused of not putting two bob's worth of cannabis back where it should have gone after recovering drugs worth millions. The organisation had turned on me.

twenty-one

ALL GOOD THINGS MUST COME TO AN END

I was exhausted. That night I went home and slept the sleep of the dead. I awoke at midday and went for a jog. I had a decision to make. I ran a route that took me through my old beats and around the area I grew up. The landscape was familiar. I still felt that territorial instinct I'd always felt over the years. From my days as a rookie copper to Operation Reverse 22. What would this all look like through civilian eyes?

About half an hour into my run, I noticed an elderly lady on the pavement up ahead. A man on a bicycle was zigzagging slowly about ten yards behind her. As I looked on, I saw her handbag hanging down by her side. I instinctively knew what was about to take place. Suddenly, the man on the bike sped up and rode past the old lady. As he overtook her, he scooped up the handbag, pulling her along until she let go and fell over. He then sped off and turned left out of sight.

I ran after him. As I turned left into a row of shops, there was no sign of him. I looked around for his possible escape route. In the middle of the row of shops, next to a small supermarket, there was an alleyway. At end of the alley, there were half a dozen industrial-sized wheelie bins that belonged to the supermarket. A mugger will often offload any evidence – an emptied purse, a wallet – very quickly, often in a public toilet, canal or a skip.

I reached the end of the alley and saw the bike propped up against the wall. The man was crouched down behind one of the bins going through the contents of the handbag. As he saw me, he rose to his feet. This was just what I needed. I kicked him in the stomach, doubling him over. As he tried to straighten up, I head-butted him on the middle of his nose, and he crumpled to the floor. I then picked him up by his coat, dragged him out of the alley and sat on him. There was blood everywhere. People began to gather around, and I asked someone to call the police. The mugger began to come round and groaned.

A police motorcyclist was first to arrive on the scene. I knew him by sight but not by name. I told him what had happened, and the mugger was arrested. The police officer said that he would be submitting a report about me for making such an outstanding arrest. I gave my details and then went home to sort my wounds out.

A couple of hours later, the telephone rang. It was the police, who said that the mugger was seriously injured. This could be considered to be more than reasonable force. Good old reasonable force. Reasonable force in law is defined by section three of the Criminal Law Act, 1967. It states that reasonable force may be used to prevent or terminate a crime or effect or assist in a lawful arrest. It is a grey area of the law, and the decision of what constitutes reasonable force can only be made by a jury.

'I'm afraid you'll have to come to the Kingsheath Police Station to be interviewed,' said the officer on the phone.

'If you want me, you'll have to come and get me,' I told him. 'You'll have to arrest me.'

I put the phone down and sat in the house waiting for the police to arrive. As I waited, it felt like the beginning of a new undercover operation just before I was to meet the villains for the first time. The rush of blood through my veins and the feeling of my own well-maintained body gave me the confidence to deal with whatever awaited me.

I sat back and thought of the only part of the Bible I knew – Luke, chapter 14, verse 23: 'Go out into the highways and hedgerows and make them come in.' I'd certainly done that.

epilogue

ONCE A COPPER...

My failure to convict the car-jack rapist we'd arrested during Operation Reverse 22 continued to bother me, long after I'd left the force. A decade after I watched a guilty man walk free, I read an article detailing how police were using new technology to solve old cases. Operation Advance was particularly concerned with using the developments in DNA testing.

I wrote a letter to West Midlands Police regarding the car-jack rapist. I gave the dates and details of the case so that they could revisit the evidence, which would have been kept in storage. The DNA was re-examined, and the perpetrator was rearrested and charged with rape. He appeared before Birmingham Crown Court, where he was sentenced to life imprisonment.

Job finally done.